M000267679

INTEGRAL
MEDITATION
THE SEVEN WAYS TO SELF-REALISATION

BY KENNETH SØRENSEN

REVIEWS

"If ever you wished to understand and bring through the power and beauty that is the full spectrum of your essential nature, then this book on the practice of integral meditation is for you.

"Meditation is an essential element of our daily life. It is the art and science of consciously building the rainbow bridge that spans and helps integrate the inner and outer dimensions and aspects of that living system we call the Self.

"Kenneth Sørensen presents a comprehensive and easy-to-assimilate roadmap for spiritual develop-ment that is drawn from his own experience, the Ageless Wisdom teachings, and fresh perspectives from the field of integral and transpersonal psychology.

"He masterfully shows how the human being is a seven-fold system of energies and offers a variety of models and meditations for accessing and utilising all the colors and qualities of this rainbow of poten-tiality and possibility."

Michael Lindfield, Board President of Meditation Mount, Ojai, California, and co-founder of the Science of Group Work Initiative

""This unique work unites personal life experiences with a clearly communicated and much-needed in-novative and visionary adventure into the practice of meditation.

"Kenneth Sørensen combines raw honesty and self-taught deep meditation skills with authenticity and a rare ability to communicate very difficult perspectives in a vibrant and meaningful way.

"The sublime and sensual meet in this intense journey into consciousness, communicated with passion, depth and heart. He shares and teaches, providing an uplifting introduction into a new, integral life perspective with a focus on meditation and spiritual practice. Old dogmas and spiritual prejudices are confronted and replaced with an integrated and fully developed paradigm for a new time. This is a bold and solid achievement which will undoubtedly stand the test of time precisely because it combines a uniquely honest and personal portrayal of a future-oriented and holistic integral vision – developed over years of deep practice."

Søren Hauge, Spiritual teacher, counsellor and author

"Kenneth is writing from a deeply authentic place. He communicates in a language that awakens the soul and opens the heart to the call to greatness. His book unites the essence of psycho-spiritual develop-ment with a brilliant and solid meditation practice."

Lene Ince, Psychotherapist and Headmaster of Tobias-skolen

"I have stretched my mind to the extreme and have been touched at the core reading this book. Along the way, I have experienced a rare clarity, both during meditation and in the course of the day."

Louise Mazanti, PhD, Psychosynthesis counsellor

Copyright: Kentaur Forlag 2017
First published in Denmark 2012
Author: Kenneth Sørensen
Translator: Anja Fløde Bjørlo
Editor: Mike Brooks
Layout: byhaugereitz.dk
1. Edition

EAN: 9788792252197
ISBN: 978-87-92252-19-7

This book is dedicated to all Souls who choose to die daily so they can live in greater freedom

TABLE OF CONTENTS

Appendix: Fifteen Meditation Outlines for Integral Meditation

The dynamic river of life: Awareness Meditation
The dynamic river of life: Power Meditation
The dynamic river of life: Dynamic Meditation on an Object
The sensitive river of life: Healing Meditation
The sensitive river of life: Unity Meditation
The sensitive river of life: Insight Meditation
The intelligent river of life: Circle Meditation
The intelligent river of life: Reflective Meditation
The intelligent river of life: Receptive Meditation
The creative river of life: Creative Meditation
The creative river of life: Soul Therapy
The scientific river of life: Reflective Meditation and Investigative Interview
The dedicated river of life: Creative Meditation with Surrender
The dedicated river of life: Creative Meditation on the Ideal Model
The manifesting river of life: Full moon meditation

Preface

This book has been in the making my entire life. For me, life started when I was twenty-four and discovered astrology. Two years later, I started seeing a psychotherapist and had begun a daily meditation practice that I've maintained ever since. It has been an incredible journey, and now, some thirty years later, I can hardly grasp how I have managed to pull my head out of that foggy, unhappy state of mind in which I was engulfed.

In hindsight, I can see two primary motivations behind my journey. One was the deep emotional pain and unhappiness I felt in relation to my life, and my sense of myself as an extremely limited person. I could not recognise myself, and this frustration around my identity troubled me until I was ready to ask the question, "Who am I?" On an unconscious or semi-conscious level, there was always a part of me who sensed I was far greater than my outer appearance. Today I call this part of me The King. It is a part of our personality that is connected to the Royal Self, the Soul in our heart. The King is in touch with our inner greatness, and this can cause great pain because of the sharp contrast it presents between our present self and what we can become. I am surely not from a royal background – my ancestors are predominantly farmers and manual workers – so this has only strengthened the contrast between my inner and outer reality.

But this pain has also been a blessing. It created a crack in my psychological defences and has shown a way out of the spiritual poverty in which I was living, opening me to the Soul's calling. This pain has motivated me to widen my inner world through meditation, philosophy and psychotherapy. This type of pain will either break us or save us; for me it became a great healing agent.

The second major motivation behind my spiritual journey was a *will to growth*, which became more serious in 1986, when, as mentioned, at the age of twenty-four I began my real life. Today I call this drive a *will to freedom*; it is an uncompromising longing for free expression on all levels. There is a voice in me that is unwilling to accept personal limitations and makes great effort to work through these limitations. This will is an expression of The King but in a more pure and direct form; it is the Royal Self fighting to manifest its kingdom.

My awakening led to a sense of vivid, immediate life and an almost unbearable feeling of ecstatic joy, a powerful, almost frightening sense of my own freedom. As with all visions or moments of ecstasy, it was temporary, but its effects stayed with me. These effects are not always pleasant. The will to be free can create a strong sense of being mediocre because the vision of what we can be always transcends our immediate experience. This is a challenge—a crisis of duality—we all must face when we open up to Spirit and its demand that we become who we truly are.

I wish to write a book for all Souls who feel the call to greatness, for those whose hearts long for unconditional love and compassion, and who desire to awaken from the dream within which most of the world is imprisoned. This book is for those who dare to develop all their resources and put them into the service of the One Life.

My message is quite simple: *meditate, love, and choose freedom every day.* This is the essence of my book.

Meditation is an effective means for speeding up our evolution because through it we shift our focus from the world of effects to the world of causes. Through meditating we have a means to help us awaken to the content of our consciousness and the stream of thoughts, images, emotions and sensations we project onto the world. Through meditation we realise that what we call reality is coloured by interpretations based on our habitual reactions, and that these reactions are illusions from the past. Meditation makes it possible to consciously choose our thoughts and emotions, enabling us to master our minds. This is the foundation of inner peace.

Meditation has two fundamental effects. It expands our awareness from the individual to the universal, a widening of consciousness through which our separate ego gradually opens into a more universal presence. We discover that our true identity is something immaterial and subtle, a state of oneness connecting us with all living beings and the whole manifested universe.

Meditation can also alter the qualities of the personality. Through the more spiritual states of mind it can induce, meditation can refine the personality, leading to visible changes in behaviour. Where before we reacted with fear, selfishness and ignorance, we can now respond with courage, kindness and wisdom. There's no limit to how far we can develop this capacity, as mystics and saints throughout history have shown. These two effects – expansion and alteration of the personality are the result of what we can call passive and active meditation. The first develops freedom of being, the second develops freedom of action.

These insights will be developed throughout this book. The fundamental message is that *meditation changes the world because, through it, you change.* The root motivation for all meditation must be for the sake of the whole because our true identity is never separate from the world.

I have called my approach *integral meditation* – integral both in the sense of something that is essential and involves all parts of us – because we must apply the whole spectrum of meditation in order to work effectively with the different frequencies of energy. A holistic attitude to meditation is vital. Our practice should suit our spiritual type. For example, not everyone benefits from the use of mindfulness, so we must adjust our meditation to the needs driving our practice. Our spiritual practice must be unique and not a standardised prescription. We should be familiar with different types of meditation so we can adopt the form of meditation most appropriate to our current life situation, our spiritual type and our immediate needs.

Meditation should also be integrated skilfully into our lives, within our particular individual, cultural and social spheres. This can be done through five integral life practices, which I discuss in this book. This approach involves understanding seven essential energies, (called the seven rays), seven levels of consciousness, seven ways of meditation and seven spiritual types, all of which can be drawn upon to establish a life of greater freedom.

Yet meditation alone is not enough. Even though meditation is an act of love, some psychic content lies so deeply in the unconscious that it is inaccessible to meditation. We have to burrow into the unconscious to uncover the repressed material that limits and inhibits our free expressions as living Souls. We must enter into a radical process of transformation that corresponds to the level of freedom we wish to achieve. This can be pretty ugly business, but we are not alone: millions of people worldwide participate in the same divine spring cleaning.

We must develop the same ideal of sustainability for our inner world as we do for our outer one, and, so to speak, cleanse the collective atmosphere of psychological smog. Many psychotherapeutic techniques can help with this process, and I will be offering meditation techniques that can supplement the necessary work we do in psychotherapy to explore our "shadow". The most effective approach to meditation is to love whatever arises in consciousness because love is the key agent when we want to transform the parts of ourselves that suffer. This means an impersonal love, an empathetic acceptance that flows from an open heart centre. When we can participate in this flow we become strong enough to embrace whatever comes up, we can rest in peace amid the deepest pain.

In each moment we can make a choice that will define our destiny. This choice determines the type of energy we choose to think, to feel and let our life be governed by. When we say yes to thoughts that enter our awareness, these thoughts become part of who we are. This is quite simple: in each moment we can learn to consciously choose what thoughts will define our state of mind. Accordingly, we can avoid what is harmful and choose what is helpful. It is crucial to choose thoughts from our highest values and not allow ourselves to be governed by habitual negative reactions. With this in mind, it is clear that we must choose freedom each day. Simple enough to say, but quite a challenge to accomplish.

I have written this book from my heart and have consulted very few external sources. You will find a few references to outer authorities, but the only authority I really want to appeal to is the intuition of your heart.

I write from my own experience, but I recognise my debt to prominent writers and teachers such as Alice Bailey, Lucille Cedercrans, Roberto Assagioli, Ken Wilber and Sri Aurobindo. All in some way have been my teachers because they have inspired my being. In one respect I can say that the esoteric heritage is my spiritual tradition. Helena P. Blavatsky, Annie Besant, Alice Bailey and Lucille Cedercrans have had an important, if unacknowledged, influence on Western civilization. They concerned themselves with spiritual evolution well ahead of its current popularity, and are in many ways responsible for the dissemination of Eastern wisdom in the West.

I have also decided to share my beliefs in reincarnation, God, and whatever else I have found to be true and helpful in this work. I don´t believe in a personal God, but in a divine being with a creative spiritual force. In its transcendent nature, this being can be experienced as a limitless, boundless awareness, which is the view of Buddhism. The Buddha did not believe in a God or a Self, even though he never directly opposed them. Equally, this divine being can also be experienced as a creator, a loving and intelligent deity who triggered the Big Bang and got the universe going – this is how more theistic religions see the divine. I believe that both perspectives can be true on different levels of consciousness.

This book is also an introduction to energy psychology, which looks at life and existence in terms of different energies. Meditation is our primary tool in getting to know and master these energies. The esoteric tradition speaks of seven rays and seven rivers of life, and it would take a life-time to understand these energies and their origin. Here I have made a start.

Finally, I must thank the people who directly contributed to my journey – you know who you are. There is no higher inspiration than the example of those who strive, love and suffer through life in order to liberate a compassionate and free heart.

Kenneth Sørensen, Copenhagen, 2017

Chapter I

Who is Meditating and Why Meditate?

"I'd been meditating for five hours, only interrupted by a ten-minute interval. My focus was on observing the content of my consciousness. Nothing specific was supposed to happen, only to be present in the moment. During the first few hours my mind was filled with a cacophony of impressions, but now a sense of clarity emerged and the many impressions no longer disturbed me. Sitting with this clarity, all thoughts, moods and sensations faded into the background, and it became obvious that only consciousness is real. I am consciousness; an awake and aware space of quiet existence.

"Then the question arose: 'What would I be without the content of consciousness?' 'Nothing,' was the prompt reply. I recognised the answer yet ... who was asking? Who was choosing to meditate? Who was maintaining the intention to sit and just observe? Who chose to stop the meditation? Who allowed these questions to arise? There is a will somewhere, who always directs energies and awareness, no matter how passive I am. This reflection made it clear to me that as long as I am in a body and have to function in a manifest universe, I must act. Not to act is also an act. Choosing not to act is an act. There is a will inside us that always upholds an intention and it is always active through our choices. This means choosing presence, a thought, a feeling, a physical act. What is this force?

Who is it? ... This question was too interesting not to pursue, so the focus of my meditation shifted character, something in me made this choice, and my journey changed."

In 2003 a new chapter in my life began. I started my own business offering astrology consultations, coaching and courses in spirituality. I also decided to start my training as a Psychosynthesis psychotherapist due to a deep dissatisfaction with myself and the esoteric milieu I was part of. Despite a regular practice of meditation and contemplation I experienced a lack of ability to walk the talk in respect to the lofty ideas I was preaching. I decided to go back to the drawing board, and to psychotherapy. I had thought I could starve my appetites and problems by not feeding them with attention, but I was wrong.

Roberto Assagioli

During my esoteric studies I had frequently come across the work of Roberto Assagioli (1888-1974), and was well aware of his close association with Alice Bailey. His writings were published in Bailey's magazine *The Beacon*; however, it was his book *The Act of Will* that piqued my interest. The book influenced me greatly, and stands as one of the best presentations of the will I've read. Delving into the studies of Psychosynthesis felt to me like coming home. His psychological model contained all that I needed to reach out to a wider audience with my teaching.

Three perspectives in Psychosynthesis especially resonated. The first is Assagioli's definition of the self as "a centre of pure self-awareness and will"; next was his idea about subpersonalities; and, lastly, his extensive exploration of the act of will. I was already familiar with the experience of being the observer of my inner world, and here was a psychological model that greatly emphasised this aspect of meditation.

Assagioli argues that our true identity is pure self-awareness and will. Decades before Eckhart Tolle was speaking of the "Power of Now", Assagioli was pioneering a psychology that had a vision of the Self as pure consciousness. The global mindfulness movement we see today has the aim of awakening meditators to themselves as consciousness itself. This awakening will change the world; it will liberate the individual from egocentric attachments and prepare her for the experience of unity and oneness. Through the individual, the World Soul is awakening to itself as consciousness. This awakening has many stages, which I explore in this book. Roberto Assagioli also provides us with techniques that help greatly with this process.

According to Assagioli we must integrate and harmonise our entire personality around the self. It was a revelation for me to see how the Eastern concept of the Self could be applied within psychotherapy practice with such skill and wisdom. I was impressed with Assagioli's self-identification exercise: "We are not our thoughts, emotions or body, but the observing and acting witness behind these instruments of action." This is pure yoga, and I was not surprised to discover that Assagioli wrote the foreword to the Italian edition of Alice Bailey's commentary on Patanjali's Yoga Sutras. It also changed my meditation practice. Whereas I had previously focused on visualisation and the contemplation of seed thoughts, I was now deeply motivated to observe consciousness itself.

In meditation I entered a place of total silence, wakefulness and peace. The sense of I-ness felt uniquely authentic. My journey with meditation changed and a completely new world opened up.

When we start experiencing the transcendent nature of our being, we need a language and certain perspectives in order to grasp its meaning. This is particularly relevant to the question of identity regarding who we are in essence. Without a good map, we can easily become lost in our inner world. Meditation is in essence an inquiry into our true identity, and a practice that can help us to manifest that identity.

I would like to describe some key perspectives that grew out of my personal experience, and the sources that helped to inspire these perspectives. Let's start with three key questions:

- Who meditates?

- Why do we meditate?

- What is spirituality?

These questions are profoundly existential in nature and cannot be easily answered. I will give a short introduction to each question in this chapter, and continue with the inquiry in subsequent chapters.

Who meditates?
Why do we meditate?
What is spirituality?

What is Meditation?

Let me begin by proposing a definition of meditation:

To be awake and present in the here and now
To focus our mind on an object

These definitions relate to two different types of meditation, both of which can create many positive changes in our character and, consequently, in our environment. The effects of meditation are physical and psychological, as well as spiritual.

Meditation can be of great benefit to the physical body, as documented in recent research, particularly regarding mindfulness. Meditation aids the development of our personality by enabling new psychological qualities such as courage, love and endurance to emerge. Also, meditation can have a spiritualising effect by expanding our consciousness from the individual to the universal, which can be experienced as unconditional love and a sense of communion with all of nature and humanity. Such experiences can offer deep insights into the mysteries of life, as well as providing artistic, scientific and ethical inspirations; the various effects depend on the focus of the meditation. While in a state of expanded awareness, we can gain insights into the meaning and purpose of our lives.

The two different types of meditation represent an active and a passive approach, and working with these we can further identify seven ways of meditation and seven paths of Self-realisation. The foundation for this philosophy is the teaching of the seven rays. According to discoveries within quantum physics, everything is energy – but some esoteric spiritual traditions argue that this energy can be divided into seven different "colours" or frequencies. The main objective of this book is to explore the seven rays and how to work with them.

In *passive meditation* we focus on the source of consciousness itself. This is often called awareness-based meditation or mindfulness. Practising this type of meditation we can experience consciousness without form, and pure awareness of our identity without thought, emotions or sensations. The practice is about letting go of all content to observe the source of consciousness itself. This can give us a sense of inner peace, a detached freedom, and clarity. The practice expands our consciousness from a separate ego identity to a wider universal presence. During these "peak experiences", our personal identity stays in the background and a timeless Now enters the mind. The basic version of this practice involves the meditator observing the breath, thoughts and sensations with a neutral attitude in order to relax the body, still the mind and reach a state of inner peace.

In active meditation we focus on creating specific changes in the personality as part of a process of purification. This practice will eventually enable the expression of Soul consciousness through the refined personality. In this way, the good, the true and the beautiful already inherent in the Soul will manifest in creative ways. This form of meditation is orientated towards the *manifestation of our Soul in action.*

Another important thing to consider in respect to meditation is the psychological typology of the individual. People are different in their psychological make-up. This variety demands that a whole spectrum of meditation techniques are required to suit the particular spiritual type of the meditator. Such a holistic approach to meditation is integral: it takes into account all individual, cultural and social dimensions of life, and includes all levels of an individual from body, mind to Soul and Spirit. To illuminate this integral perspective is one of the main objectives of this book.

Meditation is also energy work. Meditation can foster an ability to master the energies that make up who we are. Energy work is a science developed by various yogic traditions over the centuries. Everything is energy, and when we realise we live in a cosmic sea of energies we better understand that spiritual realisation is a tremendous task. We live, move and have our being within this cosmic sea, and it is only through the exploration and manifestation of this sea that we can discover our inner greatness. This perspective lies at the heart of the new energy psychology, which is based on the philosophy of the seven rays or the seven rivers of life. We can master the seven rays when we understand their qualities, and integral meditation can help in this task.

In essence integral meditation concerns:

- The seven rivers of life and their ray qualities.

- The seven ways of meditation and their paths to freedom.

- The seven levels of consciousness, from body, through mind, to Soul and Spirit.

- Five integral life practices.

The fruit of this approach emerges in the sphere of "I", "We" and "It", ie in the domains of the individual, the cultural and the physical world we inhabit.

In the following chapters, I will offer an overview of the seven energies, ways and levels. I will introduce the reader to the new energy psychology and show how it can serve as a practical guide to meditation and life.

Today, meditation is often taught with a focus on its benefits to our physical and mental health, but this comprises only the basement of an individual's "inner house", and meditation can benefit the entire house, which leads us to the next of our questions.

Who Meditates?

This is the ultimate question we can ask, and it is the aim of meditation to answer it. It is a question that points directly to the Self and our experience of being in a continual process of development. I will offer a couple of perspectives here but, from an existential point of view, it is important to note that the answer cannot be known intellectually, only experienced.

When we start to meditate, we will typically be confused because we have not yet developed a centre from which to facilitate meditation. Our focus in life is so much on the external world that a conscious exploration of our inner world is an unusual and extremely difficult task to undertake. Sensations in the body, psychological states and outside disturbances occupy our consciousness, and reaching inner clarity sometimes feels like an impossible task. Even when we are able to observe the content of our consciousness, it is difficult to find meaning amid the continuous flow of thoughts and sensations that grab our attention. At this stage, we have yet to learn how to discriminate between pure consciousness and the content we project onto the inner screen of our mind.

It is not easy to grasp the full picture and nature of our identity. Let us therefore enter the laboratory of consciousness and investigate some of the many functions and parts of consciousness that are active when we have a spiritual experience.

Consciousness and Awareness

Let's use the movie theatre as a metaphor: When we experience the content of our consciousness, we encounter it as an inner movie, or what is called the stream of consciousness. We get caught up in identifying who we are with this stream of voices, feelings, images and sensations while failing to realise that who we are is actually the light that projects the images onto the screen. This light is consciousness itself, or what Assagioli calls the centre of pure self-awareness. It is the wakefulness and awareness of the individual, the inner space where all objects of consciousness become visible.

It is self-evident that something inside us is self-aware. This is the subject, the sense of I-am-ness, the experience of being alive and conscious. We call this centre of consciousness the self, and its primary function is to be self-aware.

We cannot observe consciousness itself because the eye cannot observe itself, but it is something we can become aware of, become present in and awake to. Consciousness itself is neutral, like white light, and always carries the quality of purity. Many Eastern traditions state that from an existential point of view this light is our identity: we will always be this silent, never changing and static reality – it will always be the same, an eternal and imperishable ground of conscious being. The light is likened to a silent wakefulness out of which different states of consciousness arise.

When we learn to silence the mind by observing and letting go of its content we become aware of consciousness itself, however limited at first. We will still feel a sense of being a separate individual. This sense of separateness trick us into believing that our individual consciousness is unique and special, but at a later stage of the meditation process we realise that there's no difference between the consciousness of one individual and another – although *there is a big difference in respect to the movies each of us plays inside our heads.* To reiterate, the point here is that the movie is not who we are, it's just a temporary flow of images that we play in our inner movie theatre. This movie is important because it tells the story of our life – and understanding the nature of this movie is an initial step to further development. Our aim is to experience the fundamental and universal identity that is omnipresent conscious-

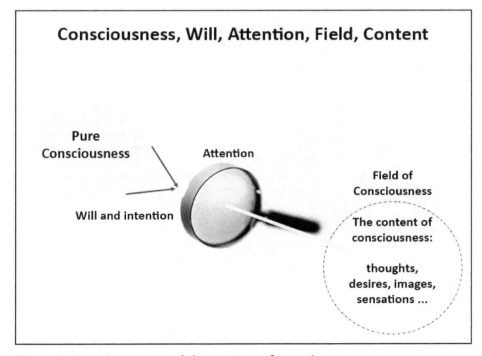

Consciousness, Will, Attention, Field, Content

Pure Consciousness

Attention

Will and intention

Field of Consciousness

The content of consciousness:

thoughts, desires, images, sensations ...

Figure 1: Consciousness and the content of consciousness.

"Our character is the effect of all the conscious and unconscious choices we have made through life"

ness – the white light that is the source of all the colours in our individual movies. We are Universal Presence having an individual experience. We are not our body, emotions or thoughts, but a centre of pure self-awareness experiencing these states. This is a radical statement that can leave people feeling uneasy because it begs the question: Who am I as an individual if I am only this static neutral awareness? I will attempt to answer this question later in this book.

The diagram above (Figure 1) illustrates some of the factors that come into play in everyday experiencing.

Consciousness is pure being, always present and aware in the here and now. It is the observer, the inner light, the Soul and the Universal Self. Whatever name we use depends on the particular level of consciousness we are describing.

Will is related to the decision-making faculty in the individual. Will gives intentionality, dynamism, direction and evolution. It is through the faculty of will that we can decide where to put our attention. Will functions primarily through the mind in relation to the personality, but it is not the mind.

Attention is the mind's eye, a tool for the conscious and acting self which is able to focus awareness onto a single object, enabling the mind to reflect upon and investigate the object.

The field of consciousness is the space of awareness in which the content of consciousness emerges. This field is closely related to the brain's physical ability to reflect its content onto an inner screen.

The content of consciousness consists of our many intuitions, thoughts, emotions, images, sensations, etc. This content is created by the activities of the observer, but also contains information and sensations from the collective unconscious. I will expand on this point later.

Consciousness is like an ocean: when we fill a cup with water from the ocean, the water in the cup is separate from the ocean but retains the same inherent qualities. Likewise, during meditation, we observe our own individual consciousness through the mind's eye – but this consciousness is just a drop from the sea of universal consciousness. This limitation is not a bad thing, it is only the mind's way of contracting around a core of consciousness which enables us to develop an individual identity and ego. We need this ego so we can assert our will through our actions in the world. This separation of consciousness – or ego contraction – serves us up to a point in our early development, but later in our spiritual journey it becomes the major obstacle for spiritual growth.

By spirituality I mean the ability and process by which we can each expand our consciousness from individuality to universality, moving from egocentric to ethnocentric to world-centric to cosmo-centric awareness. This process involves the gradual expansion of our identity and what we consider to be "I". At each level of development, we can experience the centre of pure consciousness in a more or less contracted way. Awareness Meditation, or mindfulness, facilitates this process. We are here referring to mindfulness practices as found in Buddhism, and not the practice of physical relaxation often promoted by Western mindfulness instructors. (I will describe this meditation practice in greater depth in Chapter 5.)

When we expand our awareness, we discover the ocean of consciousness. We let go of the little cup and become part of the Eternal Now, an ocean of pure consciousness that is also "I". When connected with universal presence and non-dual awareness, everything is "I", but it is a cosmic "I". This realisation is essential to the experience of oneness.

So who meditates? For now the answer is: The self as a centre of pure self-awareness.

And who am I? The answer is still: A centre of pure self-awareness.

The Will is the Freedom to Choose Our Individual Identity

The centre of pure consciousness can never be the whole story of our identity. If that was the case we would all be the same. Even the enlightened and Self-realised, such as a Buddha, a Jesus or a Krishna, express different qualities. Consciousness *manifests* in many different ways.

The awareness of pure consciousness is an existential experience for those who practice advanced awareness-based meditation, it is a state in which we are able to rest in total silence and peace. There is only pure consciousness. Not a thought crosses the horizon of mind. There is only pure, wide, empty consciousness. But the moment we decide to act and step out of the meditation, we become differentiated. When we manifest our consciousness it becomes limited – we always limit the limitless in the container of our personality. Using our will we decide to concentrate and focus our available energy in a certain direction. In the moment we think, feel or sense anything, we make a decision, and this is a limitation. We could have decided to think, feel, sense and do something very different. Every choice has a consequence; it brings energies into play and activates the law of cause and effect. But in the act of choosing lies our freedom; we can choose how we want to manifest at any given moment.

It also becomes obvious how limited and restricted we are. If we could choose to express perfect love and wisdom in any situation, we would surely do so, but we do not because we are restricted by our psychological functions. The mind, our feelings and the body are the fundamental organs of action, and they limit the full expression of our potential.

Another definition of spirituality is *the ability to express universal consciousness and all its manifestations of abundant love, wisdom and power in action.* In other words, spirituality involves the will.

The will, acting through the choices we make, is critically involved whenever we wish to show our identity in action. We act all the time, and will continue to do so as long as we are incarnated in a physical body. We are here on earth because we bring something to life through our presence and our actions. This *something* is seen in the different energies, coloured by particular qualities, which show the world who we are. These qualities determine the different ways in which life manifests itself, be it as a mineral, plant, animal or human being. There are never two identical manifestations. Each snowflake is uniquely different, and the same applies to humans.

The will is directly connected to our identity because it is an inner force, a-will-to-be-a-unique-self. When I look into the phenomenon of will, I am always surprised by its subtlety. It is a force, an intention, a purpose with a direction. The will is alive, it is a living energy, it will manifest, and it will always create a more authentic life expression. The will is in essence the will-to-be-who-you-are, and it continues to push us further and further into the greatness of what we may become. If consciousness is pure potential, the will is the urge to realise that potential in action. If consciousness is universal oneness, will is the urge to express that oneness in a unique way. When we connect with this spiritual life force, it's obvious that it contains preferences because there are some choices and directions that are more *meaningful* than others. This evolutionary life force pushes us forward from within and shows us what our true identity can be in action.

When this inner call is recognised – the-will-to-be-self – our identification with the personal will, which is usually focused on personal matters, loosens. We start to listen to the intention of the Soul, and become connected to its transpersonal will. When we realise what is motivating us our unconscious and subconscious values and needs are revealed. When we become sufficiently aware, we can use our will to choose what we want to identify with, and so identity becomes a choice. It is in the light of this perspective that Assagioli's definition holds true: "We are a centre of pure self-awareness and will." Our character is the effect of all the conscious and unconscious choices we make in life.

We now can see how *identification* is deeply related to the will – our identity is our sense of I-am-ness and identification is our ability to recognise and choose what we wish to identify with. Whenever we say "I Am" we express a choice of identification, and this will surely have consequences because it brings energies into action. Assagioli referred to the will as the primary function of the self, and even argued that "we are a will". The will is first and foremost an experience we need to explore in consciousness as a dynamic energy separate from the mind. We use the mind to reflect on different choices, but the experience of purpose, the will-to-be, is not mental. It is a great adventure to contemplate the nature of the will in meditation and to explore the question: "What force is behind our need for an authentic life expression?" This contemplation can bring us into the very heart of our existence and reveal our identity as a divine spark of fire.

The will is present at every level of consciousness. Even in a state of the most sublime transcendent freedom, the *intention* of the meditator to stay in this silent presence is residing in the background. Consciousness and will are inseparable.

We will discuss the nature of the will later, but now we will focus on the question of who is meditating? The answer as we shall see is "a centre of pure self-awareness and will".

The Stage Selves:
The Many Faces of the Personality

It is obvious that our identifications and self-images change during our life span, from childhood until our last days. Our *manifested* identity is something that changes too, and develops according to the choices we make in life. Early in life we copy the people around us, and don't make any real conscious decisions about our identity. From this point of view, the faculty of the will is something that develops as we are able to reflect with self-awareness, and this happens when we start using the mind's capacity for reasoning. The self-images and identities we create before we learn to use the mind make up a role we play, a role-self based on expectations we have internalised from our social environment and our need for survival, security and safety.

Developmental theories based on integral philosophy and the psychology of Psychosynthesis define a set of stages through which we progress as part of the self's overall development. Drawing upon these theories, I have devised a model of development comprising of seven stages or phases, whereby a different type of awareness is created at each stage (see Table 1).

Table 1: The seven stages of development.

	Stage of Development	Type of Awareness that Emerges
1	Development of the body self	Body-awareness (instinctual-physical)
2	Development of the feeling self	Sensitive-awareness (emotional)
3	Development of the mental self	Self-awareness (rational-mental)
4	Development of the integrated self (personality)	Holistic-awareness (abstract mind-Soul)
5	Development of the holistic self (Soul)	Group-awareness (intuitive-Soul)
6	Development of the sacrificial self (Soul)	Sacrificial-awareness (will-Soul)
7	Development of the spiritual Self (Spirit)	Unity-awareness (Spirit)

Essentially, these developmental stages represent the story of the self's journey from symbiotic union with the mother to profound oneness with Spirit. I will discuss this more in the next chapter.

At each stage of development, the self develops a new level of awareness, a new self-image and new identifications. Using the term stage-self, it can be seen that at each successful stage of development, a stage-self emerges that embodies the values, needs and drives relevant for that specific stage, with an accompanying self-image that gives the self a centre of gravity and a sense of continuity and stability.

Development through the seven stages is not a rigid sequential stage model. Rather, it is more a case of two steps forward, one step back, with identifications and attachments made at earlier stages needing to be re-aligned whenever a higher level of awareness and identification emerges.

This brief account of the developmental line of the self is only a part of the total picture. Assagioli has defined seven psychological functions through which the self expresses self-awareness, with each psychological function having its own developmental line. I have modified Assagioli's model slightly; the seven functions in my developmental model are will, feeling, thought, imagination, logic, passion, and action (which includes the body and its sensations).

The self-line is my term for the development of the point of pure self-awareness: how much we are aware of at a particular stage. This development is more or less concurrent with the other seven lines, with each line corresponding to a different psychological function. Intuition is also a psychological function, but a transpersonal one, which comes into play with six other transpersonal functions. These transpersonal functions are equivalent to the seven psychological functions, but manifest at a higher level. When the transpersonal functions become evident in an individual, we can say that the Soul is making its influence felt.

The personal will is for many people only a potential that remains hidden behind automatic and unconscious behavioural patterns developed during the early developmental stages. During these early stages we rely on the external world for confirmation and recognition, but we are not yet capable of making conscious decisions, therefore we rely on automatic, we might say genetic or pre-programmed, human responses. A major step forward in our development happens when we awaken to the idea that we can live an individual life based on our own sovereign decisions. This realisation marks a transition from an unconscious safety-orientated way of being to a self-aware and individualistic way of being. We become self-directed and free to choose our own lifestyle. We realise we can create our own destiny and experience the consequences of our choices. This is an important step towards the realisation of Soul-consciousness, which in my terminology involves a manifestation of holistic and altruistic group consciousness.

The discovery of the will enables the individual to integrate their personality around meaningful, self-defined goals. Accordingly, we can align our resources, needs, values and psychological functions around a planned life expression, around what we might call a vision of a good personal life. We step into character and become robust, dependable and recognisable as individuals. What we witness here is how the will is expressed through the mental and rational level – so let's see how the expression of will changes according to the level of development.

1. *The unconscious stage* is defined by a safety-orientated lifestyle. There is no individual will at this stage, no real self-awareness, so the individual is attached to living out whatever is expected of them.

2. *The rational stage* marks the first stage of the conscious will. We are able to choose new ways of being in the world based on self-reliant evaluations of our identity, needs and desires. At this stage the individual does not yet have any real power in the world, defined as the ability to make their influence known.

3. *The integrated stage* is a powerful stage in the growth of the personal self, called self-actualisation by Abraham Maslow and personal psychosynthesis by Assagioli. The individual succeeds in realising ambitions and meeting needs for individual self-expression. The will comes through as the will-to-power, and the individual naturally becomes a centre of influence. Our focus is on developing all our creative talents, and we begin to exhibit a high level of individual freedom and creative self-expression.

4. *The awakening of the Soul* generates an existential crisis. Our awareness becomes increasingly humanistic and holistic. Instead of being at the centre of the world, we start to identify with the needs of the world. This leads to a battle between the personal will with its ambitions, and the transpersonal will with its altruistic goals. We are faced with an ongoing choice between the values of the personality and those of the Soul. When the shift is complete the individual will start to make their influence known as a potent force for good in the world.

5. *The enlightenment of the personality by the Soul* is a long ongoing process of purification of the personality which shows itself in the emerging ability to express the Soul's goodness, truth and beauty. The transpersonal gives

us meaning and purpose. We let go of the smaller joys of the personality in exchange for the deep joy of bringing goodness into the world. I am not suggesting an ascetic way of life because all the smaller joys of the personality can be enjoyed in a balanced way, but the importance of these joys diminishes as we experience the flow of creativity, communion with other people, and a deep connectedness with the world. At this stage the power of the will expresses itself in individuals who are able to use their skills and talents within the spheres of politics, culture, psychology, arts, religion, science and business.

The will can reach even higher stages of development but, for now, I offer only the above description of stages to help explain the development of our psychological functions. Knowledge of the developmental stages and lines is helpful when we want to evaluate our progress. We expand our self-awareness and self-image through each of the developmental lines, all of which are connected and therefore influence each other.

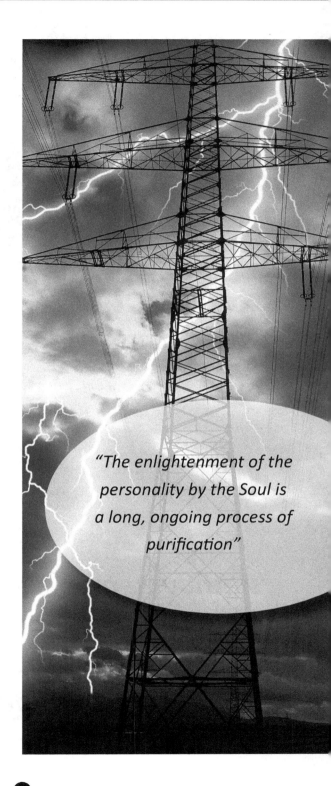

"The enlightenment of the personality by the Soul is a long, ongoing process of purification"

31

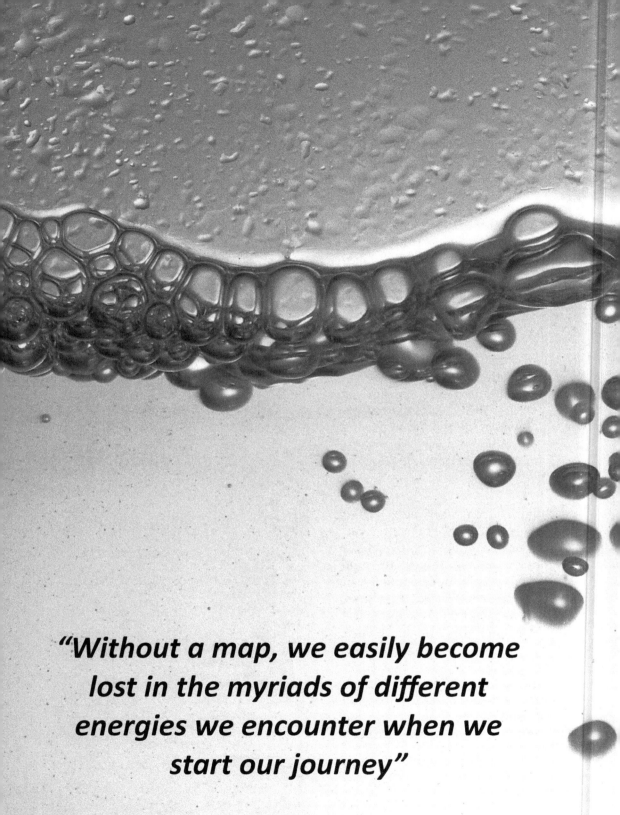

"Without a map, we easily become lost in the myriads of different energies we encounter when we start our journey"

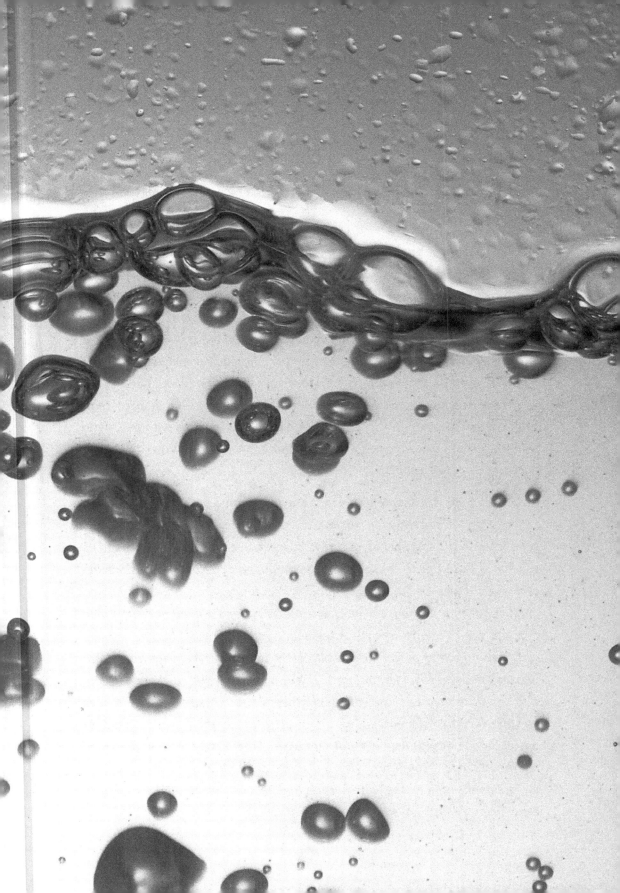

Chapter 2

Your Essence and Your Inner House

We had been meditating for an hour, sitting face to face in a lotus position on the floor. This was how we connected at the start of our friendship. The silence was intense that day, but there was no particular content in the field of consciousness. Just this inner space of being and a potent silence. Afterward we shared whatever impressions and insights had come up, trying to turn them into a deeper understanding. I remember this particular day vividly; it was at a time in my life when I was deeply engaged in reflecting on the difference between the individual Soul and the World Soul. It struck me as paradoxical that, from one perspective we can experience a profound oneness with the World Soul, the Soul of humanity, and yet from another we have our own individual purposes and responsibilities.

An intuition of clarity came to me that day that I could not fully grasp. When I started to reflect on my impressions an inner space opened up. The energy condensed into a soft field of love, it was like an ocean in its wideness and its substance was utter truth. There's no other way to describe it: it was a being and I knew it was the Soul of humanity. An immediate sense of identity left me in no doubt that this was my utter essence. My friend agreed and confirmed that this ocean of love was the essence of humanity itself. I had never been so close to another person without it being "personal". We were free of our personalities, yet strangely intimate. It was a love without need of confirmation or attachment because it had all it needed to be self-fulfilled. The love was the very air we breathed; we were WITHIN love, there was no need for any exchange. It was love without an object. "There are points of fire," said my friend. "Yes," I confirmed, "it's a gigantic network of living points of fire. We are points of fire!" We were particle and field in love, an amazing thing to experience. "We all have a cosmic address, where we belong," I said. In that

"There are points of fire," ...

"YES" I confirmed, "it is a gigantic

network of living points of fire."

very moment I recollected Ken Wilber's remarks about our having a unique
perspective in time and space according to our level of consciousness and our
individual journey.

It was wondrous to occupy this field of love and explore the particle/field nature of our being. It was like a quantum consciousness let loose in a laboratory
of the Soul. When we became particles, the energy condensed into a tight

nucleus, intense, potent, alive and full of will. The field remained in the background, but the creative impulse was very much in the foreground. Through this point of fire, the very meaning of my life emerged. Despite the profound love that merged everything into a whole, I was still an "I". I knew I was not another being; yet there was no sense of separation. My identity was no longer limited to my personal story; it was an impersonal experience beyond time and circumstances. It was pure identity without the masks personality wears. In this "I-am-ness" there was intention, power and a will to be. We understood then the unique role we all play in the cosmic drama performed in each moment.

I have spent hours in painful meditation, doing little else than observing the pain, accepting it, and surrendering. When we accept pain without identifying with it magic can happen. The pain does not necessary lessen, but a space around it expands and is filled with the love and gentleness that can heal the wound causing the pain. Intense pain can overwhelm and blind us; it's like being surrounded by a thick layer of fog, we feel ourselves pulled into the shadows of the past. Yet if our will-to-be is strong enough, it pushes us out of our comfort zones so we can realise new potentials, and here pain is inevitable. It is part of our evolution. Knowing this comforts the personality who brings new light into the world.

A psychological map is useful when we go through painful transformations. It gives us perspective and illuminates what would otherwise be dark. We can say that it shows the sun that stands behind our fog of miseries.

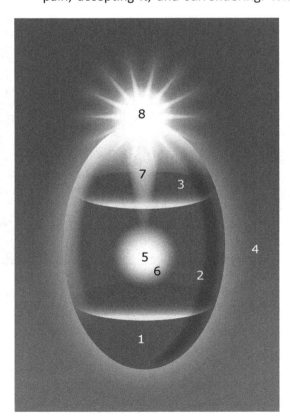

Figure 2: Roberto Assagioli's egg diagram.

Let me introduce a map[1] which has helped me immensely on my own journey, especially with the many energies that arise in meditation. We need to discriminate between these different energies so that we can master them. The map I am speaking of is Roberto Assagioli's egg diagram (Figure 2), which illustrates the relationship between the observer, the will and the different psychological processes. Assagioli had deep insight into Eastern wisdom traditions and attained a high level of spiritual development himself. He wrote out of experience, not only from theory. The diagram presents the relationships between consciousness *in-itself* and its *contents*. Consciousness is light and illuminates everything in the inner world; through this we become aware of the contents of our inner world. The content consists of thoughts, images, sensations, desires and intuitions

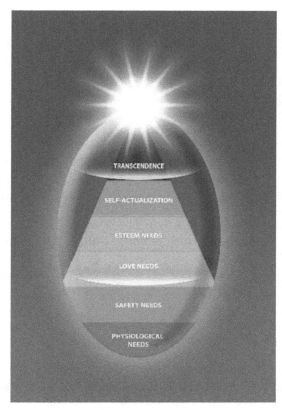

Figure 3: 'Assagioli's egg diagram incorporating Maslow's hierarchy of needs.

– different types of energies and habits that constitute our character. Through meditation we work with these energies as a *creative observer*. Everything is energy and the egg diagram presents a multidimensional model of the human psyche depicting different levels of consciousness.

These levels of consciousness resemble the *Great Chain of Being* of traditional philosophy. In Assagioli's model they represent the physical, emotional, mental, intuitive and transcendent levels of consciousness. Each level contains different energies and forms, which we experience as thinking, feeling, acting or intuition. (This model represents only a part of the psyche; much else resides out of sight, as I will touch on later[2].)

Assagioli divided his egg diagram in four interconnected levels. We are aware of them according to our level of self-awareness and where our attention is at any moment.

1 My Masters thesis on Integral Psychosynthesis contains all the relevant source notes in support of this presentation and is available at http://www.integralworld.net/sorensen1.html. See also my book The Soul of Psychosynthesis – The Seven Core Concepts, 2016.

2 Let me recommend Ken Wilber's books Transformations of Consciousness, Integral Psychology and Integral Spirituality for a further study in developmental psychology and spirituality.

The Basic Unconscious

The bottom section of the egg diagram (1) is called *the lower unconscious*. There are some concerns about using the term "lower", so I've come to use "basic". Our fundamental psychological processes are located here. According to Abraham Maslow's "hierarchy of needs" (see Figure 3), here we are concerned with our survival, security and safety. When we are hungry or afraid, the basic unconscious is active. Here we find the roots of many traumas from our childhood or even past lives. They are re-activated by different circumstances and emerge as fears, inhibitions, phobias, compulsive desires and attachments. The reactions are very often difficult to understand from a rational point of view because their very nature is pre-rational.

The energies here are *egocentric* and *ethnocentric*. They represent desires, fantasies, and memories from birth to around the age of three; some memories can reach back to past lives. When the basic unconscious is healthy, we feel safe and have a good sense of self; we are playful and open, able to be in the world and enjoy sensual pleasures.

The Middle Unconscious

The middle section of the egg diagram represents the middle unconscious (2). The need for intimacy, self-esteem and recognition is located here. Here too we find the resources and qualities necessary for a creative personality, for self-actualisation and an independent life.

Here too are the desires, dreams and frustrations surrounding our ambitions, our love life and social world. Our struggle to develop the skills necessary to live a good and successful life takes place here.

This region relates to our self-image, our theories and worldviews. It is here that we form our roles in work, the family and our social circles, as well as our political and philosophical opinions. Mature emotional energies, expressed as care for others and the need for relationships based on shared values and interests, are also located here.

Personal traumas and difficulties experienced throughout our early years also affect this region, as do unresolved conflicts in the basic unconscious.

Here we try to reach a compromise between the needs of the outer world and those of the inner. We do this by balancing our conflicting energies through dialogue and reflections. The middle unconscious is accessible to the conscious mind, although many creative processes take place below the threshold of awareness.

The upper part of the middle unconscious holds holistic energies, and informs our ability to think abstractly and create visions of what we could be and offer to the world. We can call this the integral area because here we integrate different skills, talents and qualities. Through it we organise our thoughts, focus our energies, think holistically and handle complexities, displaying solid leadership skills. These are not necessarily spiritual qualities; we are still motivated by a need for self-expression. The energies are individualistic and ethnocentric. As with the basic unconscious, when the middle unconscious is healthy it allows us to be more or less functional human beings who are able to engage in life and relationships.

The Higher Unconscious or Superconscious

Next we have the *superconscious* or *higher unconscious* (3) where we find the higher needs, talents and qualities of the Soul, which is sometimes called the transpersonal Self. The content of the higher unconscious is of an altruistic, transpersonal nature, related to that which is universal; this is what Maslow is referring to when he speaks of the need for self-transcendence.

Transpersonal energies expand our awareness from the individual to the universal, and can often bring about supernatural experiences. One of my clients experienced the physical world dissolving into energies of love. She was floating in thin air, completely at peace. It lasted ten minutes and entirely changed her outlook on life. The experience I mentioned at the start of this chapter is a good example of contact with the superconscious. These energies connect us with a larger whole with which we feel at one. This can mean a sense of communion with humanity, nature or the cosmos.

Superconscious energies bring great insights to science, art or ethics. Our ideas about human rights and welfare also arise from these energies. And it is in the superconscious that we can experience a kind of *group consciousness,* or what we can call a "world-centric awareness". We experience the world as a whole and understand the meaning of true brotherhood and sisterhood. We can accept the unacceptable and forgive the unforgivable. From here too emerge new creative forms.

A glimpse of the good, the true and the beautiful radiating from this realm of consciousness can change our life forever.

The Collective Unconscious

Outside the egg (4) we find the collective unconscious; it too reaches from a basic unconscious to a superconscious. This is the storehouse of humanity's past, captured in myths, images and memories. These collective visions enter our personal sphere through dreams and imaginations, and they permeate our cultural world.

The collective unconscious connects us to our surroundings. When we practice Awareness Meditation we see that what we thought were our personal feelings of love, fear, excitement or depression may actually be other people's feelings floating in a shared psychological world. We discover the "gates" where collective energies and corresponding subpersonalities (or archetypes) enter our personal world. We recognise that we *receive* and *project* energies whenever we direct our mind at an internal or external object (Figures 4+5).

A continuous exchange takes place between these four levels of consciousness. That is why the egg diagram is depicted as transparent.

It is also important to note that, at each level, material is unconscious to different degrees. For example, at each level there is material that is *preconscious*, meaning the material lies just below or above the threshold of awareness. As with a hard disk, the data stored here can be accessed anytime; the information lies ready to hand for whenever it is needed.

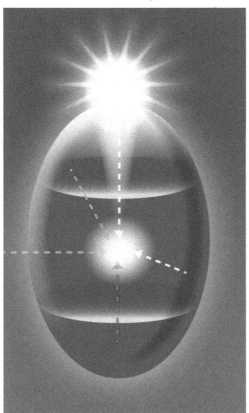

Then there is material that is unconscious because it may simply have been forgotten, rather than actively repressed.

And then, at each level, we find material that is deeply and truly unconscious. This might include material that we have not been able to contain or integrate and so it became repressed, which is often the case with material relating to intimacy, sex, aggression, power, love or even mystical experiences. The deep or higher unconscious also contains material that has never reached consciousness, such as the energies of the superconscious, with which we perhaps rarely make contact.

All of this unconscious material exists as creative potential that awaits realisation as part of our future self. We can also make the observation

Figure 4: Assagioli's egg diagram and inflowing energies.

that the basic unconscious relates to the past, the middle unconscious to the present, and the superconscious to the future.

The Personal Self – a Centre of Pure Consciousness and Will

The bright centre of the egg (5) represents the personal self, which we can call "the observer". This is the conscious subject at the centre of the personality, our source of self-awareness. Assagioli defines this as a centre of pure self-awareness and will. This centre radiates out into a shining sphere, which is the observer's field of consciousness. Through this the energies of the unconscious enter our awareness, and here we think, feel and imagine. Another input into the perso- nal self is intuition, coming from the trans- personal Self. The personal self interprets all of these energies, processing them through the seven psycho- logical functions. It is then

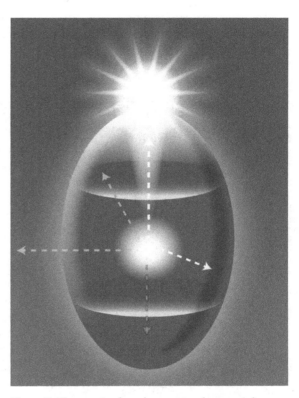

Figure 5: Diagram to show how we project energies whenever we direct our mind at an external object.

through acts of will that we decide what to *do* with this content and how to act on it. Although we are self-conscious, many of us are not self-aware. We identify with the *content* of consciousness – with *what* we think, feel or imagine – rather than with the *who* that is thinking, feeling or imagining (ie the observer). Freedom arises when we can distinguish between the observer and the observed. Such self-awareness is the aim of Awareness Meditation.

Yet the observer and the observed are linked. I am not *separate* from the content of my consciousness, yet I am *different* from it. To realise this difference is the first step in meditation. Achieving this, we can then establish a centre that is aware of the energies. Assagioli believed that *what we identify with controls us, what we disidentify from, we can master*. Dis-identifying helps us to step back and observe what is influencing us. When we feel a strong emotion, we say "I am angry" or "I am sad", and so identify with it. If we say instead "a wave of anger came over me", we are distinguishing between the anger and ourselves. From this vantage point, we can reflect upon, own and take responsibility for the feeling without being overly identified with it.

The personal self is a point of presence and clarity: when we know what we possess, and can apply ourselves creatively to how we live our lives, we become grounded and powerful.

The Subpersonalities: Our Different Inner Parts

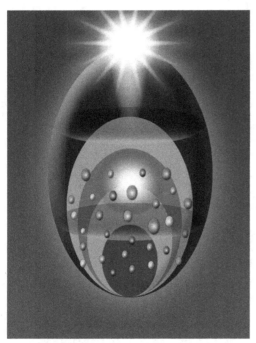

Figure 6: Subpersonalities located in the basic and middle unconscious.

Subpersonalities are found in the basic and middle unconscious (Figure 6). They are a key theme in Psychosynthesis and, as I came to realise, also in meditation. Anyone who meditates discovers the many "voices" within, our inner commentators. They appear, lurking behind undifferentiated energies of fear, anger, harmony, trust, and so on. Assagioli said our personality can be compared to an apartment building with many floors and rooms. On each floor are residents with different needs and desires. These are often expressed in our automatic responses to people and circumstances. Driven by repressed needs, emotions and thoughts, our subpersonalities inform our desires and fears, our likes and dislikes. Our inner residents do not get along; our inner child, teenager, critic and their neighbours are often in conflict.

The building therefore needs a manager, someone to harmonise and integrate the many subpersonalities around common goals and values. This is precisely the function of the personal self. The self is the proprietor of our inner house. He makes the rules and ensures that everyone follows them and co-operates. Our job is to become the master of our own inner house, through the integration of the personality – a process that Assagioli calls "personal psychosynthesis". Knowledge of the subpersonalities, together with the good, strong and skilful will, helps to achieve integration within the basic and middle unconscious parts of our self.

I vividly remember my first visualisation exercise as part of my Psychosynthesis training. It was a guided meditation which invited me to visit the basement of my inner house, where I immediately encountered a catholic priest. He had arranged for himself a cosy apartment full of books. He had retreated from the world and broken all connections to it; he was fulfilled with his books and his prayers. An atmosphere of loneliness and asceticism surrounded him.

I started a dialogue with this priest, and he told me he had created this retreat as a response to disappointment in his love life. The cosy retreat was his defence against pain and sorrows in his past. At one point during the visualisation, we were asked to find a hidden box with valuable content. When the priest opened the box, he discovered unopened letters from friends all over the world who missed him. A wave of love and appreciation hit him like a wall, and I burst into tears as the pain of isolation was released.

This insight opened a door into this aspect of my inner world, and the light of hope began to shine in my subconscious. The experience was like a dream marking the beginning of a long journey. In the years ahead, isolation, loneliness, retreat, despair and abdication were the very themes I would work with in psychotherapy. The box of unopened letters seemed to symbolise love and friendly relationships lying ahead.

A subpersonality is a living part of us, a truly *living being*. Each subpersonality has its own awareness, emotions and desires, which are expressed through actions. And as with other conscious beings, we can speak and collaborate with our subpersonalities.

They originate in the identifications we make throughout our lives, typically in connection with past or present social or familial roles. They appear when we adopt new roles in life, such as when we become parents or begin a new job. They relate to the developmental stages we pass through from infanthood to adulthood; they arise out of our identification as a child, father, mother, boss, lover. They can develop whenever we identify with a role we adopt, such as the clown, the sceptic, the romantic, and so on. For example, if we are bullied at school we can create a self-image of ourselves as a victim, and this becomes one of our subpersonalities. Each subpersonality is a character, a stable behavioural pattern, a habitual way of being.

Subpersonalities are trapped in the story relating to their role, stuck in the time the story and role were created. Through them our past lives on in the present.

We can become aware of our subpersonalities through visualisation exercises and through the recollection of our internalised images of who we are.

Psychosynthesis aims to deliberately develop our subpersonalities and harness their energies in positive ways. For example, new experiences can change or even dissolve the power of a subpersonality. I can remember when I first became a father. This was, of course, a new role to me, and I wanted to fulfil it based on my own values, and not those of my background. I asked myself: What is a father? It was not easy to see beyond the cultural expectations of fatherhood or beyond my experiences of my own father. Only after several years of working on my father subpersonality did I feel I was playing the role of a father authentically.

For several years I felt I played the role badly, and was wracked with guilt. A breakthrough came in therapy: I spoke with my inner father figure and reflected on his guilt and sense of inferiority. What ideals were behind my inner father figure's role? Suddenly an image came into mind: it was a father from the 1960s, smoking a pipe. His children were helping him clean the car. Mom was in the kitchen and everyone was calm, the atmosphere peaceful and harmonious. The environment was well-structured, the roles fixed, and the values deeply materialistic.

A breakthrough came when I realised these were not my values. They were radically different from the kind of life I wanted. I realised I had unconsciously *identified* with something inauthentic, and this had caused problems because there was a gap between my conscious aims and the unconscious expectations held by my inner father figure. But having had this realisation I was then able to begin the process of replacing the subconscious ideas I had held about fatherhood since 1968 with the values I was committed to in 2003.

This example tells us much. Along with our own subpersonalities, we also internalise the most important figures in our lives. Father, mother, important friends and loved ones are key figures found in the object relations theory of psychoanalysis. Subpersonalities founded upon these key figures not only behave like our real mother and father, they *believe* this is who they are. Many of us as adults continue to hear a parent's voice still chiding them after all these years, disapproving of some action. We are experiencing an internalised representation of our parents lives within us, influencing our actions for good and bad. Awareness of this psychodrama can help us as we try to respond to these inner figures – we can learn to deal with our parental subpersonalities, and others, treating them as real living psychic beings in our subconscious domain.

Many subpersonalities develop and become more healthy as we go through life and conquer new challenges, yet many remain stuck in the unconscious until we uncover them and begin the work of transformation.

To return to Assagioli's metaphor, we can train the subpersonalities in the apartment building to move from floor to floor and room to room, changing their roles at any given time. In Chapter 8 I will look at how we can accomplish this.

There are still other kinds of subpersonalities, ones organised around what we can call *archetypical roles*. The archetypes of the collective unconscious can draw us into making powerful identifications; throughout history we have been drawn to figures that exemplify the hero, the warrior, the trickster, the preacher, the king, and so on. Many children today identify with Harry Potter – the Magician – and this allows them to express their own archetypal sense of magic and wonder. An archetypical subpersonality is by definition an identity formation based on a collective role model.

The last category of subpersonalities is the most controversial: those related to our past lives. These subpersonalities are prominent characters from earlier lifetimes that relate to the themes of this life.

The priest I met during my guided meditation is a good example of a subpersonality from a past life. I believe that in a past life I was Father Pierre, a Frenchman who retreated into a life of seclusion. This subpersonality of mine believed he was still living in 1850 and his habits and attitudes from that period influenced my personality. I do not doubt the existence of these subpersonalities – they appear with regularity in my therapeutic practice – but how to interpret them is another question. There is no proof of past lives, so clients will often choose to interpret such subpersonalities as archetypal figures expressing authentic psychological energies.

Subpersonalities appear in the basic and middle unconscious because here they find the mental, emotional and physical energies that give them form. By contrast, the energies found in the superconscious tend to be formless, more like light than anything else, so they are less likely to manifest as personalities.

The Soul and the Transpersonal Self

Where is the personal self's source of consciousness? Assagioli called it the higher Self or the transpersonal Self (8). He may have felt his terms were more scientific, but I call it the Soul. The personal and transpersonal Self are the same Self, but at different levels of awareness. The personal self's awareness is restricted by the mental field and the brain, which causes the illusion of separation so that our self-awareness becomes contracted around an individual core. The Soul is a centre of pure self-awareness and will in the superconscious. Here our identity and self-awareness expands to include all living beings. I call this self-awareness *group consciousness* or *sacrificial consciousness*.

I prefer to speak of the Soul because of its links to love. Many have experienced the Soul as a transcendent witness free of the dramas of the personality. The Soul is not an archetype or a concept but a living divine being. The Soul knows the meaning of our lives and our tasks in our current incarnation. The Soul is an expression of the universal Self, manifesting in a unique incarnation. The Soul is able to experience the full breadth of consciousness; our self-awareness can expand to include a deep connectedness with all living beings, a sense of being at one with world and humanity. Here our sense of identity expands far beyond our personality.

The Soul is in touch with the personal self by the *bridge of consciousness* (7), linking the two points of self-awareness. This is known as the silent path because the higher levels of consciousness are accessed through silent contemplation. I call it the Soul-self connection. We can say that the Soul's consciousness descends from the top of the egg diagram through a pale reflection in the brain. This reflection is the observer, our point of pure self-awareness. It is a pale reflection until the spiritual process awakens the personal self to its higher divine counterpart. Then the Soul is able to manifest through the mind as well as the brain and the nervous system.

Assagioli's egg diagram does not show the personal self located in the brain, but esoteric philosophy describes a secret physical centre between the pineal and pituitary glands. It calls this "the cave". In the cave, Soul consciousness descends and reflects the light. Meditating in the cave can strengthen the bridge of consciousness, the Soul-self connection. The observer is not experienced as a point within the brain because we observe through the medium of the mind, and not the brain.

We can imagine the Soul as a radiant point of loving presence floating above the head. This spiritual being is often described in Eastern traditions as the "real man in the inner world". The Soul reincarnates so to develop its capacity to manifest love-wisdom. The Soul's purpose is to manifest the content of the superconscious through the personal self, using the resources found in the basic and middle unconscious. The personal self is the conductor, mediating between the Soul's vision and the needs of the personality. When the Soul is able to express itself fully through the personality, the personal self and the Soul can be said to have become one. The result is an enlightened being, someone who identifies with humanity, and can truly love his neighbour as himself.

The consciousness of the Soul and the personal self does not differ in quality. Assagioli used a helpful analogy to describe this relationship: that of sunlight reflected in a mirror. The sunlight in the mirror has the same qualities as its source: it illuminates and gives warmth. If we see only the reflection, and not the source, we can say that the light in the mirror is an illusion. The same applies with the personal self and the Soul. Meditation enables the personal self to connect with the source of light. When we do this we come to understand that the difference between the reflection and its source is one of degree, concerning intensity of light.

The star at the top of the Egg symbolises what the East calls the "Jewel in the lotus", the heart of the Soul. This is the Universal Presence in the Soul, the potential for cosmic consciousness. The Soul lives above the mental levels, a presence fully awake to the eternal Now; it leads a cosmic and earthly life. If the self is a 100W bulb radiating from its centre in the brain, the Soul is a perpetual nova radiating in eternity. Enlightenment happens when the lightbulb in the brain reflects its higher counterpart. When this happens, the creative energies in the superconscious radiate from the love, wisdom and power in the Soul. In a similar way, the personal self develops knowledge, desires and images in the basic and middle unconscious.

The Soul is also a centre of will, just like the personal self, but with a much greater scope. The Soul relates to the Spirit's overall purpose, and has a unique task in the universe. Through the evolutionary process the Soul learns how to manifest its divine qualities in the world. This is how the will plays out in the life of the Soul.

The dynamic part of the Soul is fiery. We experience its will-to-be as the evolutionary impulse, urging consciousness through all levels. Yet the Soul is dual. There is the fiery will, but also a silent, static ground. Assagioli called the Soul the "immovable mover" pointing to the paradox at the heart of the Soul.

The fire is *sacrificial* because it sacrifices minor attachments in order to realise the ultimate attachment, which is oneness. The will does away with lesser forms. This destruction means letting go of old states of consciousness while surrendering to new ones arriving from transcendent worlds.

I have experienced the fiery nature of the Soul many times. At one stage in my life I needed to surrender to the heart of the Sun, the gigantic living being ensouling the physical sun. Meditating, I connected with an enormous fiery being. I felt I had become a reservoir of living fire, abundant life saturated with power, with the potential to create all there is. From this silent will, I was already all I could hope to become and much more. There was nothing to achieve, only eternal life and being. From this solar heart, fountains of living fire produce an abundant display of pure life force – an effortless radiation of being and becoming. It was a joyful, ecstatic supernatural volcano of creativity: dynamic, unstoppable and full of love. There was no doubt that this was my true face: living fire, indestructible, eternal essence.

The bridge of consciousness has a living dynamic counterpart called the *sutratma*, meaning the thread of life, which is anchored in the physical heart. Through this living essence, the Soul is reflected on the physical plane. Through the heart centre, in the middle of the chest, we have an intuitive sense of who we are and our unique evolutionary purpose in life. The heart centre is dynamic, producing the courage to be who we truly are. Through this fiery essence we develop dignity and self-worth as a divine being.

The Soul is dual. It has masculine and feminine poles, relating to what we might call the *particle and wave nature of our being*. The silent will of the Soul patiently but insistently pushes us beyond our comfort zones so we can better serve the divine. This is our inner King or Queen, which is felt as a longing for authenticity and power. The feminine pole seeks connection and communion with society, nature and the cosmos. It knows that, despite separation and conflict, we are one. The feminine represents the love that opens hearts through kindness and generosity. The Soul's feminine side knows that the love in one heart is the same love residing in all hearts.

The Seven Evolutionary Stages

The self's evolutionary journey begins at the bottom of the egg diagram and leads through the different levels of consciousness, as defined in Chapter 1. These seven evolutionary stages create seven types of awareness: body-awareness (instinctual-physical), sensitive-awareness (emotional), self-awareness (rational-mental), holistic-awareness (personality-Soul), group-awareness (intuitive-Soul), sacrificial-awareness (will-Soul), and unity-awareness (Spirit).

Figure 7 depicts the seven developmental stages and shows how they unfold. Not all human beings go through the upper stages; for most these stages are in potential rather than reality. We have been able to describe these stages by reflecting on the attainment of some of the most realised Souls in history. It is important to stress, once again, the non-linear way that many of these developments take place in life experience. An experience of the heights of consciousness is often followed by an experience of its depths. After an experience of the heights, a process of purification will take place in the subconscious: we *have to regress for the sake of progress* because the counter pole of an experience will surface after the realisation. Similarly, whenever we act from the place of Soul, connecting with our power and integrity, we will bring out a sense of powerlessness and inadequacy from our basic unconscious. This is what we can call *the law of polarity* (Figure 8).

When we have reached the peaks, we must then descend, which means entering lower parts of the unconscious where we can then eliminate outmoded behaviour, such as attachments to early trauma which makes us reckless, greedy or reclusive. Our subpersonalities can learn to co-operate with the influx of superconscious energies, producing a spontaneous kindness and wisdom. This is hard work. Even with knowledge and skills at

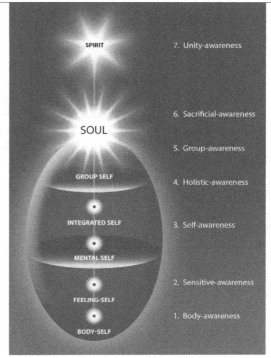

Figure 7: The unfolding of the seven developmental stages.

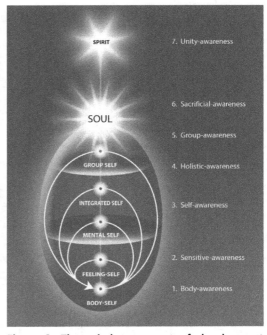

Figure 8: The spiral movement of development showing the law of polarity.

our disposal, it is a painful process. Meditation is of great help here.

The distance between what I teach and what I do can be great. Following a deep spiritual breakthrough it requires much heart to accept the immature behaviour I often witness in myself. Yet, as Ken Wilber says about spiritual realisation: "It hurts more but bothers you less." He means that we become more sensitive to pain but also more impersonal.

When growth is healthy, we see an exchange of energies between the bottom and the top of the egg. Whenever we achieve a higher level of understanding, we also descend to do some work in the basement of our inner house. This brings about changes in our relationship to sex, money and power. As we open up to the Soul, our empathy with others strengthens, and it becomes impossible to be purposefully hurtful. Barriers dissolve and our sensitivity increases, challenging us to move beyond egocentric behaviour.

If the basic energies are excluded from our development, our shadow will appear in all types of compulsive behaviours, mostly related to money, power and sex. This is common in spiritual environments where the transcendent is idealised and the material demonised. Misuse of money, power and sex by gurus or teachers is often rationalised in order to protect the reputation of the cult. This attitude neglects the role of the subconscious, whose importance in this cannot be overemphasised. Understanding the subconscious influence on our behaviour is necessary if we are to ground our spiritual visions in everyday life.

Another way to illustrate the different levels of our inner house is with the concept of a "holarchy" (Figure 9). According to Arthur Koestler, a holarchy is a hierarchical structure uniting holons, which are themselves both

Figure 9: The holarchies as they relate to the egg diagram.

"If the self is a 100 W bulb radiating from its center in the brain,

the Soul is a perpetual nova

radiating in eternity"

parts and wholes. The body (1) is a whole in itself, but also a part of a larger holon, the emotional field (2). They both are part of the mind (3), which is a part of the personality (4), which is part of the Soul (5). The superconscious emerges from the Soul and the spiritual Self is the ground of it all. Spirit is the foundation of everything and can be experienced as a Creator or a universal field.

In a holarchy, one holon transcends but includes another. In life, the process is complex because of the conflicts we experience between our egoistic (self-assertive) and altruistic (self-transcending) impulses. Holarchies are a fact but their order and harmony must be realised by us as a collective.

Summary of terms

Let me conclude this chapter by clarifying the different, sometimes seemingly contradictory, concepts of self I have been discussing.

By **the self** I mean the personal self as a centre of pure self-awareness and will. The self is not the thoughts, feelings, ideas, passions or sensations that make up the *content* of consciousness, but is the consciousness that is aware of these contents.

Assagioli calls the "I" the personal self. I prefer to use "I" to mean the self as it is identified with any particular stage in its development, what we can call the "stage-specific self". The "I" represents the present prominent identification in an individual's life. This identification could be emotional, mental, holistic or higher.

The Ego is usually a group of prominent subpersonalities, which offers a set of roles we can apply in our interaction with the world and is considered to be within normal behaviour. The ego can also be defined in a much broader sense as a contraction around self-centredness which separates us from our surroundings.

The Superego is a collection of subpersonalities that exerts a critical and a moralising influence. Its values are those of the cultural norms, what is considered good behaviour. It is motivated to maintain customs and ensure the safety of the individual within the family and society.

The Personality is the integrated, individualised expression of the talents and qualities of the basic and middle unconscious. They are united through the influence of self-awareness, the will and the mind.

The Soul, the higher Self and the transpersonal Self are all terms referring to the unique individualised expression in time and space of the one Spirit. The Jiva Atman in Hindu literature.

The Universal Self, the Universal Presence and Spirit are likewise different names for the same reality.

In Chapter 1, I asked three questions; let's see if we can answer them now.

Who meditates?

The self or the Soul according to the level of awareness defined by the stage-specific self of a particular individual.

Why do we meditate?

In order to raise our level of awareness from the egocentric to the cosmocentric, with the aim of bettering the world.

What is spirituality?

It is the expansion of consciousness from the personal to the transpersonal and beyond. It is the manifestation of our divine qualities through the body and into the world.

Now with the help of this map, let's navigate the seven rivers of life and see what kinds of energies we must master in order to become whole.

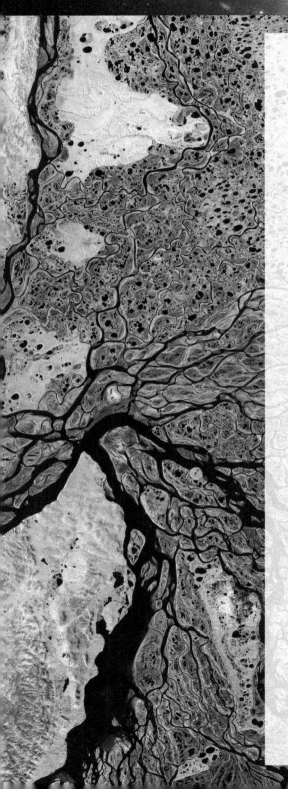

Chapter 3

Energy Psychology and The Seven Rivers of Life

We were a group of people meditating together on the theme of spiritual paths. We were receiving all the familiar thought forms relevant to the subject, but nothing new seemed to emerge. Then in a flash, my awareness expanded spontaneously into a Solar Systemic Now. A sense of clarity and a feeling of sublime love were suddenly present, connecting me to the solar system and the cosmic ocean of energy. I felt an intimate relation to the solar system; we were all brothers and sisters on a cosmic path. I felt deeply connected to the planets; they were living cosmic beings and our communion was a unity in diversity. We were one consciousness but still individual beings on our unique paths. The space was timeless and all living beings unfolded their essence in unanimity in one synchronised movement. It was as if a cosmic hand was guiding us toward our spiritual destination. I can only call this hand God, Brahman, The One Life or Spirit-in-Action.

Energy Psychology and The Seven Rivers of Life

Experiences like this are not uncommon when we expand our consciousness from the individual to the universal. And when we awaken to the fact that reality is one cosmic ocean of interconnected energies, we also realise the importance of having a map to help us navigate these waters. We work with these energies when we meditate, and Energy Psychology offers a useful map and language to understand them.

Everything is energy. This insight has become something of a cliché since books like Fritjof Capra's *The Tao of Physics* showed there were surprising resonances between some of the discoveries of quantum physics and some Eastern philosophies. But to recognise this is not enough. What we need is a language that helps us to *understand* energy, what we could call an "energy language". Energy Psychology is already well established, and I am certain that a "fifth wave" of psychology will emerge based on an understanding of energy. Many contemporary thinkers agree, for example Ken Wilber, who created integral psychology, while Sri Aurobindo, Roberto Assagioli and Alice Bailey are some outstanding exponents from the past.

In the 1990s, esoteric psychology with its teaching of the seven rays became an important source of inspiration to me. At the same time, I discovered an essay by Assagioli in which he describes his seven ways typology. It struck me that all the major Psychosynthesis schools taught Assagioli's *Seven Ways of Self-Realisation* as an integral part of their curricula. Esoteric astrology, which I have practised for several decades, is also rooted in the philosophy of the seven rays. In 2007, with my good friend Søren Hauge, I brought these different strands together and started to work deeply with the seven rays. Our research resulted in several new teaching innovations within Energy Psychology, which we called integral meditation and Soul Flow. We created a new language that helps us to communicate this psychology. We also discovered new insights and applied these in our teaching and workshops – see www.jivayou.com

Energy Psychology describes how the seven rays constitute and colour all of existence. It is also the language of integral meditation. The seven rays, seven levels of consciousness, seven ways of meditation and seven spiritual types form the basis of this philosophy, which works with five integral life practices in the three areas of I, We and It. This chapter describes the seven rays, and shows how we connect with them through the seven psychological functions.

The seven rays inform many spiritual teachings. According to the Indian philosopher Sri Aurobindo (1872-1955), the Vedas describes how the manifestation of the universe "brings down, the unrestricted downpour of the rain of heaven, the full flowing of the seven rivers from a superior sea of light and power and joy". Alice Bailey called these "seven rivers" the seven rays, and so did Aurobindo when he was quoting the Vedas.

Sri Aurobindo

These two terms – seven rays and seven rivers – are often used interchangeably to refer to the same energies, but there is a difference between them. The seven rays is a masculine expression that emphasises the will. By definition, a ray is a radiation of energy that is directed: think of a flashlight. Astrophysics speaks about cosmic radiation, and in nature scientists can measure the different types of radiation created by the colour spectrum of white light. I sometimes prefer the term *rivers of life*; rivers flow, and this seems a much more feminine kind of phenomenon. We can direct our consciousness at a target, but we can also dive into consciousness as if it were a stream. In Aurobindo's words: *"The seven Waters are the waters of being; they are the Mothers from whom all forms of existence are born."*

In the same that white light expresses itself through the seven colours of the spectrum, the seven rays are actually subdivisions of the one essential ray which contains them all. There is a close analogy between the seven rays and the seven colours of the spectrum.

These seven rays each have inherent psychological qualities. Speaking cosmologically, I will refer to rays and rivers; speaking psychologically, we can call them energy types or "ray qualities". The seven qualities are:

1. Will and power (my terminology: dynamic river of life)

2. Love and wisdom (sensitive river of life)

3. Active intelligence (intelligent river of life)

---

1. Aurobindo, The Synthesis of Yoga, p. 405

2. In his commentary on the Vedas: The Secret of the Vedas, he share his many thoughts on the seven rays as well as the seven rivers. They are expressions of the same reality but from different perspectives.

3. The Secret of the Vedas, p. 123

4. Harmony and beauty (creative river of life)

5. Scientific knowledge (scientific river of life)

6. Idealism and devotion (idealising river of life)

7. Organisation and manifestation (manifesting river of life)

Each of these rivers, and the meditations I have developed based upon them, will be explored in later chapters.

When the seven rays manifest in human behaviour they find expression in the form of seven distinct energy types, namely:

1. The dynamic type

2. The sensitive type

3. The mental type

4. The creative type

5. The analytical type

6. The dedicated type

7. The practical type

For each of us, there is a particular energy type which colours the expression of our soul and personality. It is important to know our soul type because this lets us know which ray qualities we are primarily working with to create spiritual meaning, and it is important to know our personality type so we can create a successful personal life. In the next chapter we will explore these different types in detail.

The seven rays constitute everything in existence, from the mineral world to the highest spiritual levels of being. From this perspective, there is no area of study where we cannot apply Energy Psychology.

The term "ray" should be understood to refer to the *quality* associated with it, and not the form in which it is expressed. In the mineral world, different metals have particular qualities. Metals are energy in a particular atomic pattern; their qualities emerge through the energy pattern – the "ray quality" – that created them. The same applies to human beings; it is our psychological qualities that determine our character.

An understanding of Energy Psychology can greatly benefit our meditation.

Not all types of meditation facilitate our spiritual growth. Each of our Souls is dominated by a particular one of the seven rays, which has implications for our choice of meditation. The yoga schools of Hinduism emphasise that there are different ways to connect with God. Different people need different techniques to realise the self. The same principle applies to Assagioli's seven ways and to the seven rays of esotericism. We each contain all of the seven rays, but not in equal measure; some are more important than others in respect to our individual Self-realisation. This book is about fashioning meditations to suit our own particular spiritual needs.

The Source of the Seven Rivers of Life

Spirit-in-action

SOUL

Personality

Figure 10: Diagram showing how the seven ray qualities flow into the Soul then out into the self and the personality in the form of the psychological functions.

What is the source of the seven rivers of life? Where do we come from? The energies are not outside us, they are the essence of who we are. We are energy! Sri Aurobindo poetically says that the rivers come from "a superior sea of light and power and joy" and that they reveal *Sat-Cit-Ananda*, which is "being, consciousness, bliss".

This is one of the things that makes Energy Psychology so fascinating: it provides a cosmic view of life, along with practical advice for psychological application; it is a spiritual typology made up of levels, stages, states, quadrants and types as with Ken Wilber's integral psychology.

Wilber emphasises the concept of Spirit-in-Action, which he describes as the universal life force driving the evolution of consciousness. Spirit-in-Action is the very fabric of life, the inmost power of all living beings. We all ride on the wave of this great evolutionary force: we ARE this wave – We Are Spirit-in-Action.

An important teaching in many religions concerns the transcendent, unmanifest realm that exists outside time and space. In Buddhism it is called Dharmakaya; in Hinduism it is Parabrahman; and in the Christian tradition it is God. Out of this ground of being emerges the will to manifest. The universe appears and continually actualises its potentials. We have Spirit-in-Action, we have a Big Bang, but not only the physical realm is created in this act. According to the processes of involution and evolution, our inner worlds appear before our outer one. (We will discuss this in more detail further on.) These inner worlds also constitute the manifest ground of reality; they are the source of what is known in the "perennial philosophy" as *the Great Chain of Being*. They are the "heavens" of an *interior* space.

The seven rivers of life are seven streams of spiritual force produced by Spirit-in-Action which shape and maintain creation. But how do they manifest in us? The spiritual Soul receives these energies from Spirit-in-Action and channels them throughout the personality, and continues to do so throughout our life. The three levels – Spirit, Soul and personality and the seven rivers of life – are illustrated in Figure 10. The diagram shows how the seven ray qualities flow into the Soul at the top of the egg. From here they flow into the self in the middle of the egg, and then they move out into the personality in the form of our psychological functions: will, feelings, thoughts, imagination, logic, passion and, eventually, physical actions.

The Seven Rivers of Life in Everyday Life

Let's see how the seven rivers are active in daily life. Energy can be expressed in different ways. Love can be boundless and all-encompassing or stiflingly selfish. It is the same energy but expressed in what we might call two different frequencies.

Try this visualisation exercise. Close your eyes and imagine soldiers marching across a field. Notice their expressions, the sound of their feet, the weight of their packs. How did you react to this? Now imagine a baby in the arms of a loving mother. What was your reaction then? In the first instance you experienced the energies of the dynamic quality of will and power; in the second that of sensitivity and compassion.

The same kinds of reaction appear when we meditate. If we know the ray qualities, we can work with and eventually master them. Later chapters will explore each ray in detail; here I will briefly introduce them. Remember, we contain all seven energies and we should try to understand our relationship to each of them.

The energies of will and power are the most difficult to master. They are so powerful that we often become fearful in their presence. This dynamic ray quality is concerned with the *will to power* and the *will to be self*. Many people are afraid of this power because of the responsibility it entails. Power is a part of reality, and if we don't take our share of it, others surely will.

People governed by this ray are *dynamic* types, who reach the top within their sphere of influence.

We use this power for good or bad according to our level of consciousness. This ray quality gives us focus, courage and determination. We pursue our objectives and sacrifice whatever is necessary to succeed. Dynamic energy can be destructive; it can enable us to cut through and eliminate whatever obstructs our aims. The dynamic aspect of our nature compels us to fully actualise our potential. We become pioneers and adventurers within our sphere. It gives us the will to manifest our greatness.

We take responsibility and occupy the centre of influence. We are drawn to be a leader and to use our power, initiative and drive. We love competition and want to succeed. In terms of our personality, it is the psychological function of will that manifests this quality.

The energies of love and wisdom carry a softness, warmth and sensitivity. These sensitive ray qualities lead us into the world of relationships. Like water, this energy gently penetrates rock, entering its cracks and shaping it. When influenced by this energy, we have an empathetic understanding of not only humans, but of anything we love. Here we feel a deep understanding and an urge to unite what is separate. Relationships are all; we are nurturing, calm and co-operative. We are speaking here of the archetypical energy of love. Whereas the will breaks down, love restores and unites. This sensitive energy produces patience and a desire to build relationships and heal whatever is broken. This energy is a *magnetism*, a force that connects and holds together, be it a solar system or a personal relationship. People governed by this ray often work in the helping professions where there's a need for understanding, compassion and empathy. This ray is expressed through the psychological function of feeling.

The energies of intelligence make us mentally sharp and quick. They help us to understand and communicate multiple perspectives. Here we are motivated to acquire information which becomes the knowledge necessary to act intelligently and efficiently. This energy makes us light, flexible and curious, and it enhances our social skills. It helps us to make connections with all the relevant people in our network. It may not garner the depth of understanding that the sensitive energy can discern, but it helps us to collect information and see the larger picture. This energy motivates us to think and investigate. Types governed by this ray are often astute and can handle their resources efficiently. They are suited to activities requiring bridge-building. They are great networkers and excel in problem solving. The energies of intelligence are expressed through the psychological function of thought.

The energies of harmony and beauty make us playful and spontaneous, and instil a strong desire for the harmonious and beautiful. We cannot live without beauty, lightness and balance. Conflicts and drama are ok inasmuch as they can relieve tensions. But under the influence of this ray, we can find harmony in disharmony. We can mediate between extremes and turn chaos into order. We can lose control, safe in our belief that new potentials will emerge in the process. All the rays are creative, but this one carries a gift for bringing beauty

into form. It provides insight into inner conflicting forces, helping them to reach accord. Types governed by this ray are often drawn to the arts, where imagination reigns, but also into professions where mediation and appeasement are highly valued. The energies of harmony and beauty use the psychological function of imagination.

The energies of scientific understanding make us serious, precise and attentive to facts. Practical details are important to us and we find great pleasure in learning. In psychology we analyse human behaviour in order to ensure valid and reliable conclusions. We want to know the truth so we can speak with authority. We are logical, using our intellect to discriminate, discard and conclude. We are inventive, curious and dig deep into our specialised studies. We are well suited to circumstances that demand sharp analytical thinking,

and we are drawn to be a researcher, technician and practical innovator. The energies of scientific understanding are expressed through the psychological function of logic.

The energies of idealism and devotion make us enthusiastic, loyal and earnest. We are passionate about everything we do and are committed to it wholeheartedly. We elevate the people around us and motivate them to reach for their highest goals. We are, in a word, idealists. We tend to think in "black or white" because our dedication is all-consuming. We are happy to follow a leader as long as we share his values. The cause motivates us, not the attention. We are loyal and accountable because we judge ourselves by the ideals we follow. We are born activists, zealous advocates of any cause that captures our heart. Professions requiring sincere communication suit us: sales, marketing, coaching, the helping professions. The energies of idealism and devotion are expressed through the psychological function of passion.

The energies of organisation and manifestation make us efficient, orderly and systematic. We strive for excellence, which is the central aim of this energy. We enjoy planning strategies with efficient people. Achieving concrete results and bringing ideas into life is deeply rewarding, even the planning, preparation and presentation of the perfect meal. We love to experiment with new methods in order to perfect our skills. We are creators of law and order because we firmly believe there is a right way to do everything. We co-ordinate and direct group activities where ideas are an essential part of the overall process. We recognise different qualities and abilities and see how they fit together in the bigger picture. This type of personality makes an ideal team leader. The energies of organisation and manifestation are expressed through the body and physical action.

I hope you can recognise yourself somewhere in the descriptions above. But let me give an example from my own life regarding how these ray qualities can come into play.

We all ride on the wave of the evolutionary force:

We ARE this wave –
We ARE Spirit-in-Action

My Own Energy Types

I have suggested how the seven ray/energy types can dominate an individual's psychological constitution. In Energy Psychology, we also distinguish between what we call the five dominating energy types: body, emotions, mind, personality and Soul, each of which has a particular dominant energy conditioned by one of the seven ray qualities. These five energy types influence how we experience the world. We can access all the seven rays, but some of the rays are primary and others are secondary. (Energy typology is simple but complex, and will be explored in more detail in the next chapter.)

The two most important energy types are the Soul and personality. The first influences how we pursue our spiritual path, while the second shapes how we create a successful personal life. When I reflected on how I managed my own successful professional life, the qualities that came to me were *idealism* and *passion*.

When I was 17, I joined the army, giving five years of my life to the service. Later I spent a decade working in social psychiatry, during which time I edited a magazine that was written and produced by people suffering with mental illness. Since then my work life has been focused on pursuing esoteric wisdom and exploring transpersonal psychology through teaching, counselling, workshops and education. My passion has driven me forward. This quality belongs to *the dedicated* energy type, burning with idealism and devotion. Idealism and passion for the "cause" formed my character. I have also been influenced by the shadow side of this energy type: a tendency to fanaticism and extremes, to playing the righteous missionary, sure of his perspectives in life.

I became aware of other prominent qualities in my psychological constitution: my love for the ageless wisdom and a deep longing for connection. Meditation satisfied me deeply. It felt like coming home. And teaching spiritual psychology was deeply gratifying. I found the connection with others that is afforded by the intimacy of the therapeutic space to be nourishing and rewarding. The difference between the dedicated type and the sensitive type is that the dedicated type lacks the soft, embracing and calm quality of the sensitive. However, in the late 1990s, I became aware that my sensitivity was increasingly beginning to influence my character. I was certain that I was a 2-6 type, that is, a second ray Soul and a sixth ray personality.

This perhaps needs a short explanation. My personality, which means the dominant qualities of the basic and middle unconscious in the egg diagram, was the major influence throughout my youth. The dedicated energies of the sixth ray conditioned my overall behaviour, so I was a dedicated personality type. Then, later, the superconscious energies began to emerge in my life. The dominant qualities of the superconscious and the Soul itself started to influence me. These energies were primarily an expression of the second ray in my case, so I became aware of my second ray soul type – also called the sensitive soul type.

When I started my spiritual practice in 1988, I visualised the sun in my heart centre, and continued this practice every day for the next ten years. I was so focused on my spiritual life that I never really had the time to relate to people in a deeper sense, or to enjoy a gentler, less driven way of being. I pushed myself to the limit with work, a common hazard of the dedicated type.

Around the millennium, my life changed drastically. A power struggle within the esoteric community I was involved in left me disillusioned about our ability to practice what we preached. We sought wisdom, but when everyday conflicts arose no one, myself included, was mature enough to handle the situation. This painful wake up call was nevertheless a blessed event.

Disillusionment is a common crisis among dedicated types. Their ideals are too lofty, too impractical to become realities, and that was exactly the case with me. The next few years were difficult; with no focus for my ideals, I felt my life had stalled. Yet what emerged was a more open outlook on the world. I decided to never again identify with any belief system, no matter how beautiful or significant. I would practice an open spirituality based on experience.

I would also start long-term psychotherapeutic work in order to overcome some of the problems I had become aware of, such as my tendency to isolate myself, my sense of loneliness and fear of intimacy with people I didn't know. I decided to take training in Psychosynthesis psychotherapy. Six years later, that goal was accomplished.

What really happened? Today it is clear to me that there was a conflict between my personality ray and my Soul ray. It was a deep existential crisis that took centre stage in my life and defined my new identity. In Psychosynthesis terminology, it was a phase where the personality was integrating with the Soul. I moved from holding an intellectual philosophical attitude to adopting a more intuitive "being-orientated" approach. I did not reject my intellect but I didn't need to identify with it or with a particular faith. The focus of my meditations was to simply be aware and present, silently, with no aims or goals. I also realised a need for more intimacy, more "presence", in my relationships. It was the way of love-wisdom bringing me to the Soul.

When the Soul qualities begin to emerge and we come under the influence of a new flow of energies, it's important not to forget the stage we have just left. My natural enthusiasm, drive and passion remain – they are part of my Soul's equipment and necessary for life. But instead of identifying with these qualities, I am learning how to ride their energies in a calmer and open-minded way. The second ray Soul can now start to inform the energies of the personality. The opposite could have happened. If I had been a calm, lazy type (a common trait of sensitive personalities), I would need to tap into my Soul's fire and passion. It all depends on the individual and what feels right according to the purpose we are here to realise.

What does my story tells us? Knowledge leads to mastery. When we walk in the forest, we see trees, but a forester sees oaks, green ashes, weeping willows, cedars and much more that escapes you or me. This knowledge means the resources around him are available to the forester, and the same applies to our inner energies. All our experiences are movements of energy. When we are focused we experience the energy of will, when we relate intimately we experience the energy of love, and when we organise our work it is the energy of manifestation.

Energy Psychology helps us to identify the different energies that influence us and shows us how to use them. To do this the energy psychologist identifies seven psychological functions.

The Seven Psychological Functions

Let's look at how we can work with these energies from the point of view of the psychological functions. The psychiatrist C. G. Jung wrote about four functions: feeling, thinking, sensing and intuition. Assagioli, however, spoke of seven psychological functions, which he presented in a Star Diagram. These functions are sensation, desire (passion), feeling, imagination, thought, intuition and the will. Our system follows Assagioli's with a few changes. We include logic as a psychological function. This seems in keeping with the thinking of Assagioli, who was aware of the dual nature of the mind, its ability to grasp abstract meanings and to analyse concrete facts. Also, we speak of passion rather than desire because of the negative associations with the former, and we prefer the term action to Assagioli's term sensation. Furthermore, we list intuition as a transpersonal function rather than a psychological function (there are also seven transpersonal functions – see below).

The self moves through life through the seven evolutionary stages by making use of the psychological functions. We do not consider awareness a function, but a state of being, yet we are able to expand and develop awareness, so there are eight developmental lines in all.

Assagioli depicted the seven psycho-logical functions in the form of a Star Diagram (Figure 11) and here in my modified form.

1. Action (Sensation)

2. Feeling

3. Passion

4. Imagination

5. Logic

6. Thought

7. Will (and the conscious "I")

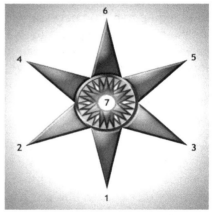

Figure 11: Assagioli's Star Diagram depicting the seven psychological functions:

Each of us makes use of these functions; they are part of normal human psychology. Through developing them we can learn to know and eventually to master the seven ray qualities. There are meditations designed to help develop these functions, but they also unfold naturally as we go through life. Meditation is a way of accelerating their growth. Different schools of yoga are aimed at harnessing different qualities: devotion through Bhakti yoga, the mind through Raja yoga, and the body through Hatha yoga. Our aim is to develop all of them through an integral approach.

The self uses the psychological functions to gain knowledge of the inner and outer world and to express itself in the world. At the centre of the Star Diagram, we have a white circle – a point of pure self-awareness, static and immovable. From this centre, the Self radiates its qualities. All the psychological functions have their respective centres in the brain.

Gradually, the psychological functions of the personality transform into the transpersonal functions of the Soul. Will becomes synthesis; feeling becomes intuition; thought becomes idea; imagination becomes vision; logic becomes wisdom; passion becomes service; and action becomes mastery. While love relates to feeling and intuition, as Oneness love is also the essence of all the seven ways: every single atom in the cosmos longs to be one with all the others.

The Psychological Functions and their Internal Relations

As an alternative to Assagioli's Star Diagram, Figure 12 shows how the seven psychological functions relate to the seven rays via the three primary functions of will, feeling and thought.

These three primary functions relate to the seven psychological functions in the same way that the three primary colours, red, blue and yellow, relate to the other colours in the spectrum. Figure 12 shows how will, feeling and thought form a triangle with action at the centre, in contrast to Assagioli's Star Diagram, which puts will at the centre. Action has been placed at the centre because we are concerned with *manifesting* our life's purpose. There will be more about this later.

Figure 12: How the seven psychological functions related to the seven rays via the three primary functions of will, feeling and thought.

The will directs energy and is expressed through purpose, choice and decision. The will motivates us, and puts life into motion, often in subtle ways; sometimes we don't even know that a decision has been made. The will confirms who we are. Through our choices and actions, the will reveals our identifications.

Feeling is our sensitivity. It makes us sympathetic to the psychological *qualities* of a given situation. It informs us of our likes and dislikes, what we find pleasant or unpleasant. It also connects us to our surroundings, so we can feel what is going on in the outside world.

Thought tells us the nature of something. It gathers information, creates categories, and weaves different perspectives into a system. It interprets data received through the other functions. Using thought we can communicate how we see the world to others.

The next four psychological functions are formed through different combinations of the primary functions. So, for example, combining thought and feeling produces *imagination*, our playful visualising faculty. Through imagination we can create images that carry an emotional atmosphere. We use imagination to visualise reality as it is or as it *could* be. We may say it is our magical faculty: anything is possible through the imagination. Though not physical, the imagination affects us just as real as the "real world" does.

Logic is produced by combining will and thought. Logic is directed analytical thinking; it gets us from A to B through the shortest route. Logic discriminates and evaluates; it is concerned with facts, certainties and objective truths. Thinking is broader and reasons inductively; logic begins with premises and follows through to conclusions using deductive reasoning.

Passion, the combination of will and feeling, focuses us intently on a goal. It includes our drives, desires, aspirations and needs. Passion moves us. It is the power we need to get things going. Passions can range from a brute survival instinct to a burning love for God.

Action occurs when will, feeling and thought inform our capacity for movement. All action involves a decision and thought about how to realise it. This puts us in motion. One function can be more dominant than the others, ie when our actions are informed by our strong will. Action means specifically physical action. We can say that all the psychological functions are "acting" simply because they are active; but what we have in mind here is when specific actions are performed in the outer world.

The Psychological Functions are Lines of Development

Meditation can help develop the psychological functions, but there are also other ways. The psychological functions provide access to the different energies, as well as to the seven rivers of life. They develop differently from person to person, so it makes sense to consider the functions separately, along with the self's own particular path of awareness and identity.

There are eight developmental lines when we include the self line (Figure 13) because each of the seven psychological functions and the self develop through their own stages of development. We have:

1. Will

2. Feeling

3. Thought

4. Imagination

5. Logic

6. Passion

7. Action

8. Self

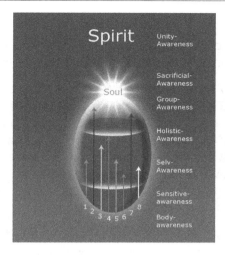

Figure 13: The eight developmental lines and the seven psychological functions:

Figure 13 shows the main stages the functions pass through, starting from the bottom of the egg moving up to the top. When the functions become open to the superconscious, transpersonal functions emerge. For example, the psychological function of feeling becomes the transpersonal function of intuition. This illustrates that while the cognitive line (thought) may be well developed, the emotional line (feeling) can lag behind; the same applies for the other functions as well. There are eight primary lines of development, but many other lines appear as the different functions form different combinations. Ken Wilber's integral psychology provides a brilliant presentation of the different lines of development. In Figure 13 the eight developmental lines, we see a hypothetical illustration of the various psychological functions and how they develop independently.

If the diagram was representative of a person, we could conclude that this individual's compassion and empathy were highly developed (line 2), more so than his self-awareness (line 8). Perhaps he works in the helping professions and is doing a great job, but his awareness does not exceed that of the average personality. He has not yet awakened to his identity with the whole. The line of action (7) is also very developed, so he is probably skilful in organising and manifesting compassion in a practical way.

Let's look at the self-line and those of the three primary functions. We need to remember how the seven functions relate to the seven rays. The self is not a function but a being of light. As the "white light" and Universal Self it is the source of all the different rays.

The self-line represents the width and height of our self-awareness. It indicates the development of how we relate to the world, from an egocentric view through ethnocentric and world-centric views to a Cosmo-centric identification, and it also refers to the levels of awareness that the self has attained, from body consciousness to Spirit consciousness. The Self enters these inner landscapes through meditation and reflection.

The feeling-line relates to the development of sensitivity. It shows our level of empathy with others and our understanding of different emotional states. It charts the development of our empathetic understanding, not only in the social dimension, but also with the higher worlds of intuition and transcendence. Sensitivity is needed if we are to embrace impersonal and boundless love. In addition, the capacity to contain painful states grows as we direct our sensitivity toward the depths of our being, into the darkness of destructive patterns.

The thought-line develops as our mind grows and we are able to entertain many different perspectives simultaneously. It represents our worldview, our understanding of social environments and the products of culture. It is also the vertical dimension, and charts the quality and validity of our interpretations of reality, how integral we are and the extent to which our perspectives are flexible.

To summarise:

The will provides the power to breakthrough and the ability to express our identity in action and continually enlarge our sense of freedom in action.

Feelings enable us to experience intimacy, connectedness, warmth and deep meaningful relationships.

Thought gives us clarity, overview and expands our horizons, so we can grasp the world and communicate.

Imagination allows us to experience magic, spontaneity, play and adventure, a space where the grey routines of the day are interrupted by dance, laughter and joy.

Logic contributes to our sense of reality and provides an ability to make judgments from a firm footing, so we can build our dreams on solid factual ground.

Passion gives us the fire we need to accomplish our dreams; it provides focus and enthusiasm.

Action offers grounding, vitality and a practical sense so we can organise and see the results of our creative force.

From these perspectives, let us now investigate the seven energy types in detail and see how they develop through the seven ways to Self-realisation.

"Meditation is energy work - We work in and with energies"

Chapter 4

Your Energy Typology: Your Psychological and Spiritual DNA

When I had come to understand the ray qualities of my Soul, my personality, feelings, body and mind – I felt I was in touch with something profound. I could see how understanding the ray qualities offered me an explanation for the good and the problematic aspects of my personality. For example, I used to get irritable if someone asked for a detailed explanation of something because it slowed down my mind. I assumed they were "idiots" and knew I had the right answer, even if I didn't. When facts showed that I was wrong I felt as if a natural law had been violated. I realised that my mental processes were dominated by the dynamic energy type (the river of will and power). The positive aspect of the will is the ability to focus, to concentrate, to penetrate to the essence of things. Will helps us to define fundamental principles, to think abstractly and see the larger picture. Its negative qualities are arrogance, impatience and inflexibility. This mental type can be more or less balanced depending on the individual's level of awareness and his mind's developmental progress. The ability to turn what is immature in oneself into one's higher talents is crucial here. Much observation is needed to clarify the five different energies within the personality and Soul. We seldom distinguish between thought, feeling and bodily energies; they are often mixed up.

It took me a lot of time to recognise my own

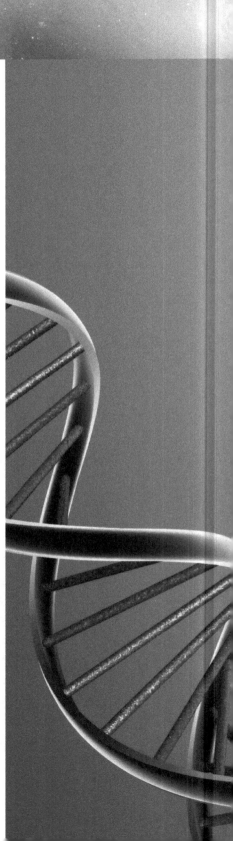

energy type profile, a 2-6161 combination; this has been evaluated many times by my friends, colleagues and students. My Soul is influenced by the second ray of love-wisdom, the sensitive energy type (2). My personality is dominated by the sixth ray, the dedicated energy type (6). My mind is dynamic (1), my feelings are dedicated (6) and my body is dynamic (1). So my energy type profile is 2-6161. This makes me a sensitive Soul endeavouring to express its qualities through a fiery and dedicated personality. There is a touch of humour: we can say that my soft wisdom-orientated Soul unfolds through a persona resembling a battle tank. My two dominating energy types move in opposite directions; no wonder my life has been a struggle against a tendency to isolate myself.

My first and sixth ray typology also gives me endurance and a will to experience freedom. Knowing my typology helps me accept my DNA on all levels, and to realise my inherent potential. It highlights the qualities I need to develop for my psychological make-up to become whole.

Our primary energy types warrant a great deal of focus in our meditations because they are what enables us to experience our joy, meaning, talents and motivation. Integral meditation balances and develops our psychological and spiritual DNA. I have meditated extensively on the psychological qualities of the sensitive and creative ray qualities, and this has given my character more flow and freedom. Meditating on the creative energy type, radiating harmony and beauty, added lightness, grace and spontaneity to my personality. It has curbed my tendency to be overly serious and single minded; I now achieve my objectives more easily If I "go–with–the flow". It is not always good to force our will onto people and situations, and this has been an important lesson for me. If we identify the qualities we need to become whole, we can design meditations to bring this about.

It's important to stress that a meditation not suited to your spiritual type can have negative consequences. Mindfulness meditations are very popular to-day; yet research has shown that they can create a passive and dispassionate character. This may have advantages in some cases, but in others it may not. We should be aware of the effects of our meditations in order to practice the right one at the right time.

Each of the seven energy types expresses a particular ray quality. Table 2 shows the correspondence between ray, function and type.

Table 2: The seven rays, seven psychological functions and seven energy types.

	The Seven Rays	The Seven Psychological Functions	The Seven Energy Types
1	The dynamic ray one	Will	The dynamic type
2	The sensitive ray two	Feeling	The sensitive type
3	The intelligent ray three	Thought	The mental type
4	The creative ray four	Imagination	The creative type
5	The scientific ray five	Logic	The analytical type
6	The idealising ray sixth	Passion	The dedicated type
7	The manifesting ray seven	Action	The practical type

If we observe human behaviour, it is easy to see how different we are. Different typologies have been devised to classify these differences, for example Gurdjieff's Enneagram, C.G Jung's *Psychological Types*, the Meyers Briggs test, astrology, psychiatric classifications, and so on.

Energy typology is unique because of its vertical levels of types from the body to Spirit. There are also the possible energy types of Spirit, of which we have yet to speak. It is such an advanced study that hardly anyone expresses these qualities. For practical reasons we work with the five levels of body, feelings, mind, personality and Soul based on the development of the seven psychological functions. The possible combinations here are many. When we add the introvert and extrovert version of the types, their 63 talents and 56 shadow parts, we have an enormous variation. Simple, but yet so complex. This is the foundation of our online identity profile – Jivayou.com

These variations safeguard us from narrow categories. The different levels also explain the vertical conflicts we can experience between our mind and emotions. When we begin to understand the different levels, we can help them to co-operate. *However, no one is only a type.* There is an X-factor, a unique pattern within us, which transcends all systems and classifications. This is the evolutionary stage of the Soul – the development of consciousness-will. This is expressed through the degree of wisdom with which the Soul applies the different energies and informs our life and actions.

While we've seen that the rays and types are the same, it is still important to differentiate between the energies of the rays and the energy types, and the ways they manifest. The seven rivers of life are ever-present in the great universal ocean; they flow through every manifestation of the All. An energy type, however, is an energy bound to a particular vehicle, what we call the physical body, the emotional body, the mental body, the personality field and the Soul body. Along with the physical body, we have subtle bodies, or "sheaths" as they are called in yogic literature. Each body has a particular energy type coloured by one of the seven rays. I will speak more about them in Chapter 9.

When we speak of the five individual energy types, we mean how the seven ray qualities are expressed in our lives through the five bodies. How do we seek meaning? What is our character? How do we think, feel and act?

Figure 14: The five levels of our inner house, also known as the five layers of our body, emotions, mind, personality and soul.

Figure 14 shows the five levels of our inner house, which is made up of our Soul and our personality. We are not aware of all the rooms or floors in our inner house. Some have never been inhabited, and few of us know the layout of all the rooms. In the diagram we see the different holarchies (wholes within wholes) symbolising the five layers from the bottom up: the symbol of the energy types is illustrated at each level. An exchange takes places through these levels between the environment and the incoming energies of the different rays. Moving down from above this diagram depicts a 7-2521 profile: a *manifestation type* on the Soul level (7), with a *sensitive* personality (2), an *analytical* mind (5), a *sensitive* feeling nature (2), and a *dynamic* body (1).

The seven different energy types combined with the five levels make up a kind of physical, psychological and spiritual DNA in each of us. The seven ray qualities that are influencing us all the time are coloured by, or filtered through, the different energy types and bodies that express them. It is through this process that variations of personality develop. We can see that:

Body types are different, some are slim, fast, light; others are strong, slow and heavy ...

Emotional types are different, some are calm, others fiery, and some are stoic ...

Thinking types are different, our thought processes can be dominated by analytical, associative or abstract thinking.

Personality types are different, some are dynamic, some are sensitive, others are creative in the way they create success in life.

Soul types are different, some express their spirituality through politics, others through science, teaching or art …

Energy typology helps locate different types on the appropriate levels, and applies methods to develop each to the fullest potential. When we understand our types, we can harmonise them, which is key to the integration of the personality and Soul-realisation, which is what we mean by personal and transpersonal Psychosynthesis respectively.

Here is a brief run through of the seven energy types and their characteristics. As previously described, each type develops in keeping with its corresponding psychological function.

 The dynamic energy type is often found in the archetypical roles of **Hero**, **Manager** and **Pioneer**. If you are influenced by this energy you will seek a position of power, that of a leader. You enjoy competition and thrive on challenges. You embrace the role of the hero, who puts things into order. *The manager* expresses the introvert aspect of the will through endurance, and as the one who upholds purpose and protects values. *The pioneer* expresses the will's extroverted aspect, its power to make breakthroughs. This person leads people to the horizon and beyond; he can overcome any obstacle. *The Hero* balances both sides of the will and leads through inspiration. The hero does not want followers but is committed to the idea. The Hero inspires through charisma, magnetism, integrity and courage, leading others to unite their efforts. Those strongly influenced by the archetype of the Hero can shape the future by uniting all available resources around a common goal. The Hero takes risks and goes where angels fear to tread. He knows that at the edge of the unknown much power can be found.

The downward pointing red arrow symbolises the dynamic energy type, which is fiery and strong. It illustrates its power to stimulate greatness through bold decision-making, like a lightning bolt from the sky. Sudden decisions and quick actions are an expression of this creative and powerful life force.

Virtues: Strength, one-pointed, focus, liberation, courage, forceful, pioneering, steadfast, simplicity, impersonality, boldness, directness, truthful, self-esteem, empowerment, fearless, authority, impartiality, decisiveness, break-through power, immovable, sovereignty, authenticity, centredness, will to victory, trustworthy, broad-minded.

Vices: Ruthless, hard, domineering, insensitive, cold, isolating, power hungry, destructive, prideful, arrogant, violent, suppressive, impatient, stubborn, tyrannical, self-centred, cruel, control freak.

The sensitive energy type fills the roles of **The Illuminator, The Guide** and **The Helper**. Your life is motivated by what we might call the intelligence of the heart. Your deep insights help you understand your own psychological life as well as that of others. You excel in building good human relationships. A sense of belonging and community is important to you. The ability to empathise and understand the psychological world of others comes with the influence of *The Guide*. This is the introverted aspect of the feeling function, which enables you to develop a profound insight into the causes of suffering and separation. This can be a great help to the people around you. *The Helper* expresses the extrovert qualities through compassion, warmth and heartfelt understanding. You are attracted to people who suffer and need your protection. You can be a true healer, a person who cures physical illnesses or psychological wounds. *The Illuminator* masters both sides and aids the enlightenment of others through teaching, mostly through personal example. Your presence is calm and peaceful, and you are an authentic expression of the Soul's light in the world. The Illuminator brings new revelations of what we can accomplish when we unite our common forces, and it is this that lies behind ideas of sisterhood and brotherhood.

The blue counter clockwise arrow symbolises this type: blue is calming and peaceful, the circle embracing and inclusive.

Virtues: Wisdom, calm, unity, love, compassion, holistic, connection, appreciation, healing, co-operative, inclusiveness, insight, warmth, forgiveness, strength, endurance, patience, magnetism, openness, love of truth, acceptance, intuition, serenity

Vices: Sentimental, victimised, naivety, vague, passive, oversensitive, indifference, self pity, fear, love of being loved, attachment, overprotective, fear of conflict, powerless, impractical.

The mental energy type enjoys playing **The Genius, The Thinker** and **The Strategist**. The skilful use of the mind motivates those who feel this energy. You love to think, to develop new perspectives, to communicate and to foster new understandings. *The Thinker* expresses the introverted aspect of thought through an ability to gain an overview of his field of knowledge. You can acquire much knowledge, get to the point and create new ideas. *The Strategist* expresses the extroverted aspect of thought. Your plans succeed because you make the best use of whatever is available. You handle financial and other resources intelligently to secure practical output. Because *The Genius* combines these aspects he or she is a true innovator who knows how to create new ideas by thinking outside the box.

Here we find the open and free expression of a mind that plays with ideas but is not attached to them. Through this, new inventions and theories enter the world.

The yellow arrows symbolise the mental type: like the mind, the arrows move in many directions, linking thoughts together. Yellow is traditionally thought to stimulate the intellect.

Virtues: Mental understanding, abstract views, strategic, communicative, oral skills, curiosity, sincerity, clarity of intellect, originality, foresight, caution, planning, flexibility, intelligence, quickness, impartiality, economic, high activity, efficiency, alertness, concentration, skilful, understands complexity.

Vices: Mental pride, cold, calculating, hyperactive, veiling facts, spin, over-complicated, manipulative, devious, scheming, inaccuracy, obstinacy, critical, treacherous

 The creative energy type gives us **The Artist, The Aesthete** and **The Transformer**. Harmony and beauty are essential to types informed by this energy. *The Aesthete* expresses the introverted side of imagination. You can create images of harmony and beauty, which are expressed in your life and work, through your relationships with others or through your surroundings. *The Transformer* expresses the extroverted aspect of imagination; he is the dramatist, actor, psychotherapist or mediator. You are attracted to the light and dark sides of life and can foster harmony through conflict. You make peace through shadow-work with an open heart. *The Artist* combines both of these aspects creatively. You are able to play with opposites and create new levels of design, beauty and inventive life forms. Your intuitive lifestyle inspires new cultural and social values and outlooks, which in turn inspire new communities and holistic awareness. Your spontaneity, joy and unorthodox behaviour invigorate the social atmosphere, so we can discover a new way of being together.

The two green connected arrows are an appropriate symbol for the creative type because imagination helps us to unite opposites into wholes, and green is the colour of harmony.

Virtues: Beauty, vision, humour, mediating, peacemaker, balance, affectionate, conflict resolution, artistic, spontaneity, aesthetic, joy, play, entertainment, improvising, presence, sympathetic, courage, clarity, generous, quick intellect.

Vices: Worrier, exaggerated, muddy, agitating, daydreamer, inaccuracy, theatrical, lazy, unstable, self-centredness, cowardice, extravagance, moody, dramatising.

The analytical energy type appears in the archetypes of **The Explorer, The Investigator** and **The Specialist**. This type has a strong motivation for objective knowledge; they have a great need to know with *certainty*. For them knowing the truth and having all the facts is important. *The Investigator* expresses the introverted aspect of logic. She skilfully collects and systemises facts so as to arrive at an accurate picture of whatever is under scrutiny. Those influenced by this type will excel at discriminating between true and false knowledge. The Investigator cuts through assumptions to reach the core. *The Specialist* expresses the extroverted aspect of logic; this type uses knowledge in a very practical way. Inventing new products or improving the practical world with technical skills is common to these types – perhaps through psychological methods, green technology or crafts such as carpentry. *The Explorer* combines both skills in a spirit of invention, extending the boundaries of what might be thought possible. This type researches deeply and uncovers everything necessary to get to the truth. Possibilities abound in all areas of study, and will be discovered.

The orange arrow pointing right symbolises the analytical energy type because logic moves from point to point. Orange is the colour of the dynamic mind.

Virtues: Insight, revealing, know-how, knows cause and effect, perseverance, discrimination, inventive, verifying, scientific, just, common sense, fair, accuracy, impartiality, rational, uprightness, objective, experimenting, independence, precise, clarity, keen intellect.

Vices: Dogmatic, arrogant, dry, over analytical, narrowness, harsh criticism, unsympathetic, pride, prejudice, suspicious, hard, narrow-minded, cold.

The dedicated energy type takes on the roles of **The Visionary, The Idealist** and **The Advocate**. Whatever your other roles, with this in your psychological makeup you will be motivated by ideals. Something in your life demands your passionate, enthusiastic devotion. *The Idealist* expresses the introverted aspect of passion through seeing the potential goodness in the projects in which you are involved. This brings great loyalty and dedication. You motivate others through your optimism and steadfastness. *The advocate* displays the extroverted aspect of passion, and produces the skilful activist or motivational speaker. You love to infect others with your enthusiasm. You radiate love by giving projects your all. *The Visionary* is a dreamer who makes dreams come true. You see into the future and have great faith in what you see. Through your insight and hard work you make your visions available to others.

The purple upward pointing arrow symbolises the passionate heart, which lift the spirits of those around it. Purple suggests movement into the world of ideals.

Virtues: Idealism, devotion, strength, perseverance, one-pointedness, dedication, faith, optimism, humility, loyalty, purity, seriousness, intensity, courage, courtesy, motivation, fiery, self-reliance, inspiration, seeing potentials, futuristic, sincere, loving.

Vices: Naive, impulsive, formal, extreme, jealous, bigotry, pride, opinionated, fanatic, superficial, blind faith, judgmental, impractical, narrow.

 **The practical energy type** meets us as **The Creator, The Systematiser** and **The Organiser**. This energy motivates us to achieve concrete results through whatever is available to us. *The Systematiser* expresses the introverted aspect of action; through it you can turn chaos into order. Through your controlled actions and performance, you exude efficiency, reliability and skill. You lead whenever there's a need for order and structure. *The organiser* embodies the extroverted aspect of action, the energy to order your environment to optimum efficiency. You love to organise people and resources. *The Creator* is a magician when it comes to great ideas. He can plan and execute large projects, manifesting an inventive spirit. The Creator fashions new organisations, buildings or projects, expressing and mastering the divine fire within.

The dark red converging arrows symbolise this practical type; they focus the will, mind and feelings around a single goal. The dark red colour anchors and grounds the will through the body.

Virtues: Organising, strength, creative, timing, coordination, perseverance, courage, courtesy, detailed, self-reliance, practical, nobility, sense of order, ritual, synthesis, integration, elegance, co-operative, self-mastery, action, transformational, mastery of skills,

Vices: Power-greedy, hard, formal, bigotry, materialistic, pride, fixated, inflexible, opinionated, judgmental, narrow-minded, superficial.

The Seven Ways to the Soul

There are seven ways to the Soul, and each way benefits from certain meditation styles. The Soul's "way" is the process of bringing its qualities and aims into our lives. This does not mean a system of meditation in which, for example, you meditate solely on the will if you are a dynamic type. Dynamic types and all the others need to integrate all the different energies. Nevertheless it can help different types to follow a meditation that explores their specific qualities and develops their primary energies.

Energy typology embraces an evolutionary perspective, with a progression from awareness of the body to that of the Soul. The Soul's way of being becomes available to us depending on our level in this progression. The Soul opens our awareness beyond the self to others and the world, even to all of humanity. Soul qualities are always present in an indirect manner through diffusion through the personality and the types. An analytical personality will appear differently depending on whether he is wedded to a sensitive Soul or a dynamic one because the Soul quality conditions the energies of the personality.

The Soul manifests in the body through the personal self, which is a reflection of its luminous source. The awakening to the Soul often accompanies an existential crisis, when the Soul's values slowly begin to motivate the personality. Our earlier values, needs and habits don't necessary disappear but become secondary to those of the Soul.

It is important to remember that the seven ways are like the rainbow, with one colour passing into the other. One path will always attract us more than others, and this is our own way to the Soul. Piero Ferrucci's wonderful book *Inevitable Grace* presents the seven ways through accounts of the lives of famous men and women.

Below I will describe some well known characters from history who infused their personalities with the altruism, dedication, goodness, truthfulness and beauty of the Soul.

1. The Way of the Hero

The hero's way leads through the will, so meditations emphasising the will are important here. We can think of heroes who showed courage during war. Others were pioneers who showed moral courage to resist mainstream opinion and open new ways to freedom and justice. They had the power to stand alone, fortified by a calm certainty that their actions were correct. They sustained and defended their vision and values. The American President Franklin Delano Roosevelt, who suffered severe physical handicaps, led his country out of depression and came to Europe's aid in World War II. Winston Churchill's spirited resistance to Hitler is another good example. But there are also inner wars that require heroes too. Here we find many religious pioneers. Very often these are sensitive or dedicated types, with much of the leader within them.

Franklin Rooosevelt

Winston Churchill

The hero's way is that of the leader because through leading one can develop the strength and power needed to perform heroic deeds. The leader is guided by a purpose that defines the law of his or her life. This purpose is often expressed in a new vision of freedom and justice for the people they serve. Leaders are moved by an evolutionary impulse and initiate new developments in society. A true leader empowers those around them. Such leaders give us the courage to step into the unknown and inspire us to embrace lofty visions of humanity.

Queen Elisabeth I

The hero can also be a reformer. Heroes often bring a sword, and not peace, because the old order seldom gives up without a fight. They sow new ideas that eventually inspire humanity. England's Queen Elisabeth I brought England into a Golden Age and was a true reformer. The greatness of the hero manifests as a bold, daring spirit that serves the love that motivates them. This is the mark of a true hero.

The diamond symbolises the hero. It is strong, yet transparent, allowing light and inspiration to shine through.

2. The Way of the Illuminator

Meditations on the ray qualities of love and wisdom are important for this path. Let's see who we find here.

Who am I? Where do we come from? Where are we heading? Human beings have asked these questions for millennia. The spiritual illuminators have answered them through their own enlightenment. The illuminator is called to seek an answer to the big questions concerning life and death through their own lives. They are

Maria Montessori

motivated by a deep need to end suffering. They develop their understanding through a kind of wisdom that comes from contemplating the question and acting from this inner knowledge. They feel a love for all humanity in its misery and become a channel for boundless compassion. The Dalai Lama and the South African bishop Desmond Tutu are contemporary examples of the illuminator. Christ was one and so was the Buddha; each in their own way showed the world that love and wisdom are the ultimate goal of humanity.

Desmond Tutu

The archetypical role of the teacher is typical for this path. He teaches best by example, and through a deep sympathy with the people he is able to enlighten. Teachers understand the need for education: children are like flowers – anyone who wants to learn is like a flower – and education is sun, water and earth. True education

Dalai Lama

stimulates our inner light; through this our awakening to knowledge, wisdom and love is made possible. Good teachers know this and bestow empathy, understanding and kindness on their students. They are the light that awakens light. On this way we find many influential teachers and educationalists such as the founder of the Montessori Method, Maria Montessori.

The sun symbolises this way. Those who have developed their light illuminate all around them.

3. The way of the Genius

The Genius realises himself through intelligence, ideas and abstract thinking. Meditations aimed at reflection and reception are important here.

Albert Einstein

The eagle-eyed can see through complexity and confusion. This is the way of the genius and the philosopher. I offer Albert Einstein and Ken Wilber as examples. Genius penetrates the mystery of creation and grasps the purpose behind the forms. They translate the complexity of evolution into theories and weave these theories into an integral pattern. They are in search of a theory of everything because they know intuitively that everything is interconnected. For them separation is an illusion.

The way of genius follows the *path of ethics* Societies and cultures change quickly: new

Ken Wilber

Simone de Beauvoir

technologies, discoveries and values emerge and trigger a re-evaluation of our ethical frameworks, such as in human rights, animal rights and gender equality. The genius is more than an intellectual; she forms the avant-garde creating new cultural patterns through being a living example of the change. These are the writers, thinkers and philosophers who raise our level of consciousness. These are the trendsetters who offer themselves as examples for how to pursue the true, the good and the beautiful. In her life, the French existential thinker Simone de Beauvoir pioneered new possibilities for modern women.

Thinkers and the geniuses formulate the ideas that direct the evolution of culture.

The eye symbolises the way of genius, ever on the lookout for new evolutionary perspectives.

4. The Way of the Artist

 The evolution of the artist requires the qualities of harmony and beauty. Imagination dominates in him, so meditation based on visualisation is important for this type.

Artists occupy all the rays, but here is an artist of life. The artist can harmonise contrasts and unite conflicts. By enduring chaos, darkness and drama they can distil their particular wisdom. When they succeed in balancing opposites, great beauty is their reward.

The way of the artist is often the way of *suffering*. The true artist embraces painful oppositions in life; by doing so, she becomes a true representative of humanity. Artists mirror imperfection and grace, dramatising our inner lives. A longing for harmony and balance sustains them through their struggles, which the artist presents to us through dance, music, film and theatre, showing us life in the form of great dramas and their resolution. The great composer Richard Wagner is a good example.

The psychotherapist or mediator also moves in this way, helping people to find harmony through their conflicts. C.G. Jung, founder of analytical psychology, is an example. The

C.G. Jung

Richard Wagner

Georgia O'Keeffe

way of the artist is also the way of aesthetics. Beauty is the artist's polar star. Without beauty this world cannot truly reflect Spirit. Someone who set new standards in this way was the American painter Georgia O'Keeffe.

The Soul is beautiful, and contains all that is good and true. Meditation can be an inner atelier where we beautify our personality using the qualities of the Soul. This is the importance of visualisation.

The Chinese symbol of *Yin-Yang*, linking light and darkness in a unified whole, can represent this way.

5. The Way of the Explorer

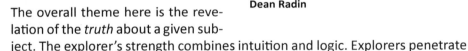

The explorer illuminates through the concrete mind. Through intuition and analysis the explorer investigates the mysteries of life. Focused reflective meditation is an important practice for this way.

Dean Radin

The overall theme here is the revelation of the *truth* about a given subject. The explorer's strength combines intuition and logic. Explorers penetrate the facts and get behind a mystery that requires resolution. The explorer goes where others do not. New discoveries, technologies and possibilities fascinate them. They explore subtle realms: the quantum physicist is an example here, but also those who study life after death and the reality of the Soul.

Explorers map new territory; their research brings new technological, psychological and spiritual innovations that change our understanding of the world. The Swiss psychiatrist Elisabeth Kübler-Ross, well-known

Elisabeth Kübler-Ross

for her research into the near-death experience, is an example for this type.

The explorer is a man or woman of science, exploring not only the physical sciences but also the mental and spiritual realms. Only through comparative experimental studies within all three areas will true knowledge of the world emerge. It is not the subject matter that makes a study scientific, but the rigor that is applied to the research. The American psychologist Dean Radin, one of the leading explorers in contemporary parapsychology, is a good example of this kind of science.

Madame Curie

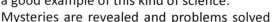

Mysteries are revealed and problems solved through the explorer's reflective, focused analysis, which is a kind of meditation. The practical value of their research is important for the explorer. Madame Curie, who developed the theory of radiation, is an example of the true explorer.

The key of wisdom, opening the doors of the mysteries, is a good symbol for the explorer.

6. The Way of the Visionary

The idealising ray informs the way of the visionary. Visionaries access spiritual dimensions through their surrender to the passionate heart. They are the world's true mystics. Appropriate meditations here focus on devotion and passion.

A longing for the transcendent leads the visionary on his quest. In search of perfection, supernal light or boundless love, the visionary is always on his way to the Promised Land. His visions are not necessary religious. As Carl Sagan puts it: "The

Mahatma Gandhi

cosmos is all that is or ever was or ever will be. Our feeblest contemplations of the Cosmos stir us—there is a tingling in the spine, a catch in the voice,

Mother Teresa

a faint sensation, as if a distant memory, or falling from a height. We know we are approaching the greatest of mysteries."

Visionaries like Mahatma Gandhi risked their lives for their cause. Their focused, passionate love led them to their goals. Within religion, visionaries are the introverted mystics or the extroverted saints. The mystic wants to illuminate the divine and bow to it in humble surrender. Through purification of the heart and dedication to the One, visionaries unite with the source. Here we can think of Saint Teresa of Avila.

The saint is motivated by a desire to be a true representative of the divine. If God is love, our duty is to bear witness to this and be an example through the consecration of our life. Saints follow their divine passion with utmost dedication. They care for the sick, help the poor and embrace the outcast, all of whom are children of God. Mother Teresa devoted her life to walking in the footsteps of Jesus. The same love can be directed at all of life, even the planet.

The flame symbolises the visionary: it is the fire that burns in their heart.

7. The Way of the Creator

The manifesting qualities of the seventh ray motivate this type. Meditations leading to well-structured rituals are important for this way. The Creator brings ideas to life through organised and collaborative processes.

Herbert von Karajan

The true creator follows a higher purpose that transcends personal ambition. Creators turn their resources towards a great goal. This requires psychological insight and great skill. Human and other resources are put to the test in the service of art, architecture or society. The creator organises people, formulates detailed and intelligent plans, and systematises everything to get the best results. An orchestra conductor is a good example of this type. He orchestrates a collection of musicians to create a musical masterpiece. *Herbert von Karajan* is a role model in this regard.

Creators bring law and order through new social systems and methods of administration. Great architects exemplify these ray qualities. Through their unique skills they manifest grand designs seen with their inner eye. As Spirit-in-Action created the manifest universe, so can we manifest our creative ideas (as above, so below). Jørn Utzon, designer of the Sydney Opera House, is an example of this type. *The six-pointed* star is a good symbol here because it represents the unified triangles of Spirit and matter.

Jørn Utzon

In Tables 3 and 4 I have represented all the energy types discussed so far.

Table 3: Personal energy types

	Function	Name	Drive	Roles
1	Will	The Dynamic type	Power,	The Manager, The Pioneer
2	Feeling	The Sensitive type	Heart,	The Guide, The Helper
3	Thought	The Mental type	Intelligence,	Thinker, The Strategist
4	Imagination	The Creative type	Harmony,	The Aesthete, The Transformer
5	Logic	The Analytical type	Knowhow,	The Investigator, The Specialist
6	Passion	The Dedicated type	Ideals,	The idealist, The Advocate
7	Action	The Practical type	Results,	The systematic, The Organiser

Table 4: Transpersonal energy types.

	Function	Name	Drive	Roles
1	Synthesis	The Dynamic type	Freedom	The Hero
2	Intuition	The Sensitive type	Love	The Illuminator
3	Ideas	The Mental type	Clarity	The Genius
4	Vision	The Creative type	Beauty	The Artist
5	Wisdom	The Analytical type	Truth	The Explorer
6	Service	The Dedicated type	Perfection	The Visionary
7	Creation	The Practical type	Manifestation	The Creator

This concludes our introduction to integral meditation. We have met the traveller, the Soul, the seven rivers of life, the seven energy types, the seven ways to the Soul and the seven levels of consciousness. In the next seven chapters we will travel on the seven rivers and feel their flow. By focusing on the most useful meditations, we will learn how to harvest the qualities of the rivers.

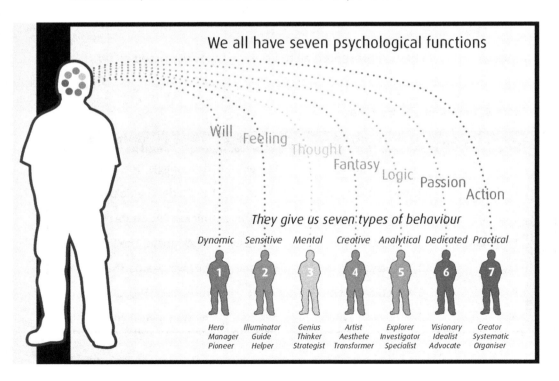

There are seven ways to the soul

... One will dominate your way

Chapter 5

The Dynamic River of Life:

Your Way to Freedom, Greatness and Power

The dynamic river of life is the way of the will, the omnipresent life force driving evolution – it's the essence of our being, life itself, but not everyone is aware of its power. In this chapter we'll look at the role the will plays in integral meditation and the process of Self-realisation. Leaders, pioneers, revolutionaries and authorities of all kinds are governed by the energy of the will: it pushes us forward with authenticity and force, continuously creating space for new life.

We all have power, yet we often disown it and relegate it to the shadows. Power is linked to sex, money, knowledge, beauty and physical strength. We often think about it in terms of having power over others, but we can also have power over ourselves. However, due to a lack of self-knowledge, our decisions are rarely based on our true needs. Most of our choices are unconscious and based on emotional material determined by our family and cultural background.

For more than a decade I've worked very closely with the will, which is a central theme in Psychosynthesis. Personally, I've never felt powerful. I come from a humble background and these roots affect me still. It's difficult to think big having grown up in an environment that inhibited such thoughts, but it's

not impossible. I've come to understand that it's only by daring to be ambitious that we can draw upon our power.

Power has always been a controversial topic because it can be so easily misused and abused, so we must certainly be cautious. Yet it is a topic we cannot avoid: when repressed, the will continues working in the unconscious, sparking one power struggle after another. Often, our need for acceptance and recognition means we are afraid to use our power in case we might upset others or earn a reputation for being domineering. But if we do not learn how to own and use our power we might find we are vulnerable to being dominated by others who are not afraid to exert their will at others' expense.

Precisely because the will is powerful, it's often the last function we learn to master. It is not power itself that's problematic, but the way we manage power. The Soul wants power in order to bring love and wisdom into the world. I want power in order to spread energy psychology as far as possible. These are good uses of power.

Greatness is related to the will. Through the will we can free ourselves from bondage and embrace our power. The will is a primary force, pushing us beyond our comfort zone when it is necessary to grow – this can be painful, and we often kick and scream when forced out of our secure little worlds. The will can also be used to cut the ties that diminish our lives. By using our will, greatness can be found; we must dare to listen to its call and throw ourselves into life. With this in mind, it is important to recognise the difference between two types of will: there is the *will of the personality*, which can be self-assertive and domineering, whereas the *will of the Soul* wants to make a difference in the world.

It will take time to learn how to use our will and our power, and even as we do so we will need to fight feelings of inferiority and negative self-images which require great effort to overcome. It is a never-ending struggle. The One Life's will, which means the Universal Life drives us toward greatness, yet too often we are satisfied with mediocrity and ignore the gold hidden in our hearts. Mediocrity insults our divine core, but even the most inert mediocrity eventually gives way to the piercing force of the Soul. Something in us insists on the freedom to realise our potential for the good, the true and the beautiful. And the good news is that many are now waking up to this freedom.

No one can be great without a vision of greatness. What is our personal vision of greatness? What do we want to achieve so that our lives can be a true ex-pression of who we are? Small achievements are sufficient for the little self, but the Soul requires something more – yet becoming aware of this ambition can be frightening.

In late 2011, I was on a meditation retreat, meditating ten hours a day for five days. On the third day I noticed a shift in my being. An intense, tightly focused energy surrounded my head. I felt like something was pushing me – a vacuum that wanted to suck me out of myself and into the cosmos. I could see a light at the end of a long tunnel. I gathered my strength and focused on this light, then suddenly found myself in a kind of birth canal, a narrow passage that I had to force myself through. How long I stayed like this I do not know because my awareness was so fixed on the light. Finally I emerged into what I can only describe as a "cosmic intention", a force field of will, more powerful than any I have ever known. Its message was simple: the intention demanded that a number of meditation schools be established over the world in order to forge a link between the divine will and humanity's collective will. The message was wordless, an intuitive awakening to my part in a global, even cosmic project. I had long felt this calling and worked towards it, but never before had I felt in possession of such a grand vision or of the feeling that the cosmos was working with me.

The universal will manifests in us as the will to love. The World Soul is awakening so quickly that it needs help in reaching humanity so we can play our part in its emergence. This work needs to take place all over the planet, and I felt awe and pride in recognising my small role in this noble task.

I have learned that intuitions that arrive during meditation can be filled with intention and power. They are not merely mental images but fields of living energy and determination. The personality reacts to these forces differently, depending on its readiness. Opposition to the new will rises from the subcon-scious, ready to defend its territory. A power struggle begins. Who will occupy the throne in our inner kingdom? Here we discover what kind of hero we are. Our choices and actions reveal who we are, our values and needs, and the powers we serve. In this struggle we need to learn forgiveness. We invariably make mistakes and let ourselves down. Befriending our inner and outer com-batants helps. We are never alone, however isolated we feel at times.

In my experience, as an old wounded warrior, gentle love is not enough. We need a fiery dynamic love – a *will* to love. The dynamic river leads to the Royal Road and the way of the hero. We are all kings and queens of noble birth, des-tined to rule over our personal kingdom. The purpose of life is to realise our talents and actualise our Soul's vision in the world. By conquering ourselves we enter the kingdom of heaven – which is the Soul – then we can share the treasure we find with the world. This ongoing struggle requires much blood, sweat and tears, and our later moments of spontaneous flow come about as a result of our work on integrating our will and power. What does it mean to be a hero? It means realising our inner nature and expressing it in action, thereby bringing greatness to life.

An appetite for freedom is characteristic of the dynamic river of life. At first freedom was not that important to me, I only wanted love, or to be free in the sense of being free *from* something. This was partly because I misunderstood the meaning of freedom. Most commonly, freedom is often associated with boundaries – which are, of course, an important aspect of freedom because they help us to assert our sovereignty, to stand up for ourselves, and to develop the resilience we need to face life. But this is only one aspect of freedom . Freedom also means expressing our divine potential through will, love, beauty, genius, and our power to create. Freedom means embracing life and investing our power and abilities in creative expression. Some religions speak of transcending the world we find ourselves in – but this is not the way of freedom. It is certainly true that we can be free by running from our conflicts, but we can also access the freedom to stand and confront our conflicts. So while the ascetic rejects the world, the new spirituality urges us to actualise our highest self *in* the world, pursuing higher levels of consciousness in order to embody them in the here and now.

Happy was the day I discovered my deep longing to be free. It was as if I had woken up to life itself. A dynamic impulse in me longed to conquer every physical and psychological limitation. I reflected on why I was so unhappy with my life, despite my achievements. Something inside me revolted. My life had become a prison, a place of limitations. The frustration of being so irredeemably mediocre obsessed me. This was not self pity, but the pain of being unable to express myself fully, whatever my inadequacies. A wall separated me from the world. I am happy to report I have made great progress, although there are still times when I feel inadequate. However, the difference now is that I am now aware that there is a divine freedom motivating me, driving me forward through layers of resistance. My inner king wants to be free – and this will never change. There will always be pain because this coat of flesh is too small – if it isn't my personal life that's too small then it's my contribution to the world – but I truly believe our outer life is a reflection of our consciousness, which means there is always something we can do to change our circumstances. So, if I'm unhappy with something in my life, I can change my situation by changing the quality of my consciousness. Let me clarify. Whatever we are identified with, this will be reflected in that events happening in our lives. However, most of our identifications are unconscious which means to change our circumstances we must go deep inside our minds to remove old and outgrown identifications in order to master our lives. We are also part of a collective reality; this means that what we meet in the outer world is often a direct reflection of the collective awareness of the people around us. Our task here is to identify with the higher frequencies of the collective consciousness to shift the collective toward World Soul consciousness.

The Delphic maxim "know thyself" relates to the will because we are who we *choose* to be. The will directs our energies and determines the true expression of our identity. Every choice shapes our character and destiny. We can say that the will is the Soul's executive power.

Self-knowledge brings power but is difficult to achieve. Our consciousness and identity fluctuates. Who are you *really* as a man, woman, father, mother, professional, friend, son, daughter, and other roles? But we are *not* our roles. Our roles are steps towards our ultimate identity, and we cannot do without them, but we are something else. We can call these roles our "stage-selves" – our selves at different stages, which in time lead us to the Soul and the absolute universal Self.

Let me give an example of a false self from my own life concerning gender identity. Our gender identity is influenced by our parents, our earliest role models. Later, during puberty, this identity is tested and develops as we become sexually active. In my own life, I was deeply confused during my teenage years because the role models in my life did not reflect me truly: I was sensitive, taught to hide my feelings, and a bad case of acne made me afraid to approach women and lowered my sense of self as a man. To protect myself, I internalised a stereotypical notion of masculinity based on the idea of the "strong man". This gave me a socially acceptable identity but left me feeling inferior because it did not provide space for my sensitivity. Adopting my "John Wayne" persona left me feeling completely alien, and alienated from myself. Only later, after relationships, much meditation and years of psychotherapy, did I realise that women appreciated my sensitivity. Gradually, this recognition dissolved my earlier identifications and I changed. I felt more at home with myself and with women. I started to love myself as a man. There was a new, more creative balance between my action-orientated masculinity and my empathetic, easy-going side.

The dynamic river leads to the path of self-knowledge. When we awaken to deeper aspects of ourselves our subpersonalities evolve and we can create a firmer self-image based on our true nature. This will be refined and reshaped as we ascend to higher levels of consciousness, to new values that transcend and integrate previous levels.

Awareness Meditation and the Will

As we know, the will is closely linked to choice. Without choices, we cannot direct our intention towards a goal. When we exercise free choice we access the power of the will. It is true that in some situations our only choice is to accept our destiny. Nevertheless the act of choice is empowering and prevents us from becoming victims. Illness and death are not welcome experiences, but we can choose how to respond to them. As Viktor Frankl shows in *Man's Search for Meaning*, even the horrors of a concentration camp can be endured through the power to choose.

But how often are our choices *really* free? Are we free to choose a different life if we want? For many of us, the answer is no. We are bound by all sorts of attachments that limit our freedom: to people, money, beliefs and convictions. We may be ignorant of our bondage until life challenges us. Most of us change only when something external interferes with our lives: we lose a job, a partner, a home, our status. Meditation can help us recognise our attachments and lack of freedom, and this helps us to change. Practising Awareness Meditation can help us to disidentify from restrictive attachments. Assagioli said: What we identify with, controls us; what we disidentify from, we can learn to master. In his Psychosynthesis model, Assagioli's offers a dis-identification exercise based on Eastern ideas about consciousness. We've already spoken about the self, but let's look at it again in the context of meditation.

The self is not the voice we hear in our head, analysing everything. We must ignore this if we are to discover consciousness as awareness.

The self is the observer, the calm centre of consciousness. It is from this centre that will and choice arise. By disidentifying from the contents of consciousness and observing them instead, we can learn to access our will and choose *what* we identify with. Hence Assagioli's belief that the will is a direct function of the self; the will is the captain on the ship of the self.

If we want to be free to live a life according to our deepest values, we must also have a psychological practice that can help us to become aware of these values. We must recognise the forces that enslave us to an inauthentic way of life, and Awareness Meditation can help us with this. It may sound paradoxical to those who practice Awareness Meditation (mindfulness) that this particular type of meditation is associated with the will, but this meditation can help us to discover our will *if we look for it*. A traditional Eastern practice teaches us to let go of all striving and all contents of consciousness. We can then experience the self as the observer and pure open consciousness without content. This state seems to be without will, because it is effortless, but in order to disidentify (from the contents of consciousness) we still need to use our will by *choosing* to let go of our attachment to the contents of consciousness.

All action requires will and choice. Freedom is always limited by the choices we make. Even in a state of pure observation, without effort or focus, there is still the choice to continue meditating or not. This effortless intention is the will: it is the underlying motivation governing the act of withdrawing from the content of consciousness – emptying the mind, as they say. The will does not always exert itself forcefully, just as the captain lets the ship's engines do the work. But before we can reach a state of effortless intention we need to employ a radical form of Awareness Meditation that demands a tough will that can uphold a clear space in consciousness. Any trained meditator knows this to be a fact.

It makes a difference whether we direct our awareness towards the *source* of consciousness, the Self, or toward its *content*. Following the source, we find our inner witness and recognise that *we* are the awareness running through all existence. This is precisely the intention behind the dynamic river of life: to reveal our true identity.

Let me give an example from my own practice. In 2011 I led a one-day Awareness Meditation workshop. We began by observing the breath – this helps the mind to gradually relax and become quiet, leaving a calm, relaxed presence (I can recommend this practice as very rejuvenating) The next stage involved disidentifying from the body, emotions and mind to recognise that our essential self is something other than these entities. I let the content of my consciousness pass like clouds in the sky, letting go of thoughts and sensations. As my consciousness grew empty, a quiet neutral centre appeared. In this state, when our consciousness has quietened, we are often tempted to do something because the sense of emptiness seems too detached – there is no colour or emotion, only neutral observation. I had experienced this before; I knew my consciousness had not yet transcended my mental field because I still felt myself to be a human being separated from other people. This state is important: through prolonged practice we can create a place of stilness and

peace inside; when we disidentify from everything in the mind. In this state we make better choices because we are less affected by fear, desire and other impulses. We start to master our behaviour from this center, and accept what is and choose to stay with it.

During the third stage we turn our attention to the source of consciousness. Now we observe the observer. The eye cannot see itself, but if we meditate long enough our separate personal consciousness begins to dissolve. During the last hours of the meditation I managed to let go of everything; my awareness rested in an open presence. Then something familiar to anyone who has practised this type of meditation happened: spontaneously my consciousness expanded. It felt like I had escaped from a prison. I was free to join the wider impersonal consciousness because I was released from my mind and personal history. Experiencing no-thing-ness, we have the opportunity to be everything. It is perhaps more accurate to call this expanded presence a "universal presence" because the awareness itself suggests a self that is awake. In any case, the experience of a separate self disappears and we awaken to an expanded, larger self.

The no-thing-ness contains the potential for all possible actions. Yet once we act, our limitations and lack of freedom become obvious. I cannot choose to create a supernova the way Brahman can. I also cannot solve complex mathematical equations, unless I have studied a great deal. Transcendence cannot change these limitations. So even transcendence has its limits. The movement from potential to actual is always one of limits.

Our freedom will always face limitations. Those who withdraw from the world in pursuit of transcendence will achieve only relative freedom because they have given up the freedom to create and manifest their will in the outer world. An old Zen saying illustrates this: "Before enlightenment I chop wood and carry water, after enlightenment I chop wood and carry water." Transcendence may not make us free to act in the world. Rather we may give up our freedom to act in the world because we consider physical existence an empty illusion. This is not the way of the bodhisattva, who forgoes nirvana in order to remain on earth to help his fellow beings; he does not seek to escape to heaven from earth, but remains on earth until everybody has become enlightened.

Some so-called enlightened masters have successfully transcended everyday existence, but they still had to live a personal life in the world, and some have done so in a manner that lacks ethics and integrity. Such people might have experienced freedom and detachment, but psychologically they were immature and unable to manifest this freedom in the form of physical action. Enlightenment is a relative concept with different aspects to it: it partly involves transcending the world, but it can also mean bringing God, with in all his might, into the world.

In the experience of timeless being we still retain an "I". The feeling of "I" is always present. I experience it as an indefinable golden thread which stays constant throughout my life. The perspective of *who* I am changes, but the timeless "I" does not. In my meditation I wanted to explore this transcendent state. I looked into the void and examined if I really should be free of will. While passive, there was no apparent will beyond the intention to meditate. But as soon as I contemplated action, a dynamic force emerged – a psychological electricity – urgent and full of meaning. I realised that I could not do whatever I liked in life; I could not go against the strong sense of purpose and meaning emanating from this electric force field.

I could not choose to live a different life. My life with all its restrictions was perfect as it was, and I could sense a powerful will that wanted to incarnate as "me". Through this life, my "I" can be liberated, set free to manifest the wisdom, love and light my experiences could provide. The suffering I experience is entirely impersonal; the higher order at work is far more significant. Each Soul's journey is important to the whole of humanity; each Soul participates in the redemption and resurrection of humankind. My personal will is a point of life and a dynamic intention that travels through time and space. In Eastern terminology, I had an experience of Jiva Atman, what we call the Soul.

Is there anything beyond this transcendent emptiness? Is nirvana the last stop? I was able to recognise that the experience of the Soul's will is clearly a contraction, and therefore operating at a lower frequency of consciousness, but I can't say what lies beyond it. However, many esoteric sources suggest nirvana is only a step on the way to higher levels of consciousness. Sri Aurobindo, a great enlightened Soul and one of my main sources of inspiration, describes his experience of nirvana and its underlying levels as follows:

"Now to reach nirvana was the first radical result of my own Yoga. It threw me suddenly into a condition above and without thought, unstained by any mental or vital movement; there was no ego, no real world – only when one looked through the immobile senses, something perceived or bore upon its sheer silence a world of empty forms, materialised shadows without true substance... I lived in that nirvana day and night before it began to admit other things into itself or modify itself at all, and the inner heart of experience, a constant memory of it and its power to return remained until in the end it began to disappear into a greater Superconsciousness from above. But meanwhile realisation added itself to realisation and fused itself with this original experience. At an early stage the aspect of an illusionary world gave place to one in which illusion is only a small surface phenomenon with an immense Divine Reality behind it and a supreme Divine Reality above it and an intense Divine Reality in the heart of everything that had seemed at first only a cinematic shape or shadow." (Sri Aurobindo, On Himself, p. 101)

Aurobindo's description resonates deeply with me. I am convinced there is a divine source behind creation. This raises the question of what it means to be enlightened. An enlightenment that only involves transcendence seems partial to me. If there is only one Self, and the same consciousness looking out from my eyes is also looking out from yours, then enlightenment will remain partial until all sentient beings are enlightened. Seen absolutely, individual enlightenment may be an illusion. But not individually, and here evolution is relevant. Evolution shows that all human beings are of equal value, but all are not equally developed, ie in terms of the degree of love-wisdom a person has realised.

The will is associated with death. According to esoteric sources, when the universe collapses and goes into pralaya – a period of un-manifested rest – it is because its source, the cosmic Logos, wills it so. It withdraws the life energy from the cosmos which then collapses and dissolves into its component parts. The same process happens when we die. The Soul draws back the consciousness and life energy from the physical body and the physical form perishes. The process of transformation is governed by the same principle. When we decide to stop a bad habit or leave a relationship, we withdraw the energy from the habit or relationship and it dies. Desires linked to the relationship or habit gradually dissolve. This can be painful but it will eventually release us from the attachment.

This is the way of the will. It shows that we keep something alive by giving it our attention, consciously or unconsciously. If we take life away from whatever no longer serves our higher purpose, it dies. I like the metaphor of "the will swinging the axe" because it shows the will's ability to swiftly cut away constraints. In practice it is very difficult to drop old habits without the support of psychotherapeutic techniques. Many habits hide behind defences and we do not see them during Awareness Meditation. Nevertheless, Awareness Meditation is invaluable for eliminating destructive desires and unhelpful behaviours. It shows us that we suffer when we cannot fulfil our desires, but it also reveals the impermanence of our desires. I am not a Buddhist, but the wisdom of the Buddha is fundamental to integral meditation.

Awareness Meditation leads to the development of three qualities, which esoteric philosophy identifies as detachment, dispassion and discrimination: the three Ds.

By letting go of desires, we achieve *detachment*. We do this by disidentifying from the attachments we recognise in meditation. Gradually we find the quiet and open centre, leading to transcendent awareness. This is freedom *from*.

Dispassion means that we are not *controlled* by our desires. We can enjoy them without being engulfed by them. Desire is a powerful force that can be put to creative use. It can be a source of pleasure if we learn how to enjoy our desires without being used by them. Desire, or passion, is a focused energy that we can experience as sexual energy or the devotional surrender to the divine. Our task is to cultivate our desires, to accustom them to a taste for higher qualities and values.

We learn how to *discriminate* by observing the energies arising in meditation. We can free ourselves from desires by breaking them down into their constituent parts. Jealousy, for example, consists of greed, anger and ignorance. By consciously observing a desire, we can examine its essence and understand its function and see how it is restricting our freedom. Then we can let it go.

I have spent hours contemplating some of my painful reactions to life, especially my tendency to isolation. In my case, layers of self-protection had crystallised around hatred, anger, hurt, ignorance, self pity, despair and, underneath them all, vulnerability. Awareness Meditation uncovers these elements and prescribes the psychological medicine necessary to cure the condition. In my case, I discovered that beauty and the qualities of grace, harmony and lightness could lead me away from a negative tendency to seek isolation.

Beauty defeats all my defence mechanisms, allowing the vulnerable core to meet the beloved. Beauty is an important part of the creative visualisation techniques used in meditating on the creative river of life. Given integral meditation practice this makes sense; it shows how different problems require different kinds of meditation.

What is the role of the will here? The answer is inner freedom. Awareness Meditation can lead to greater inner freedom, but not by itself. The will must be combined with other techniques before true freedom in action can be realised.

Power Meditation and Dynamic Meditation

In Chapter 2, we examined the consciousness bridge, which is a channel of pure consciousness connecting self and Soul. But it is also a bridge of being and life through which we can experience our I-Am-ness: identity without interpretation. In fact, the consciousness bridge keeps the incarnated part of the Soul alive and can recognise itself as a divine being. The Soul's greatest task is to strengthen this contact so that the being-life connection can develop in the personality. Life and being are both an expression of the dynamic river of life which directs us toward our ultimate identity.

Meditation aimed at developing the consciousness aspect of this bridge strengthens the contact between self and Soul and gives greater clarity and insight into ourselves and our life purpose. This is accomplished through Awareness Meditation, with its focus on the observer. In relation to strengthening the life aspect of this channel, many forms of meditation are effective here, particularly in strengthening what we can call "standing power": the ability to stay centred in our hearts no matter what. Through standing power we are able to rest in a sense of being which gives an intuitive knowledge of our divine inner nature. Standing power gives us access to dignity, nobility and the integrity we can connect to by serving a purpose that is grand, noble and mighty. This being-life bridge links the heart centre, the cave in the middle of the brain, the heart of the Soul's presence above the head, and the heart of the great solar being, the creator of our solar system (there are also other minor "stations" or points along this energy channel).

My understanding of standing power grew out of the practice with my "sun in the heart" meditation. When we meditate on the sun in the heart (ignoring the vertical connection with the sun above the head and beyond), we can learn to hold whatever emerges in our consciousness. (As mentioned earlier, we can also use this meditation to focus on developing particular Soul qualities. However, note we don't connect to the vertical masculine energies if we don't incorporate the vertical aspect of this meditation.)

I have used the vertical meditation for many years now. I call it the "Power Meditation" or the "I am who I am meditation" (see Appendix). You visualise the sun in the heart. Then you raise the sun's golden energy up to the sun in the head, and then to the sun over your head. You can even extend this energy to the heart of the great divine sun. When the connection between all the points is established, depending on your typology, you can anchor your awareness in the heart or the head centre (the heart develops its contact with Soul through the calm emotional field, the mind through the still mental field). I personally tend to focus in the mind, with a being connection in the heart that operates as the base or foundation for the meditation. In the next stage of the meditation, we rest into the phrase "I am who I am". Without thinking about the words, we maintain the *intention* to merge with this inner identity. The key word here is identity – with a focus on the will. We explore our identity as it opens to the source, the divine core of the Soul. We must keep alert, open and alive during the entire meditation because this allows us to sink deeper into the silence, the inner source of power and strength. Here we are able to surrender to our true nature, which in essence is the One Self, full of life and creative power.

Such meditation strengthens our sense of authentic identity. Archetypal images may emerge, showing us the ideal model our Soul seeks to achieve through our personality. I've even received two images simultaneously: one for the perfection of my personality, another showing my Soul's goal in this incarnation. This latter had a name and was associated with the image of a yogi. This image was so charged with intention that I was compelled to meditate on it until I understood my mission and my identity. Such images ignite our dedication and determination, but they also set very high standards which demand complete dedication to achieve. Without the heart's burning aspiration we cannot get far in this meditation.

Standing power represents the Soul's sovereignty and, as with all kings, the Soul has a sceptre: the spine. The spine conducts life energy from its base to the Soul above our head, the spine carries the Soul's intention to control the forces of our personality, to introduce the law of the Soul and the power of its will. Power Meditation literally strengthens our backbone so we can say no to desires, fears and to people and situations that diminish us. Life will test us to see if we can stay the course and stick to our truth. We may fall, but our standing power will enable us to rise again. Our standing power provides the courage and persistence to affirm the good, the true and the beautiful, even if this means painful sacrifices.

The mature will is ready to sacrifice whatever is necessary to achieve its objectives, even to kill what was once loved. This is not easy. Anyone who has tried to leave a dysfunctional relationship, or stop a bad habit, knows this. Our intention may be strong, but there is always the inclination to carry on as before. As we know, the spirit may be willing but the flesh is weak.

The Dynamic Meditation aims to develop the extroverted pole of the will, which is the will's break-through power. Increasing our standing power develops the will's introverted pole. Dynamic power breaks through whatever stands in the way of new life. The new life in nature that we see appearing in the spring is a symbol of our own spiritual power which can liberate us from old habits, from slavery to fear, and from old desires. We can see how the two poles of the will work together: we first breakthrough, then we stand firm on our decision. Or we slowly build up our intention and then actualise it.

Given the many limitations we face, the power to break through is essential. It gives us the strength to claim new territories, to realise our talents and potentials. This capacity for directed will, together with the heart's redeeming love, has been central to my own development. I've often had to force myself to think bigger, to pull myself up by my hair, as it were. The sense of inadequacy and inferiority that characterised my life was like a clammy fog extinguishing a heroic flame. Its advice to "be satisfied" and "fly no higher than the wings can carry you" justified taking no risks and the acceptance of a dull life. The acceptance of mediocrity and bland normality is the greatest obstacle to the living force of Spirit.

Nothing has ever been given to me, or so it seems. I used to lament this fact, but now I appreciate it. Working hard to achieve a goal makes us capable of creating something solid from scratch. Desert landscapes and barren rocks represent great natural beauty for me. To conquer life despite all obstacles is a basic impulse. We have many goals. We may desire more money or the love of someone; we may want to explore our sexuality, or have greater influence at work. To achieve these goals requires courage and the will to maintain an intention strong enough to overcome fear and laziness. In-tention means inner tension; it is a force that accumulates before it is released. We all know the feeling of momentum that follows a decision. When we say A, we must follow with B, and it is from here that the action starts. We then find ourselves in unfamiliar territory, facing the unknown and the loss of what has been abandoned. But there is also the vitality of our courage, its boldness and will to freedom. Through our will to freedom we realize that we are far greater than we believed. Daring is the prerequisite of heroism. Not Hollywood heroism, but that of everyday life; the heroism of an oppressed woman who finds the courage to leave her abusive husband. When we fight for greater freedom in our lives, we are heroes. We are often afraid of this uncompromising urge because we fear that it may kill us, but what really dies is the small part of ourselves that is not up to the challenge. It is, in fact, through this death that we can move on.

An Eastern teacher describes the Dynamic Meditation as "intense focus, the overwhelming determination that eliminates all barriers and literally forces a channel". Through the dynamic will the world becomes our oyster. We can project our consciousness towards our goals. The Dynamic Meditation always begins with the mind's targeted focus. In the world of the personality, the mind is the will's primary tool. We can apply our directed focus in different ways, depending on our purpose.

During one Dynamic Meditation, the will to manifest my vision for establishing a network of meditation schools (mentioned earlier) was so strong that I felt I had been pushed through a channel at the top of my head into a cosmic force field. I have also used the Dynamic Meditation to eliminate unwanted emotions. This technique consists of "staring" the emotion or situation "in the eyes" to drive it out of my energy field. (I should say that it helps if you have had experience in energy work.) This must be done correctly, otherwise it will only repress the material, which will return even stronger at a later date.

A few years ago I was hit by strong feelings of inadequacy, self pity and despair that emanated directly from my solar plexus. It was unusual for me to feel self pity so I was anxious to rid myself of it. I meditated in order to understand and eliminate this condition. This decision alone developed a force in me, a strong intention to be free. I observed the condition and found its source in the solar plexus. A hole in my energy system had allowed in a stream of self pity, despair and "wet" sensitivity, as if someone *outside* of me wanted to force weakness into me. Once I discovered this pressure, I stared it in the eyes intensely, focusing all the strength of my Soul on this invader as if I was throwing an intruder out of my house. Gradually the weakness left. I closed the gap in my energy field, then located the part of me that had opened this gap (when negative energies enter us, some part of us has allowed them in). This illustration of how I managed to fix a personal problem by drawing upon a number of different meditation techniques is illustrative of how integral meditation works.

In the Appendix you will find an example of Dynamic Meditation which can be used by readers who want to develop their break-through energy. The meditator begins by defining his purpose. He may want to focus on a particular quality that he would like to develop, such as beauty, freedom, courage or love. Or he may focus on an object, such as an image or a thought, which he wishes to understand. Then the meditator penetrates into the heart of what is desired in three stages. The first stage involves remaining disidentified from the object of meditation and all associated thoughts, ideas and feelings. The second stage involves entering into the quality of what is desired, merging with it while continuing to penetrate its essence. In the third stage, the meditator becomes one with the object of meditation in a state of non-duality

In his book *The Act of Will*, Assagioli describes different kinds of will: strong, good and skilful. Strong will is the one-pointed dynamic force we have discussed above. Good will is motivated by love and is holistic and collaborative. Skilful will is strategic, like that used by a chess player. The combination of these three wills makes for effective action. Assagioli's also distinguishes between personal, transpersonal and universal will, with each relating to different levels of consciousness. Ultimately there's only one will, the universal will that arises from Spirit-in-Action.

We can say that Dynamic Meditation suits all who need to strengthen their identity and achieve a breakthrough of some sort.

We should study all the dynamic river's positive qualities, yet we need to remember that if we are not mature enough to handle the energies there can be unwanted consequences. Energy is impersonal; playing with it foolishly is inadvisable. Sensitive, mental and creative types should pursue this meditation because they often lack direction and "break though" power. Others, who do not need this, should perhaps leave it alone. For example, this meditation will of course appeal to dynamic types, as this is their primary style of personality. However, for these types, it might be wise to work with less strenuous forms of meditation, focusing instead on the sensitive, creative and idealistic rivers of life. This is because wills that are already tough can arouse resistance in those around them, so some softening of the will, rather than strengthening, might be desirable.

Will is important, yet the will alone cannot lead us to our journey's end. We must enter other rivers, some of them formed out of much gentler waters.

"The power of the soul is the will to love"

Chapter 6

The Sensitive River of Life:
Your Way to Love, Wisdom and Unity

This chapter will look at the sensitive river of life, which is the river of love and wisdom. Love is an essential part of our lives, but do we really under-stand it? We've all had some difficulties with love; I am no exception. I have loved wholeheartedly and unreservedly and I write these words with pride because my life has proven a difficult terrain for love to thrive in. Alongside love, the sensitive river of life also concerns the wisdom we develop as we go through life's many experiences. The sensitive energy of this river is available to help us develop relationships within the spheres of I, We and the World. The I-zone concerns our relationship to ourselves; the We-zone concerns our relationships with others; and the World-zone concerns our capacity to bring love to the world at large. These three zones are an important part of integral meditation and form an important area to master.

Through the growth of sensitivity and our feeling function, our ability to love develops. But what we think of as love is often just a faint reflection of love's true nature, which is unity consciousness, or love without object. Without the lover or the beloved, love is like an ocean: we no longer give or receive love, but are *in* love. We breathe love – together. This omnipresent love can hold and be with everything just because it *is*; it understands the other so deeply that we *become* him or her through empathetic love. At the level of personality, this love makes us aware of the differences between self and other, yet we also see that because of this difference we are *more* complete while in relationship. We can learn to let go of barriers and be fully present with the other. This is a self-sacrificing love. Such a love has acquired nega-tive connotations because of its association with hidden agendas, which are self-serving, calculating and conditional. But by accessing the energy of the sensitive river such covert motives can be converted into their opposite. In this way we are able to experience love in its highest expression, which is an example of non-dual consciousness, a union between ourselves and the ob-ject of our awareness.

To really understand love we must distinguish between its different expres-sions. What is the difference between paternal love, maternal love, erotic love, possessive love, altruistic love, love of God, or the love of nature, culture

or beauty? There are also unhealthy expression of love – if our self-love is ego-centric and narcissistic we cannot truly love anyone else. When love is sealed off and isolated it can turn to hatred, which is really protective self-love. By contrast, healthy self-love is based on a deep appreciation of our basic identity and gives us a sense of dignity, self-esteem and responsibility.

Whereas the dynamic river of life insists on greatness, the sensitive river of love-wisdom helps us to accept our many imperfections. When we achieve a balance between love and will we can reach beyond our habitual selves and integrate those parts of us that shy away from greatness. A love of the perfect only is an impoverished love, whereas love that can reach into the darkness and embrace hatred, jealousy, greed and aggression – without succumbing to these states – is great. This is the love I focus on in many meditations. It asks us to *love everything that is!*

I recall that during an experience of meditation in which I was focusing on loving everything that is, I had an insight that proved central to my understanding of the meaning of life. As will be familiar to many of those who meditate, I was feeling frustrated by banal thoughts and images that filled my mind. I visualised a stream of acceptance flowing through my heart, but this made no difference because I realised I had a hidden agenda. Pure acceptance is about *not* trying to change anything. I had a choice: I could stop meditating or accept the banality and frustration. I abandoned my expectations and gradually embraced the content of my consciousness, including my identification with mediocrity.

This surrendering to my situation altered my consciousness, as if an inner cell had been illuminated by my Soul, completely changing my perspective. This was not about me! What was happening was far greater than my ego's need for convenience. Two phrases came to me: "All is teaching" and "All is service" (for some reason my most powerful insights during meditation come to me in English). I realised that these difficult conditions were teaching me something; they were direct reflections of my false identifications. I understood that as long as I believed these thoughts were a part of my identity, they would imprison me. Once more I could see that "my" thoughts were merely one frequency of a collective consciousness; anyone who had tuned into that frequency would feel them as well. Trivialities occupied my consciousness because I had insisted they had something to do with *me*. Seeing them impersonally revealed that they were only a frequency creating a kind of psychological smog – *which I needed to love!*

The message I received was that I was not meditating for my own sake. Rather, I was an "energy renovation worker" contracted to purify an area of the collective consciousness using the transformative power of love. Seeing this, I could release my victim consciousness and egocentrism. In a flash I shot from the basement to the rooftop, and then I received the next transmission: "Agony or Ecstasy – No difference!" I realised that whether I felt I was in contact with a cosmic love or whether I felt like a victim, it made no difference because neither feeling was about me. *Everything* was about service and teaching. The lesson was to love everything that is. With this came a sense of overwhelming freedom. I could have been surrounded by the walls of a prison, nevertheless I was completely free, as I am always. I can always choose to love, to be a brilliant light of consciousness in a dark place.

We can love our way through a brick wall or use willpower to knock it down.

Love dissolves, the will breaks through. Let me explain: the brick wall is my sense of being imprisoned by feelings and thoughts that stop me from engaging with life and freely expressing the creativity I feel inside.

Freedom and love are perfect partners. All of existence yearns for love, belonging and unity. Within every thing there is this longing, and when we touch it through love a process of liberation is initiated. This sounds abstract, but in reality it is a kind of alchemy: we can transform lead into gold through love. Each of the elements represents a state of consciousness associated with survival, safety and primary relationships, and gold represents the divine essence. As Aurobindo said, this divine essence is the One Life that lives in the heart of all states. Lust and fear trap us in addictions; we cannot be free until we liberate their essence. This is what "kissing the frog" means in fairy tales: at the magic touch, something lowly becomes a prince or princess. Let us explore this transforming power of love.

Through love we can increase the frequency of any state of consciousness. Through it negativity dissolves like ice in the sun. If we direct love to our feelings of hatred, they will gradually be released in love. This is a scientific fact anyone can verify. Love dissolves hatred into its component parts, releasing the light and life it has captured. Quantum physics tells us that, in a sense, everything is light. That's why meditation is about *enlightenment*. By becoming enlightened, we raise the frequency of everything around us. Meditation, aided by psychotherapy, can, in a short time, change consciousness significantly. Life itself provides opportunities to transform consciousness. But this journey can take a long time because we tend to repeat certain patterns, which meditation and psychotherapy can help us to avoid.

Feeling pain is unavoidable when working with love to create transformation. If we cannot contain the pain, we block our access to its source, which means we cannot increase its frequency. Pain activates defence mechanisms which protect us from our vulnerabilities through the instinctual responses of fight, flight or freezing on the spot. Most of us have felt the painful loss of intimacy with a partner, a friend or some significant other. Like the rest of us, I have ex-perienced this several times and when it happens, love is tested. It is difficult to love when a paralysing pain emerges. Our solar plexus becomes a black hole, our heart screams out, and old coping strategies resurface. In these situations we may need solitude, or contact with the other, even if at first you thought otherwise. Anger, aggression and irritation invade us. After one break up, thanks to my daily meditation and psychotherapy, I avoided most of the flight, fight or freeze responses through focusing on the vulnerable parts of my psyche that cried out for love. This is what is known as *withdrawing our projections. Let me explain.* Needs we cannot meet in ourselves, we proj-ect onto others in an attempt to make them our "love suppliers". When this umbilical cord is cut we feel intense pain; there is no longer a projected love to surround and protect our vulnerable parts, such as our inner child, our inner teenager or other fragile subpersonalities. When we withdraw our pro-jections, we consciously abandon trying to have our needs met by the other. We take responsibility for our own needs and become our own love supplier. Parts of us that had tried to steal energy from others begin to mature and be-come self-sufficient. This is not to say that we now meet all our needs alone, which is impossible – in our essence we are whole but as physical beings we are dependent on each other, which is something we need to understand if we are not to end up like North Korea, isolated and undeveloped. If we are to be mature adults we must learn to be able to stand alone and meet our basic needs for security ourselves.

After a break-up, we may obsess over our ex-partner as a way to restore our love supply. Meditation gradually stops this as we turn our attention to what is suffering *in us*. We focus on our own pain rather than thinking about the other. Of course, often we lose focus and let our coping strategies take over. We try to escape the pain through entertainment, sex or food (flight); or we can attack the pain with hateful thoughts and fantasies of revenge (fight); or we can do nothing, going about our daily life feeling dead inside (freeze). These strategies change nothing; through them we do not heal, we merely repeat old routines. Our friends may support us, and our work may give our life perspective and direction, but if we want to turn the crisis into a radical process of growth that makes us stronger, meditation is indispensable.

During one break up I meditated three times a day, just observing the pain. I sank into it and identified with the parts of me that were suffering. This can be challenging. Initially the pain is almost unbearable, like stepping into a very hot bath – only gradually do you get used to the heat. But staying with the pain can also be a beautiful experience if we understand there is a void within that yearns to be filled with love. This offers an opportunity to allow what is fragile and vulnerable to mature. When I had located my inner wounds,

I visualised a stream of loving acceptance and empathy radiating from the sun in my heart chakra to heal the pain. The relief was immediate, as if I had applied some kind of ointment. In this way, we can gradually work with our vulnerable parts, layer by layer, healing each wounded psychological state. As we do so, initially we will notice a vague pain somewhere inside, but through observation we can discover the source of the pain. We can then go deeper into the pain, seeing what it needs, which is perhaps affection, beauty, security and care. The quality we need to heal the pain that has been exposed is typically the quality we had been receiving in the partner we separated from. From this position we can let the needed quality flow from the heart, where the universal Soul qualities reside, to the suffering part.

This work shows us how to initiate new frequencies and qualities by replacing black holes of pain with love. In the beginning there is nothing but pain, but gradually we learn how to contain it. The pain does not disappear but the pain takes up less space as sensitivity penetrates our suffering, and love and acceptance flows into the place that pain used to be. This practice heals on several levels. We disidentify from our vulnerability and identify instead with the strong, loving observer who remains centred and contains the pain. We avoid becoming the victims of our suffering. Instead, we take responsibility and know that it is our own vulnerabilities that are causing the pain. Being the observer empowers us, and we can choose to *act* on the situation. Love's power unifies what is isolated and separate and makes it whole. Our vulnerable parts are met by a new inner source of love and compassion, and as projections are withdrawn and replaced by self-love, the pain diminishes. Self-care gives us the strength and courage to love again because we know there is a safe place within to which we can always return.

Whatever dark and self-destructive forces we find in ourselves, they always contain hidden possibilities that can be triggered by the transforming power of impersonal and unconditional love. This love is love beyond likes and dislikes, an empathic love that can contain everything simply because it exists, flowing like a quiet stream in every human heart. We can encourage this flow with practices such as the heart sun meditation. When we are closed off and identified with our vulnerable, egocentric tendencies, we can try to open our hearts to this healing river. Love transforms our vulnerabilities in the way that sunlight melts ice. It activates a process in the *heart of the suffering part* that lowers our defences. We become more stable, self-regulating and less dependent on others for love.

Healing Meditation

The purpose of Healing Meditation is to send positive energies to the parts of ourselves that are suffering. In the Appendix you can find a version of this meditation that I work with myself. I begin with an integration exercise, connecting my heart, head and Soul, before moving into the meditation itself. It is important to work with the vertical axis between self and Soul as doing so aligns and strengthens the connections between the different levels of our being. The Soul and the superconscious must be connected before beginning the meditation so we can draw on the universal healing energies of the collective unconscious. Spirit-in-Action and the World Soul want us to release old painful conditions. It doesn't matter who is suffering because all suffering is collective. What matters is that the suffering is redeemed. All is teaching – All is service.

I continue this meditation by invoking the Soul's wisdom and love through prayer in order to show my commitment to co-operate with the Soul's energies. This prayer also encourages our inner helpers (angelic beings and souls on the inner planes who work according to our free will) to intervene.

When we understand that transforming our individual pain is part of a larger global process of transformation we are released from our limited personal perspective. The pain then becomes impersonal and universal, as we see ourselves sharing in the suffering of others. We are all in the same boat. When we freely share our experiences, other people can bring compassion and positive energies into our work, expanding our consciousness and making it more dynamic. We simply have more energy to draw upon. Obviously we should only involve the helpful people in the process, otherwise we risk getting a supply of unwanted negative energies.

Connecting our personal healing to that of humanity is an important part of the Healing Meditation. We do this by letting healing energy flow from the Soul, through our hearts, and out to everyone suffering from the same problems. Channelling this energy on behalf of all humankind creates a strong flow. There is a risk that we could become overstimulated, but connecting our own energy to the collective will prevent this from happening. The energy we channel flows through us and flushes out our entire system. Impersonality is key when working with the collective – we don't focus on any person or people in particular. Instead, our only intention is to heal ourselves and our surroundings. The atmosphere we create is available to everyone, but we impose it on no one.

How we connect to the collective field is up to us. Sometimes our focus must be on our own individual pain. In these cases we can send healing to all of humanity before closing the meditation. I recommend this: it protects against overstimulation, maintains our impersonal perspective, and helps the environment.

A variation on this meditation is to directly involve others subjectively in the work. If I am angry with someone, I can benefit by involving him or her in the inner healing. If we feel betrayed or offended, we have opportunity for inner healing by absorbing the hurt this person has caused us. This is not a substitute for whatever outer actions we must take, but it's easier to establish healthy boundaries if we are not overwhelmed by negative emotions.

Anger and vindictiveness create a highly toxic psychological atmosphere (ie aggression). When we identify with anger unconstructively we allow collective anger to enter our system, exacerbating the problem. Angry energy also induces other negative states, making it hard to think clearly. The anger helps neither those who feel it, nor those at whom it is directed. It creates imbalance and discord. If we are directed by spiritual values, we do not want to cause destruction in ourselves or in others. We must find another way to deal with anger.

Anger is natural and valuable, and if we are able to contain it we can transmute it into our standing power. When fully accepted with an intention not to harm, anger can be a powerful force aiding constructive action. Healthy aggression is non-violent; it helps us to set boundaries and assert our interests. As in many things, our motivation is key.

The aim is to bring the aggression within the control of the Soul's love and wisdom. First, we accept that we are angry. Next, we accept that the target of our anger acted out of ignorance. We neither approve of nor excuse their action; we merely accept that, like ourselves, they are fallible. This is the message of Nelson Mandela, Gandhi and the Dalai Lama: meet your "enemies" with loving kindness, but do not compromise your own values.

From the Soul's perspective, at some level we attract everything that comes into our lives. We can call this karma, the law of cause and effect. But no matter how we choose to interpret an action, we can always learn something from it. All is teaching.

During the first stage of a Healing Meditation we can send a stream of loving acceptance to the people we are angry with, and to anyone whose behaviour upsets us. This empathy and acceptance helps us understand whatever lies behind people's bad behaviour, and can make us wise. Accepting our own aggression helps us to see that it protects something vulnerable in us, a pain we cannot contain. Anger is a technique we use to protect ourselves by trying

"A love only of the perfect is poor.

The love that can reach into the dark and embrace hatred,

jealousy, greed, aggression - without succumbing to these states

- is great"

to give our pain to someone else – we try to pass on our pain like a hot potato. But this technique doesn't work; the pain will returns to us repeatedly until we learn that our pain is not healed by attacking someone else. We must mature beyond our vulnerabilities; doing so will help us to withstand future slights. Accepting anger transforms the feeling into inner strength.

To direct loving acceptance at someone who has hurt you is a radical act. Love widens our perspectives until we can understand the other's motivation. We see that we might have done the same thing ourselves. The Dalai Lama was once asked what his greatest concern was about the Chinese takeover of his country. He replied: "Losing compassion for the Chinese." Forgiving such terrible violations puts our own suffering into perspective. With loves comes humility. We no longer judge others as harshly as we might have. This does not mean that we become a pushover – we must still maintain our boundaries – but it can become easier for us to put ourselves in someone else's shoes.

The dynamic river of life leads to our inner core, while the sensitive river of life insists that we find ourselves in our encounters with others. Love is expansive. When we love others, we love ourselves through them. This interpenetrating consciousness is central to Unity Meditation, something I have practiced for a long time and that I call *The Great Silent Heart*.

Unity Meditation: The Great Silent Heart

During the great silent heart visualisation we visualise a deep blue, indigo ocean of love in our heart centre or in the centre of our brain. With the help of the imagination, visualisation opens the door to the energies we visualise.

We begin by focusing on the heart, visualising a deep blue ocean of love. Imagine this deep blue love energy expanding through you, and then to your family, and then out through wider and wider connections until it sur-rounds all of humankind. Extend the love further, to all living beings. This deep compassionate love can penetrate the essence of all existence and melt all barriers.

Over several days during a retreat, I had the opportunity to study the effect of this meditation. Meditating on cosmic love, I felt that after a few hours my personal boundaries had dissolved into a soft field of impersonal embracing love. Over the next few days the silence intensified; I felt connected with all living beings. I sank into a great silent heart that held all of existence in its compassionate embrace, as if I was at the bottom of a deep warm ocean of benign awareness. I realised that here was the bass note of all other states of consciousness, and I began to explore these states.

By somehow undoing the contractions and spasms in consciousness triggered by our defence mechanisms, this indigo-coloured cosmic love dissolves the pain of separation. We may soon return to "normal", but nothing is quite the same again. The memory of what happened reminds us that there is a way out of the prison. By consciously working on ourselves, and changing our lives, we can map an escape route.

While meditating on the great silent heart I felt completely identified with humanity. I was humanity, not a part of it, but its living Soul. I've read much about the World Soul, but had never before had such an immediate sense of being humanity itself. Christ's teaching to "Love your neighbour as yourself" suddenly had new meaning. My *neighbour is myself*, yet, as I've discussed previously, we still maintain our uniqueness.

Practising the great silent heart develops our empathy. We must be sensitive so we can understand the true nature of everything we encounter, even what we fear or hate. We begin by reaching those emotionally blocked areas in ourselves and embrace them with love and sensitivity. This can hurt, but feeling nothing is worse. Empathy and compassion aid our ability to register the multiple worlds of consciousness around us. Our sensitivity to different states of consciousness increases and we begin to distinguish their *qualities.* Our psychological taste buds become discriminating, and we can detect psychological qualities just as a master chef can identify the ingredients of a dish. We assess different people through identifying with their multifaceted nature. Barriers and conflicts indicate where our sensitivity could be extended, even to ourselves. The world around us serves as a giant mirror, showing us who we are through our *reactions to what we see in it*. These may or may not be a valid expression of what we identify with at any given moment. To become aware of our reactions without getting lost in the mirror is an art. In reality, we do not see other people as *they* are, but as *we* are. What we know is our subjective interpretation of them. A true meeting with the other can only take place when we become aware of our own reactions and appreciative of the other's qualities.

The sensitive river of life and an empathic understanding of ourselves and the world can guide us into our own and others' psychological DNA. It helps us to distinguish our unique energy types. We can then start to work with ourselves and others according to our unique typology on five levels, which is the goal of integral meditation.

Wisdom is Knowledge, Love and Purpose

The sensitive river of life develops the intelligence of the heart. In the personality, this energy unfolds through our feelings. Yet the love and wisdom we seek transcends likes and dislikes of the emotional body – true love is impersonal, universal and unconditional. It is only when our emotions are stable and free of egocentric desires that the love energy can *reflect* itself through the emotional field as intuition.

Intuition is an awareness of the whole. It helps us to understand reality by seeing into the heart of everything through the eyes of the divine. Intuitions are often beyond the intellect's comprehension and are difficult to describe with words. Most intuitions are brief glimpses into our inner connection with the world. For lack of better terms to describe this sense of unity, we speak of intuition and universal love. Ultimately, intuition and universal love are one, but they can be expressed in different ways: as love in the heart chakra and as wisdom in the brow chakra.

What is wisdom? It is difficult to define, but it seems connected to our empathic understanding of the underlying causes of what is happening around us. Wisdom seems to be a blend of experiential knowledge, love and purpose. Lacking one of these, one falls short of wisdom.

Much of our knowledge concerns how to do something, but not why we should do something. For this reason we must seek the deeper reason behind someone's actions if we want to truly understand them. This requires love, empathy and purpose.

Wisdom is always practical. It refers not so much to metaphysics as to a practical knowledge that is rooted in metaphysics. Buddha was a practical man whose aim was to develop an effective solution to the problem of suffering, to develop a knowledge concerned with concrete reality and actual experience. Basic practical knowledge can be very effective, but it is also partial – hence the saying that one can know a lot, yet understand little. For this reason, Buddha and others understood that it is important to go beyond practical knowledge to wisdom.

A loving, empathic consciousness is also an important aspect of wisdom – and has been crucial to healing my own wounds because it offers an inner container into which the pain can be released. However, empathic love without knowledge can be confusing. For example, we might love blindly if we lack the psychological knowledge to discern the deeper patterns involved in a relationship. Love can make us naïve, so we also need a cool and rational approach to understanding how love works.

The third aspect of wisdom is an awareness of the Soul's purpose. Purpose offers a "bird's eye view" of our situation and helps us to approach a problem with true wisdom. Purpose reveals the meaning behind a problem or crisis so we can understand the reasons why we suffer. We can then see our suffering as part of an evolutionary journey and recognise the next steps we must take.

Awareness of purpose relates to the vertical dimension of our being, to what gives us perspective and direction, offering glimpses of underlying meaning. The purpose behind my personal struggle with isolation was to show me (and the world) a way out. I learned how I had created my own isolation by identifying with idealised love, which is not an uncommon experience. Many people are isolated because they hold onto an idealised vision of perfect love and become stuck at this level, or frequency, of consciousness.

As mentioned, *only loving the perfect is an impoverished form of love, whereas a love that can accept conflicts and limitations is great.* Realising this was a major break though for me; it allowed my journey out of isolation to begin. This insight gave me a purpose. I learned I would rather be free than comfortable. I learned that I could aid the liberation of humanity through my own example.

Insight Meditation

Insight Meditation, my own preferred approach, is orientated toward love and wisdom. All true meditation should lead to wisdom because through it we come into contact with the Soul. This practice focuses on the energies in the head, specifically in the brow chakra or the Cave, where the third eye is located. There are three key aspects to this meditation: observation, love and exploration. We choose a problem we want to find a solution for, and position ourselves as the observer. Detached observation is essential in order to work with the energies that arise during this meditation. This is stage one. We need to accept and empathise with all aspects of the challenge facing us; that is, we need to love it. This provides a deeper understanding of things, and greater patience with what we cannot understand. This is stage two.

In the third stage we investigate, asking what, why, how? We draw back to *see* the larger pattern, the meaning within the problem, making it a friend who can guide us, rather than an enemy we must overcome. We creatively explore all aspects of the problem. If we see that we lack some basic knowledge, we must supplement our meditation with concrete study. Insights can come in bursts or the illumination can be more gradual.

Here is an example of an Insight Meditation that focuses on a concern of my own: I am frustrated that my teachings are not reaching a wider audience. I would like my work to have more notice, since my primary vocation is to teach energy psychology. First, I formulate a question: "What stands in the way of a greater flow?" As my outer life is a reflection of my consciousness, I understand that some inner block must be standing in the way of abundance.

I centre myself (see "Outline for Insight Meditation" in the Appendix), then observe who or what is frustrated. It can't be me. *I* am the detached observer, pure consciousness, so it must be something else that is acting up. I explore the frustration, ask what is motivating it. I sense restlessness and pain in my solar plexus. Other "voices" join in: a hunger for popularity and economic security, the joy of working with something I love, my meditation group, and the desire to make a difference in the world doing something I am passionate about. I can hear these different voices and I accept them all. They do not surprise me, and I continue my exploration.

There is meaning and purpose here, a reason why my teaching is not as popular as some part of me would like. There's a lesson for me to learn. *All is teaching, all is service*, I remind myself. This helps with the frustration. I am now willing to learn something new that can benefit others struggling with the same problem. I focus with empathy in my brow chakra and examine what inner assumption is blocking my progress. It takes as much energy to manifest loss as it does profit, this much I know; somewhere some unconscious conviction that I am lacking something must be jamming the works. I move from thinking about a problem to seeking wisdom about myself. I know I am more than capable of teaching, so the problem must lie somewhere else. Where is the resistance? There is something in my solar plexus. It is a desire not to get involved, to be left alone, to be safe. It is a desire to avoid conflicts and, paradoxically, a fear of rejection and isolation.

So it is that old thought form again: a defence mechanism to avoid situations associated with pain. This kind of ignorance can be illuminated by shining wisdom into the darkness. I am wise. I know my purpose. I acknowledge my growth and development, and all that I know about the transformation of the unconscious. Now wisdom must reach that part of my unconscious where the refusal to engage with people is blocking my abundance.

Inner resistance and "voices" present situations that must be met in a new way, and it is through this that our wisdom develops. Meditation reveals something in my unconscious contrary to my evolutionary purpose, which is to introduce energy psychology to large numbers of people. The Soul's wisdom makes this collaboration possible, with the inner flow allowing an outer flow of teaching. One can work with different types of visualisations in order to make the unconscious conscious, and a skilled psychotherapist can help with navigating through the defence mechanisms associated with this specific area.

I've given an example of a meditation working with the basic unconscious. There are other meditations that focus on the Soul's transpersonal qualities. What is universal love, power, beauty? Regarding such a question, we would proceed in the same manner: observe, love and investigate, relating what we find to our evolutionary purpose. This is an important part of integral meditation, seeing that the intention behind it is to serve. The Soul's primary aim is to make a difference in the world; the intention to serve evokes the strongest co-operation from the essence of our being.

Insight Meditation is a creative process. It offers new perspectives on the

object of our meditation, and is another example of how integral meditation combines different disciplines and techniques: observation, reflection, visualisation, radiating love, empathy and determination. Insight Meditation works by activating our ability to recognise inner realities, something that is said of the third eye.

Meditating on the sensitive river of life facilitates healing, understanding and enlightenment. The self is revealed and subpersonalities are brought to light. The sensitive river of life is essential to integral meditation. Love and wisdom are prerequisites for our very existence. Healing Meditation also supports shadow work in psychotherapy.

Sensitive types will naturally feel at home with this practice, but dynamic, analytical and practical types need it even more. These latter types have a tendency to isolate themselves from others and can adopt a dry approach to life which the sensitive river can moisten. That said, it should also be noted that indulging too much in this meditation can make one too introverted and oversensitive.

Now let's move away from these warm waters into the cooler stream of the intelligent river of life.

Chapter 7

The Intelligent River of Life:

Your Way to Higher Perspectives, Inspiration and Creativity

In the early 90s, I attended a satsang with Isaac Shapiro. Shapiro was a student of Sri Poonja, whose own teacher was the renowned Ramana Maharshi. I sat in the first row, directly in front of Isaac. I had no expectation about coming to the satsang, which I had not attended before. But I was intrigued and when the opportunity came I joined the dialogue. Isaac looked at me with his piercing gaze and focused on one central question: Who are you? Whenever I replied, he asked what was behind my answer. Eventually my answers ran out; I felt empty, having exhausted all definitions. At that moment my consciousness expanded into a wide open space, boundless, undefined. Something in me said, "I am nobody," and a blissful sense of freedom swept through me, unlike anything I had experienced before. Being free of identifications allowed me to be anything. There was only NOW, without qualification, pure, naked, beyond words. Isaac smiled and everyone in the group knew that I had had an opening because I was beaming like a jewel.

I sat like this for half an hour before I began to examine my state. It felt somehow familiar, as if it came from another time, another life. I was indifferent to everything and there was nothing to do. My commitment to everyday life was dissolving. It was linked to my old identity, but did I really want that? After an hour I became aware that I was regressing to a past life. It was in India, by the Ganges, where I lived a life of transcendent awareness. It was freedom, but not liberation. It was bliss, but uninvolved in life. It was enlightenment without commitment. My Soul called, and I answered. This was not my way in this lifetime.

Dialogue is an expression of the intelligent river of life. Integral meditation is about changing our perspective, and that is exactly what dialogue is about. Meditation helps us to see our life from many perspectives; through this we realise we are a part of a greater whole. We can infuse our work and life with the ideas and inspirations gained through meditation. Ourselves, others and the wider world form an integrated whole. Conversely, what we experience in life informs our meditation. This is the essence and quality of the intelligent river of life.

If Spirit-in-Action is one great living reality connecting all of existence, we must be able to understand and articulate this. There must be a kind of "theory of everything". Imagine what such a meta-perspective would give us, perceiving the world as an all-seeing eye, observing life's complexity with a 'bird's eye view.

We can achieve such clarity by letting go of our familiar perspectives, our handy definitions, and stepping back from our experience in order to observe our situation objectively. In this way we can recognise the difference between reality and our interpretations of it. In order to *know* we must be able to see phenomena as they are without our personal preferences. We have to see reality as it is, not as we wish it to be.

The universe is intelligent. All life pulsates and is governed by an extraordinary precision and order, from the smallest particles to dazzling supernovas. The unfolding universe is a great living being, evolving from imperfection to perfection.

Let's look at this. An important expression of the intelligent river of life is our understanding of the symbolic meaning of "the heights". The ancient gods lived on mountain tops, and we can access these peaks through ideas and the higher, integrative powers of consciousness. When we grasp an archetypal idea we can use it to create new products, knowledge and insights.

According to esoteric philosophy the primary emanations from the One are the dynamic, sensitive and intelligent rivers of life. The creation of the universe was an act of will. The will of the One initiated the Big Bang and dynamic life poured out from a divine ocean, setting primary matter in motion. Through the magnetism of the sensitive river of life and the creativity of the intelligent river of life the universe came into being. Because of this all existence is life, consciousness and intelligence.

Life is dynamic. Life manifests through the will, actualised by Spirit-in-Action. Everything is alive, everything evolves, even minerals, as the ancient alchemists thought.

Consciousness is the magnetism and the sensitive awareness that fosters conscious relations. Through varying degrees of awareness, minerals, plants, animals and humankind share a common sensitivity to the environment. Everything is conscious to some extent, but only human beings, and beyond, are self-aware.

Life's intelligence is the inherent ability in all matter (on all levels) to be moulded and created in order to manifest the purpose of Spirit. We see this through nature's complex ecosystem and humankind's creative activity.

We can say that life creates evolution, coherence and diversity through the will, emotions and thoughts of human beings. Will, love-wisdom and creative intelligence are the three fundamental forces in the universe and man. From a cosmic perspective, the creative, scientific, idealising and manifesting rivers of life are combinations of the three primary rivers of life. They help the intelligent river of life to release the creativity that Spirit-in-Action – evolution – seeks to manifest. (The same principle was discussed when we described the psychological functions in Chapter 3. Will, feeling and thought are the primary functions, and the four secondary functions of imagination, logic, passion and action are combinations of these three primary functions.)

The intelligent river of life seeks wise relationships and good connections. Intelligence runs through all levels of existence – our bodies, emotions and imagination are expressions of intelligence – yet intelligence is primarily manifested through thought and the mind. This is so because everything starts with an idea, a blueprint that will eventually lead to its realisation. All forms of creativity can be traced back to a vitalising archetypal idea.

Where do ideas come from? Some might say from God, others from a universal mind. The intelligent river of life is linked to an omniscient level; this suggests that somewhere a kind of cosmic hard drive contains all the answers to life's mysteries. Those who access this cosmic cloud may share in the omniscience of Spirit-in-Action. A master plan drives evolution and humanity, part of which entails the possibility that each of us can become aware of our role in this great cosmic drama. Through this awareness we can begin to co-operate with Spirit-in-Action, which we do every time we manifest new ideas. These ideas emanate from the superconscious, and inspire humankind's discoveries and visions, from ideas to further human rights to the invention of the internet.

Meditating on the intelligent river of life focuses and develops the mind. We have seen how the dynamic and sensitive rivers of life develop different qualities in consciousness. God's all-seeing eye is the archetypal symbol of this process, which in man correspondences to the mind or thought. The mind is like an inner eye through which we can focus on abstract ideas and intuitions. We can look at practical matters or explore the unconscious. Thought is symbolised by Mercury, the messenger of the gods. We are the god that is enlightened, and who in turn enlighten the world.

"The abstract mind is the mother of creativity. All creativity begins with an idea"

Our Perspectives are Windows to Our Reality

The intelligent river of life is largely associated with the development of abstract thought and our ability to adopt higher perspectives.

Our perspectives, ideas and theories form our understanding of ourselves and the world we live in. These maps of reality help define our experience of life and allow us to shape our destiny. Is the glass half-full or half-empty? Our perspectives determine how we interpret reality. When we believe in our ideas strongly, they become convictions. These arouse strong feelings, motivate our actions, and condition our path in life.

Our perspectives inform the narratives we use to explain our lives and the world around us. Abstract thought may not seem to resemble meditation, but *contemplating* life's great questions is a meditation in itself. By doing so we approach the unknown and may even experience a kind of pain, similar to birth pangs, as our mind expands. But we also experience the sense of satisfaction when something we thought was beyond us becomes comprehensible.

Abstract thought allows us to access the universal mind. The knowledge we acquire through study and thought becomes available to those aspects of the superconscious that are preparing new ideas. When Einstein formulated the theory of relativity he had already accumulated the knowledge necessary for his insight.

Meditating on the intelligent river of life differs from contemplating the dynamic and sensitive rivers of life. The primary aspects of Spirit-in-Action – will, love-wisdom and intelligence – create three different perspectives, which can be understood as being first, second and third person perspectives. From a first person perspective everything that exists is ultimately me, there is no duality, everything is an expression of the One, the source, the Cosmic Self, Brahman. But we can also experience reality as dual. This is the second person perspective when we are in relation to God and our fellow human beings, and through love we can unite with them. We can also experience reality from a third person perspective when we observe it impersonally, from a distance.

Meditating on the dynamic river of life develops our unique identity; it informs our will-to-be self. It shares in the authority of the One Self, through whom we become *empowered.* Meditating on the empathic, sensitive river of life fosters intimacy, unity and harmony with the object of meditation, developing our capacity to give and receive love. Meditating on the intelligent river of life gives us a wider perspective, allowing us to step back and observe life from a distance. Through this we can achieve a greater *clarity.*

Circle Meditation in Groups

How can meditating on the intelligent river of life provide us with this greater perspective? For several years I led a number of full moon meditations. We met to meditate on themes related to the astrological sign of the month, asking questions like: What is a spiritual path, What is group spirituality, or What is the love of the Soul?

During the first hour, we sat and quietly contemplated the energies and themes corresponding to the astrological sign. We then entered a Circle Meditation. Here participants are led through three stages of meditative group dialogue where their ability to sense the field and communicate what they hear sharpens.

The process involves three concentric circles or stages: the outer individualist circle, the middle group circle (the group relation stage), and the inner unifying circle. Each stage provides a different perspective, a window through which we can examine the field.

This work shows that to a great extent, our perspectives determine what we experience. But it also makes clear that each perspective leads to the next, rather like a natural progression of consciousness running from the individual to the group and on to the unifying stage. This resembles the developmental stages in psychology and seems to correspond respectively to the personality, the Soul and consciousness of Spirit.

A skilled guide can lead a group through these stages, depending on the group's ability to access the field and adopt the right perspectives.

The group forms a circle, placing candles, flowers and a talking stick at its centre. Following an initial meditation, someone takes the talking stick and begins to speak, replacing it when finished. If someone wants a short break for contemplation, they tap a singing bowl or ring a bell, asking for silence. Then the group dialogue starts, the objective being to penetrate deeper into the topic of meditation. In the individualistic stage, people share their own impressions from the meditation. Impressions vary, each participant having their own thoughts, feelings and bodily sensations in connection to the subject. Each individual's perspective colours the way they express themselves.

Moving into the next stage, the participants consider the material arising from the dialogue. Inspired by what is said, the group focuses on the impressions being shared in the group, and the field begins to change. As different ideas and perceptions cross-fertilise, the perspective changes from an individual to a group consciousness. The group begins to think and sense *together*. Here the leader's job is to maintain the focus on group consciousness, and prevent participants from reverting back to their individual perspectives.

During stage two the group as a whole discovers new perspectives and connections, an experience that is very joyful. We realise it is possible to gain new knowledge and insights *together*, rather like weaving a tapestry of insight, with each participant making a unique contribution.

Sometimes in rare cases the field leads to an almost ecstatic communion, creating an electric atmosphere where each individual consciousness fades into the background. In such cases, stage three begins, what can be called an experience of the higher We. This is difficult to define, other than to say that *something* wants to come through. We can think of a higher Self, a more comprehensive, loving intelligence that wishes to manifest. When the group succeeds in accessing this field of higher inspiration, it will for a time unite in a higher consciousness. This is often associated with feelings of universal love and power, and insights into the destiny and development of humanity.

My group had a few peak experiences where, as a shared ecstatic eye, we looked into the deeper mysteries. A prerequisite for stage three is the courage to reach from the known into the unknown. We must surrender to the vague thoughts and intuitions that appear. When this happens, we must listen, remaining alert, allowing whatever arises in the space to manifest, again making sure that we do not revert to an earlier stage.

Intuitions arising from the intelligent river of life help us to understand the great connectedness of all things. The meditation I've just described is not the only expression of the intelligent river of life. All the rivers of life we have looked at are closely interwoven. But the ability to disidentify from our limited perspectives, as individuals or in a group, characterises the intelligent river of life.

Circle Meditation is a *reflective group meditation*. In formulating abstract thoughts or intuitive impressions we activate our mental body. Language gives these subtle insights structure and form. The intelligent river of life helps us to gain greater perspectives so we can develop our understanding of connectedness. The internet is an example of how technology can be developed through the use of the intelligent river of life. Another clear expression of this river is language. Language disseminates awareness (second river) so that it can manifest in culture and develop our lives (first river).

Meditation is most often pursued silently, but the kind of spiritual dialogue involved in Circle Meditation can be a powerful aid in the quest for higher consciousness. Language gives form to our inner worlds, allowing us to share them with others. Circle Meditation highlights the delicate balance between open listening and the practice of finding just the right words to express our intuitions. When we manage to do this we can say that we have achieved an expansion and enlightenment of the mind to a degree.

With our minds we can organise our lives intelligently and also access arche-typal ideas. When we behave unintelligently and act against universal laws and natural relationships, we suffer the consequences of our actions. This can mean physical illness or psychological problems. One aim of meditating on the intelligent river of life is to develop our thinking based on the principle that energy follows thought.

Discovering the World of Thought

I clearly remember the day I became aware of the content of my *thought life*. It happened in the late 1990s. An inattentive driver almost ran into me as I was cycling home. It was a shock, nothing more, and I cycled on. But soon afterwards I realised that my pulse was pounding and my body tense. This led to an insight into my thoughts. I was imagining a physical fight with the driver. My anger had exploded in my imagination. I observed this from an unusual calm, impersonal place, as if I was watching a film. I realised that my thoughts were thinking *me* rather than I them. Until then I was unaware of this separate reality existing in my mind. At that moment a great peace came over me. I could reach into my imagination and calm my inner voices. The fantasy dissolved, my body relaxed and my pulse returned to normal.

This experience changed my meditation practice. I shifted my focus from the sun in the heart, to my head. Through Reflec-tive Meditation I saw that I could control my thoughts. A vision became clear to me, no longer should my thoughts think me; *I* would consciously choose them. At that mo-ment I first truly understood the meaning of dis-identification and detachment.

Once we grasp that *everything is energy* and that *energy follows thought*, we can use the mind to take charge of our lives. We can be the captain of our ship and master of our house. This experience led me to experiment with the idea that energy follows thought. I would focus on something positive and then observe how this affected my thinking, my emotions and my behaviour positively. I observed the same law with negative thoughts, and saw that there, too, energy follows thought.

It became clear to me that when old emotional states, thoughts and beliefs were re-activated, I could observe them, but rarely control them. By becoming the observer I could disidentify from old programming. I could consciously accept the condition and my powerlessness, creating a distance that lessened the power of the negative state. When I started studying Psychosynthesis, I saw how central this practice is. These methods strengthen the centre of awareness and will in our personality around which we can integrate our many parts.

The abstract mind is the mother of creativity from the personality's perspective. All creativity begins with an idea, the initial impulse behind an action. The idea may be unconscious and first act upon the body, or it might stir the imagination. Creative activity can always be traced back to an archetypal idea, that is, to the mind. But if the thinking mind is so crucial to our development, we might wonder why it is so often discredited, especially in spiritual environments. There is often an impression that thinking is non-spiritual, despite the fact that great discoveries, ideals and humanitarian values are based on ideas. This reticence is probably a reaction to the hyper-rational, overly reductive thinking that has dominated in the West for centuries and has led to a devaluing of the more intuitive qualities, such as empathy, trust and imagination. Yet the fact that thought can be misused, or over-used, does not mean that thinking in itself is evil. There are equally many examples of how emotionality has fed fanaticism, stifled thought and promoted superstition. Thinking is not the villain, but rather the thinker who abuses it.

Reflective Meditation

Reflective Meditation works directly with the intelligent river of life. In essence it is a way of meditating on a subject until you have exhausted the intellect and are available for inspiration, which comes from the superconscious. Reflective thinking can open a door to the superconscious just as emotional aspiration and devotion can. The mind is an inner eye able to recognise the different phenomena inhabiting our inner worlds.

Reflective Meditation also helps in communication by leading us to choose our words wisely. Words are powerful and affect those who read or hear them. If we understand their power, we can influence how people react to our message. People with strong minds are often good communicators.

Reflective Meditation is helpful in many ways. The mind can illuminate our inner world, bringing unconscious and superconscious material to light. Reflective Meditation can also bring forth new knowledge and new thought forms which add to the data banks of our internal hard drive. And it is through the mind's ability to integrate its contents that our perspectives and outlook can develop.

Through years of practising and teaching Reflective Meditation, two key topics have always intrigued me: astrological symbols and psychological qualities. Through studying symbolism the mind enters a world of form, light and inspiration. Symbols are doors to the superconscious; here the intellect must abandon literal explanations in order to grasp the deeper meaning. The world of symbols is immensely rich, encompassing practically everything. For example, borrowing from nature we can see the mountain, the elephant and the oak as symbols of the strength that is necessary to realise the One Universal Force.

Through studying symbols, their relationships and combinations, the value of the meditation increases. Let's take a closer look at astrological symbols – the circle, dot, cross, the wavy line, the arrow, the half arch – as well as mythological figures and imagery of all kinds. Symbols can be interpreted in three ways, corresponding to the first, second and third person perspectives mentioned earlier. A good rule is to start from the outside in, a process we can refer to as 3-2-1.

From the third person perspective we examine the symbol's outer form as a way to create more *knowledge*. This will reveal the outer layer of understanding and knowledge, such as the traditional understanding that the circle and the cross represent the planet Venus. Why is this so? The circle symbolises wholeness, connectedness and love – its soft inclusive curve encloses everything it contains. The cross is associated with manifestation. The vertical line represents the force connecting heaven and earth. The horizontal line connects man with his environment. The intersection of vertical and horizontal lines represents humanity, crucified in the material world yet connected to the divine source. Therefore, we can see that the symbol for Venus of a combined circle and cross reveals that love (the circle) seeks to manifest in matter (the cross). This is what Venus (seen as a universal force) both in mythology and in our inner world seeks – she is the goddess of love and beauty who leads us to a higher world of harmony and balance.

Symbolism provides knowledge out of which we can develop a language to articulate our vague intuitions. This is necessary when we reach the symbol's second qualitative level, which refers to the symbol's emotional impact.

To gain knowledge from emotion we must have a language subtle enough to capture its fleeting impressions. At the first stage of Reflective Meditation (the third person perspective) we look at what we know about the symbol, ie the role Venus plays in mythology and esoteric philosophy. Preparing questions in advance may help. So, in the case of Venus we may ask: What is beauty? Of what beauty am I aware? What role does beauty play in the world? How does beauty affect me spiritually and personally?

You can ask similar questions about love. This kind of meditation can show us the superficiality of our ordinary everyday thinking, showing us that our intellect is undeveloped. Unless we are awake and vigilant, our thinking becomes dull. We prefer the warm sensations of feeling or the playfulness of imagination to the hard work of thought. This regression into the fantasy world of the unconscious lets us play around in a self-centred atmosphere. There is nothing wrong in exploring the unconscious – I give this full attention further on. But if we want to enlarge our perspectives and become aware of wider, more abstract connections, we must go in another direction.

When we successfully focus on the object of meditation (Venus) we create a magnetic sphere tuned into a particular frequency of consciousness. We only allow what is relevant to the object to access the field of consciousness. By bringing everything together the knowledge we already know about the object and new knowledge then creates a cross fertilisation that can nurture new understanding and connections. At some point the mind will have exhausted all its possibilities at that level of consciousness, while still in the third person perspective phase.

The technique we use is to force the mind to become quiet and vigilant, so a kind of vacuum will be formed which will attract new ideas from the superconscious. When this happens, our Reflective Meditation becomes receptive, with the still mind awaiting the birth of a new idea. From here we can go on to the second person perspective.

To return to our example of the symbol for Venus, if we choose to meditate on this from a second person perspective we can surrender to Venus and beauty as living realities with which we can communicate. Our focus will be on the qualities arising in the meeting between ourselves and the goddess. It doesn't matter if you conceive Venus as an impersonal energy, a state of consciousness or a divine being. The important thing is to empathically engage with the energy that arises while maintaining an impersonal distance. This allows the intellect to adopt the perspectives that arise in the meeting. We primarily *look* at the energy as if we were face to face with it. Regarding the second person perspective, asking questions and listening for the answer *inwardly*, as if in telepathic communication, can be of help. This kind of dialogue can spark many insights. When we have exhausted these possibilities, we can move to the receptive stage or turn to the first person perspective.

In the first person perspective we *become* the energy, fully and wholly identified with it. We become Venus. We see through her eyes, we think like her. How does the world appear when we are identified with perfect beauty and love? We reflect on the new energies we meet while meditating from this perspective. We ask our questions once again, or perhaps we have new questions.

Meditating on the intelligent river of life will always bring clarity and new perspectives, providing insights into and overviews of our subject. For an illustration, I used an astrological symbol, but we can meditate on anything we like. Politics, business, religion, economics, ethics, philosophy, aesthetics, science: all suit this kind of meditation. Similarly, meditating on virtues such as wisdom, confidence or courage will give us insight into their nature. This form of meditation can also help when we want insight into our personal lives.

Once we understand how something works – whether physical, psychological or spiritual – we have gained a knowledge that can help us to take action in the world. Knowledge is power because he who enjoys an overview can see how the details fit together to form a pattern. Strategic solutions to human problems are one important outcome of this form of meditation. We must remember that the purpose of the intelligent river of life is to manifest whatever the dynamic and sensitive rivers of life have prepared. We do this through creativity, through new thoughts and ideas.

Practical intelligence – or knowhow – is neutral and can be used for anything. Reflective Meditation enables us to change the world. We take what we learn from the world of ideas and transform it into intelligent solutions.

Reflective and Receptive Meditation

Reflective and Receptive Meditation (see Appendix) form two stages of the same process – one active, the other passive – representing two different ways of using the mind. I have described the active reflective function above. During Receptive Meditation the still mind receives abstract ideas and intuitions. Receptive Meditation requires a quiet and alert waiting. The senses await impressions from the higher sources of inspiration, such as the Soul or some extrasensory reality. During Receptive Meditation we become like a radio

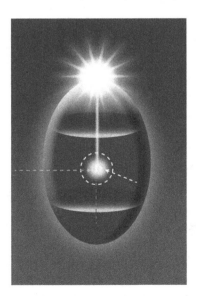

telescope looking for signs of life in outer space, or like a pilgrim who has climbed a holy mountain and now sits in silence and prayer. There is nothing to do, our awareness has transcended everyday trivialities. During this silent meditation we listen and observe the subtle currents of inspiration.

This meditation is difficult. The mind craves activity and constantly seeks new experiences, images, thoughts, emotions and sensations. Quieting the mind is difficult, but if we do not we will only receive impressions from our usual frequencies (Figure 15). Receptive Meditation changes the frequency of our awareness, moving us to a higher level that enlargens our perspectives. This transition is silent as we keep a dynamic but relaxed focus guiding us into the higher reality.

Figure 15: Impressions being received from the usual frequencies of normal consciousness.

An element of contradiction seems at work

here. On the one hand, the will is active, informing the intention behind the meditation, which is to become receptive (passive) to a deeper presence of light, love and power. Our focus is strong and specific, zeroing in on a spiritual quality, a symbol, a divine being, or one of the seven rivers of life. On the other hand Receptive Meditation is effortless. The mind remains quiet, relaxed and open to impressions coming from above. Sometimes the mind expands into the infinite, uniting with the collective mind. In this way we reach a group meditation, collectively surrendering to a greater life, to Spirit-in-Action.

We can illustrate what happens during Receptive Meditation in three ways. The first diagram shows the thoughts and sensations that are related to our everyday consciousness – these are the typical needs that drive us and their energies. Here we do not control our minds, we simply receive impressions from our usual level of consciousness. We occupy familiar rooms in our inner house: the furniture can be moved around, but there will be no significant changes in the *quality* of consciousness (for our perspectives to change we need to reach a higher level of consciousness). However, in this frame of mind we can become more efficient by understanding things in a new way. Receptive Meditation here shows us how to better express our current needs. We can make slight improvements, but no major changes. Problems created on one level of consciousness need a higher one for their solution.

Figure 16 shows how dynamic silence can enable us to draw inspiration from the superconscious. This spiritually-motivated silence creates a kind of vacuum as the thoughts and emotions that normally consume our energy are relegated to the subconscious, leaving a space for the energies we are meditating on to flow in.

Acting through the superconscious, the Soul sends ideas and energies related to the subject of meditation. We may experience this as an inspiration which changes our understanding of ourselves and our lives. This can be artistic, ethical, political or religious. In any case, it infuses a certain pursuit with fresh creativity.

More than once during meditation I have received archetypal symbols that have provided fresh insight relating to my potential development. In one I saw myself as a yogi with a special name. Because of its power,

Figure 16: Impressions, energies and inspiration being drawn from super consciousness.

this image quickly gave me insight into who I truly am. When hit with a negative mood – often because I demand too much of myself – recalling this image is of great help. Through it I receive a wisdom I know to be true, but which I can forget when caught up in negative thoughts.

Inspiration uses the seven psychological functions as channels, but inspiration also makes use of the consciousness bridge between the self and the Soul. Although our psychological functions are simultaneously active, one function usually dominates and influences the inspiration. For example, the will function dominates with our heroic impulses; the feeling function can skew any new inspiration towards experiences of love and union with something greater; a dominant thinking function tends to create new ideas and perspectives; imagination reveals mystical visions, and so on.

The different impressions of the superconscious often demand interpretation. We must interpret our thoughts, feelings and ideas, just as we do our dreams. Some distortion can occur when higher energies express themselves through the psychological functions. Discrimination is needed in assessing the value of these impressions. We might wonder whether these impressions are authentic or just wishful thinking. Such discrimination is difficult but, as a rule of thumb, impressions from the Soul generally inspire something positive.

When the impulse comes directly through the consciousness bridge the situation is different: then the inspiration comes to us something like a revelation, as if a flash of lightning suddenly illuminates the darkness. An indisputable sense of certainty accompanies such a revelation: it is direct knowledge about the meaning and purpose of the Soul.

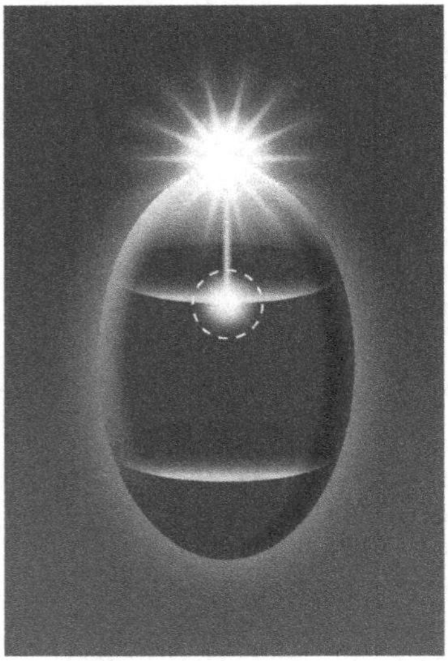

Figure 17 The ascent of the conscious "I".

Figure 17 shows how the silence of Receptive Meditation allows the personal centre of consciousness to ascend and expand from individual to holistic consciousness; we can ascend to the level of the superconscious. Our sense of "I" change. We usually live within the boundaries of our personality, and feel a sharp difference between ourselves and others, but when we ascend to the superconscious the boundaries between self and other are dissolved and we become part of a universal being. We step into a new dimension, one that is truer than our usually fragmented reality. Here we awaken to a new level of being, infused with Soul, connected to a dimension where all energies are available. The silence expands into an eternal Now containing everything. This is also what happens during Awareness Meditation when we meditate on pure consciousness without content, but in this case, we are connected to the consciousness bridge that exists between self and the Soul. Both experiences are induced by silence, and during the entire process we retain our cognitive functions and can reflect on the process if we wish to. Usually it is more interesting to pay attention to what is going on beyond our ordinary level of reality. During the interpretative stage, when we try to articulate our experiences, our intellect must be awake and well-functioning. Co-operation between the abstract and concrete mind helps us to translate inspirations into theories and understandings that can be expressed creatively in life. Without the intellect, we only have an unexplainable mystical experience. Without the ability to communicate our experiences our opportunity to make a difference in life is limited. It can also be useful to see Reflective and Receptive Meditation as representing the masculine (Reflective) and feminine (Receptive) applications of the mind, working together to enlighten the self through our intelligence.

Summing up, we can say that the intelligent river of life develops our perspective so we can understand life's complexity and find our place in it. We can become a creative force bringing new ideas to life, creating new realities. Reflective and Receptive Meditation naturally attract mental personality types, but it is important that all personality types learn to sharpen their minds. Sensitive, creative and dedicated types often want to stay in their feelings. By doing so they will have little impact on the world because they are not able to communicate their feelings clearly. Reflective Meditation can help us to dis-identify from our emotional life and provide the clarity, insight and overview needed to help communicate our life purpose. Conversely, types that easily get stuck in their heads must be careful not to overdo this form of meditation as it may increase an already existing imbalance. The mind is a good servant but, if allowed to run riot, it can be a cruel master. The best advice is to study the positive and negative aspects of this river of life, and assess the opportunities and dangers for yourself.

For integral meditation, learning from this river of life is invaluable because it develops our ability to think and provides a multidimensional perspective on our experience.

Now let's visit the last four rivers of life which, in their own way, complement and anchor the inner work done by their fellows.

Chapter 8

The Creative River of Life:

Your Way to Beauty, Transformation and Harmony

The creative river of life has been important to me for many years. As the river that channels harmony, lightness, beauty and grace, this river embodies precisely the energies I need to balance my particular typology. As mentioned, my personality combines the qualities of the dedicated type (6) in my personality and emotional life and the dynamic type (1) in the mental and physical functions. This rather extreme combination means I am a strong, dedicated, goal-orientated personality, who tends to be isolated, rigid, serious and inflexible. Without the joy and lightness that the creative river of life can bring to our social interactions, my ability to express myself was limited. Happily, though, the creative river of life provided the medicine and complimentary energies I needed to balance my personality. We can integrate its qualities in different ways. Meditation is of course the primary method, but it also helps to develop close relationships with people who embody this energy. I've done both, and fortunately my approach has been successful. In this chapter I would like to share my experiences.

People in spiritual communities often become stuck in idealistic, ascetic ways of life. This makes it difficult to live creatively and benefit others. The creative river combines the sensitive and intelligent rivers of life; the psychological function associated with it is the imagination. The aim of the creative river is to bring *beauty* to life. Spirit-in-Action wants to manifest, and because the One *is* sublime beauty, its beauty is reflected in creation. We see the beauty of nature expressed in the plant kingdom, and as humanity we must in our own way express beauty.

The Soul *is* beauty. It contains what is good, true and beautiful. I realised this some years ago during many meditations on beauty. In my experience, beauty is love's messenger, opening and uplifting whatever it touches. In this openness, love can unite whatever is separated. As Plato tells us, there are different kinds of beauty and each can awaken different types of love.

During meditation, I had at this time a powerful realisation: I saw myself as a life artist. Bringing beauty into my life became an important motivation for me. This meant fostering beautiful qualities in my own personality and appreciating these qualities in others. I think beauty became particularly important to me because in my teens I struggled with severe acne that disfigured my face. It was perhaps a karmic lesson, teaching me how to appreciate beauty. It has helped me to transform aspects of my nature, to soften an ascetic negative attitude towards beauty that I had held for too long.

The personality is both the temple and the mask of the Soul. Ideally, the personality should express the essence of who we truly are. Through meditation and self-transformation work, the inner artist beautifies his inner temple. We can reach for beauty by looking after our bodies or by wearing clothes that suit us, but we can also nurture beautiful inner qualities by thinking harmonious and positive thoughts. One difficult area that I will look at especially is the beauty we may find hidden within the darker side of our natures.

The creative river unites the new and the old. It is the river of change and transformation, of clashes and conflicts between what was, what is and what may be: past, present and future flow together. This law of change is universal and takes place in our own lives. We must adjust our reactions and behaviour constantly. This requires openness, flexibility and a playful, detached attitude towards life. Nothing lasts forever, so why not go with the flow? For the sake of beauty we choose to die daily by letting go of the old. Something within us is so large and beautiful that we have no choice but to surrender to it. Such an attitude creates lightness and spontaneity. It helps us to be in the moment, at life's epicentre, where we feel the tremors of the new. A sense of greatness is also connected to this river, embracing and expressing the rich and vast diversity of life. Every shade of beauty is an indispensable aspect of light and colour that is a part of the whole. This is also the river of suffering because achieving harmony and balance for the sake of beauty often demands that we reach into the depths and into darkness.

When we meditate on this river the psychological function of the *imagination* facilitates the arising of creative energy, and imagination itself is further developed. Imagination, of course, is associated with superstition, naivety and unreality, notions such as Santa Claus and other childish ideas. But like all psychological functions, our imagination is as mature as our level of consciousness. It is important to distinguish imagination from fantasy.

Imagination is a powerful creative force. Many spiritual traditions use visualisations as part of their contemplative practices. Advertisers know the psychological effect that images have, especially when shown repeatedly. Energy follows thought, but it also follows images. This brings us to the topic of Creative Meditation.

Creative Meditation is based on visualisation and draws on the energy of the creative river. My practice with the sun in the heart is an example of this form of meditation. Through visualisation we form images in the psyche that carry the energies attributed to them. It is one of the most important tools that our inner life artist can use to decorate the temple of our personality. This practice is necessary for the Soul to manifest as through it a new personality can be slowly formed in which a higher consciousness can express itself.

Visualisation is particularly important during certain stages of this meditation. One is the pre-contemplative stage when meditating on a specific topic. Metaphorically, this is similar to hiking up to a mountain top to sit in silence – the aim is to still our thoughts, feelings and sensations so they might be harmonised and made receptive to the Soul's inspiration. There are many ways to do this, but the essential elements of this process are balance and harmonisation.

For most meditations I follow these stages: *centring, ascension, meditation* and *anchoring*.These stages ensure that we meditate from our highest level of consciousness. We begin by raising our awareness to the superconscious realm, for which we can utilise the image of hiking up a mountain. This incidentally helps communication between the brain, our emotions, our mind, the conscious observer (or self) and the Soul. Visualisations help develop this communication, and gradually our conscious connection with the Soul is strengthened.

Centring

Here we quieten the body, the emotions and the mind so they might be harmonised with the Soul; we can then adopt a conscious position as the observer. Here is an example of a creative approach to make use of before the actual work starts.

I start by visualising a sun in my heart that emanates an acceptance of all being, and anchor myself there. This provides standing power and lets me rest in the loving centre of being. I then visualise a golden stream of energy ascending from the heart and circling my neck and throat. This stabilises the mind, the area which controls concrete thinking. I now visualise this energy moving up to my brow, where the integration of the energies of the personality and Soul takes place. I focus on a point in front of my forehead, seeing it as a bright white-gold light. Then mentally I say: "I integrate my three bodies and make them available to the service of the Soul." I say this with authority. I finish by focusing in the centre of my brain, saying: "I am the conscious soul incarnate." Then I open my mind to a global awareness, feeling the same consciousness alive in all incarnated Souls. This conscious identification with the World Soul unites me with other awakened ones. It is a very powerful experience. My personality is brought into harmony with the alert observer. I'm on the mountaintop, at the tip of my consciousness pyramid.

This is just one example of a centring visualisation. There are different types and it is important to find one that suits you.

Ascension

Here we create a channel between the incarnated Soul and the higher Soul's field of inspiration. I visualise a white-gold light streaming from the centre of my brain up to a brilliant light above it. Then I open to the Soul's wisdom and inspiration. I can send the stream of light into the cosmic being connecting me to a brilliant star-like radiance. This ascension brings a sense of meaning and harmony, connected to my spiritual purpose. It gives strength and a sense of greatness.

Centring and ascension can take no more than five minutes – less if you are experienced. (Sometimes I omit ascension if a particular meditation does not require it. Awareness Meditation do not require an ascent because our primary objective is to let go of all forms and identify with pure consciousness.)

Meditation

This is the central stage. We have already selected a theme to focus on. We can meditate on anything we like, but it is a good idea to meditate on a quality in our personality that needs to be strengthened. This links our integral meditation with the creativity we want in our life. This motivates us to practice meditation and subsequently develops our ability to manifest the Soul. Developing the qualities of the creative river also helps us to meet the challenges in our personality.

If we visualise a brilliant white lotus in the heart centre, emanating peace and harmony to all living beings, a mental lotus will develop transmitting peace and harmony from the superconscious. We create a vessel into which higher energies can descend. Experienced meditators who know the impact of a long-term visualisation practice will recognise this vessel: returning here is like visiting a house you have built and where all the created energies are at your disposal.

Through visualisation a channel to the energies of the superconscious is slowly formed. In our everyday lives we will soon notice a flow created by these energies, and the subpersonalities that resist peace will also surface in order to be transformed – this is a natural consequence of the meditation; hence this river is also the path of "harmony through conflict".

Anchoring

This is an important stage. It ensures that our energies do not accumulate, clogging our system, but are channelled into the world. Accumulations constipate our energy centres, which can lead to headaches, burning sensations, fatigue, irritability and restlessness. We therefore finish our meditation by making this energy available to everyone. We do this by saying OM out loud three times. With each OM we visualise energy flowing out into the world, to the people we know. The Soul wants to bring light to the world, and this work initiates a powerful purifying stream of light that uplifts and strengthens the social world in which we manifest. Intoning OM deepens the energies on which we mentally focus.

Creative Meditation develops our fantasy and imagination. The imagination is both an organ of vision and a creative tool. With the organ of vision we look into the inner world and see its immensity. We could become clairvoyant; we can see auras, spirits on the astral plane, and other inner beings. However, we must be careful on this path. The imagination brings us into contact with whatever we tune into or imagine. We must be able to distinguish between objective inner realities and our own subjective imaginings. A good example is angels, or devas as they are called in the East. The reality of angels is attested to by many enlightened people, but they do not necessarily look like their popular representations. These familiar images are created by fantasy and will be kept alive as long people invest in them with their thoughts and feelings. When they no longer capture our imagination, we withdraw this life energy and they will fade away. Real angels have their own life energy, development and place in evolution.

A New Relationship between Soul, self and Subpersonalities

Let's look again at working with subpersonalities. This is what Lucille Cedercrans calls Soul Therapy and Gordon Davidson Joyful Evolution. Earlier, I described how subpersonalities are created and their role in our lives. Here we will look at the transformations that are possible when we engage in subpersonality work. This technique is the closest we come to shadow work – one of the five life practices of integral meditation – and it is the most effective I know. Our personality contains different psychic self-images that we have acquired throughout our life. These subpersonalities are like real living beings, with their own internal representable images, ideas and histories, that we keep alive when we repeat the specific roles and behavioural patterns they represent.

There are four categories of subpersonalities:

1. **Age-related**: Images of ourselves from each life stage.

2. **Relationship-related**: Representing our major life relationships.

3. **Archetypical**: Talents and energies organised around an archetypal role, for example, the hero, clown, critic, and so on.

4. **Past life personalities**: Dominating self-images we have brought with us from the past into our current incarnation that form the karmic material we need to work with.

Subpersonalities evolve through challenges and new situations. We are forced to adopt new roles and new ways of being, and through this our subpersonalities come into being and evolve. Often a conflict between external demands and our struggle to meet these demands triggers a change in our ways of being, in our subpersonalities – this was the case for me when becoming a father forced me to change.

Subpersonalities from our earlier life can influence the present and future, the three dimensions of time through which the self must navigate. Here and now we have the chance to connect the past with the present and so shape the future. The creative river runs deep in this work; ultimately it will bring about a balance of opposites.

However, I am not suggesting we have no choice but to live through one crisis after another, projecting our subpersonalities onto those around us. Once we realise the reality of subpersonalities, we can withdraw our projections. We can stop acting out our inner conflicts in the outer world. We see that the outer world serves as a kind of mirror, reflecting our subpersonalities. We become more interested in changing our own reactions and subpersonalities than in changing other people. We focus on the beam in our eye, rather than the speck out of our brother's or sister's eye. We can learn to look at life as a stage on which we all play important roles. Over time we can develop a repertoire of inner roles that in their own way contribute to humanity's great drama, the realisation of Spirit-in-Action. This work of integrating the Soul, the self and the subpersonalities is best expressed through metaphors, and we chose the metaphors that best describe life's various situations. In my work I use the following:

- The Scriptwriter, Director and Actors

- The Captain, the Mate and the Sailors

- The Board, the CEO and Staff

- The Composer, Conductor and Musicians

The Soul is the inspiring force; it sees the big picture and can communicate its meaning and purpose. This is the role of the Scriptwriter, Captain, Board and Composer.

The self is the guiding force. It organises, facilitates and coordinates work among the subpersonalities. This is role of the Director, Officer, CEO and Conductor.

The subpersonalities, with their many talents and skills, implement the work. This is the role of the Actors, Sailors, Staff and Musicians.

In reality, for many people this co-operation is practically non-existent because their connection to Soul has not been developed so their inner house is not in order. With an un-integrated personality, subpersonalities run free. Our inner house is divided. The needs of different subpersonalities conflict and waste energy, or they get locked into rigid patterns. Or subpersonalities may not have the skills to carry out the plans that the Captain requires. Whatever the reason, we will be frustrated in trying to realise our needs and dreams.

The creative river of life can help in other ways. If we have a negative relationship with the basic unconscious, the energies of the creative and sensitive rivers can change this. The sensitive river helps us to develop an empathetic understanding of the unique role of the basic unconscious. And through the creative river we can learn to appreciate the darker sides of our nature and see that they hold hidden treasures that can rise to the surface.

We must realise that the basic unconscious is not an enemy that must be defeated or repressed. We know that some spiritual traditions urge us to deny our basic drives in order to transcend them. But to me this seems more about avoiding life, rather than developing it. The new spirituality wants to bring heaven to earth. This means we must befriend the basic unconscious which houses the energies we need to realise the Soul's vision.

What we need is a practice that will enable the Soul, the self and the subpersonalities to collaborate.

The relationship between the Soul, the self and the subpersonalities is relevant to a particular level of development, namely for those who are not yet advanced, fully realised Souls, which would of course mean most of us.[1]

Soul Therapy: A Joyous Transformative Practice

Most work with the basic unconscious involves pain and drama. We know from experience that we develop slowly through painful, emotional catharsis. I have worked in psychotherapy for many years, using many different approaches, and until recently I shared that view. But then it changed.

In 2011, I discovered a new method, and I have been practising it ever since, first with Gordon Davidson as a guide and later with others. It is without doubt the most effective method I have come across. It has proved its usefulness throughout hundreds of hours of therapeutic sessions so remarkably that I have come to consider it revolutionary. Tests on students and clients have produced incredible results. I have also made it part of my meditation and invariably it has had a good effect.

The method is easy and joyful and with it our problems dissolve. My claims might trigger alarm bells with my fellow therapists: surely this is too good to be true?! Let me say first that I am not proposing a miracle cure that can resolve deep trauma in a few sessions. Nor does my method suit everyone.

My method entails being able to disidentify from whatever problem you are facing. I encourage the client to develop an ability to visualise and adopt the role of the observer. It is a spiritual approach to psychotherapy that helps the client to connect with their Soul. If these conditions are met, the method can have a significant effect.

As mentioned. Gordon Davidson calls this work Joyful Evolution; for Lucille

---

1. At some point in the future there will no longer be a duality between self and Soul, but only a fully awake and manifested Soul consciousness. This is someone who is fully identified with the needs of humanity and dedicates his life to service. They will experience the continuity of consciousness, where they are constantly awake as a connected non-separated consciousness, embedded in a single dimension, while unfolding their function through the personality. However, few people live in this dimension and show this kind of global creativity. Therefore I do not take account of it in this book. For these people, Spirit will be the inspirational centre, the Soul the managing centre and subpersonalities the executive.

"Beauty is love's messenger; it opens and uplifts whatever it touches"

Cedercrans it is Soul Therapy and in my own work we call it SoulFlow. The method presented here is inspired by Davidson's work, and I warmly recommend his book *Joyful Evolution*. I have though made a few changes to his approach. I prefer Cedercrans' term Soul Therapy – and I draw upon the ideas that can be found in her books and in her Wisdom Training, but also on the developments my colleague Søren Hauge and I has created. Soul Therapy is an apt term because in practice the Soul is doing the work with the basic unconscious, with the self operating as the observer. Yet, as the work is full of joy, Joyful Evolution is also a good term.

Most psychotherapists may see this method as classical visualisation work, involving subpersonalities like the inner child, the critic, the single parent, and so on. Yet there are key points where this method differs from those I have tried or am aware of, and I speak of these below.[2]

---

2. An outline to the stages of Soul Therapy can be found in the Appendix.

1. We begin with a brief meditation connecting the client's heart, head and Soul with the world mother in the middle of the earth, where she serves as the feminine pole. This erects a strong vertical axis of healing energy. We then invoke the Soul's healing powers. This pillar of power provides enough energy and consciousness to carry out the transformation. A trained guide is helpful here, and I would suggest that only experienced meditators should attempt this exercise alone. This deliberate, methodical development of healing power is not often seen in psychotherapy.

2. Next we connect the healing energies, which are centred in the heart, with the client's basic unconscious by sending a wave of love and light to the solar plexus. Here we include the unconscious as an equal partner in the process, making the Soul, the self and the basic unconscious ready to co-operate. (Including the basic unconscious as an equal partner, and seeing subpersonalities as living beings instead of impersonal and remote, is also a new practice.)

3. Therapeutic work with the subpersonalities is essential: we engage all the subpersonalities with unconditional love and offer to work with them. We trust their Soul potential no matter how destructive and dark they seem to be. This approach is based on the belief that everything in the unconscious has the potential for light. In order to meet their needs subpersonalities may develop strategies that turn destructive. This must change. When the deeper needs of a subpersonality are identified and met, it will be transformed and adopt a new, positive function.

An attitude of love and appreciation towards our subpersonalities is unusual. We see that the destructive strategies of our inner persecutors are based on ignorance, and that through the love and wisdom of the Soul they can be transformed. In the unconscious, subpersonalities are often driven by the need for survival, security and self-esteem. When we recognise the value of these needs, the subpersonalities will understand their role in our lives, and co-operation between "top and bottom" becomes easier. You may not ask your inner child questions about the cosmos – this is the Soul's domain – but the inner child's innate joy and spontaneity may help you develop good relationships, which the Soul needs to manifest its vision. This brings me to the next point, an important one.

4. In Soul Therapy, when subpersonalities are met with love and appreciation, their identity and self-image changes. A subpersonality is a *living being*, stuck in a repeating loop of behaviour learned in the past, recreating old situations and moods. When they realise how they came into being, their true nature and the role they play in one's present life, an awakening occurs *in the subpersonality*. A subpersonality that was captured in the past can now become a player in the present. They discover that:

a. *They are a loved and valued living* part of the client's inner universe. The client communicates this to the subpersonality (or subpersonalities, if, for example, they are working with a "family" of them).

b. *They are stuck in a past time.* They must realise that the client is an adult living in the present. This may come as a surprise to many subpersonalities, rather like the Japanese soldier found in the jungle long after World War II had ended but living as if the war was still raging. When a subpersonality realises that the present offers many new opportunities, it is motivated to release its identification with the past. Subpersonalities live in a universe where everything imagined is real, so we can promise them anything as long as it is consistent with our values. Once identified with the new imaginary reality they start to create a corresponding psychological atmosphere: we become what we think in our hearts.

c. They are told that *they share the Soul of the client,* which means they also share the same light in the heart. Knowing this can be transformative. Not all subpersonalities co-operate initially. You can meet their resistance with the radical message that all their essential needs will be met. This is an offer no subpersonality can resist because they are often in pain. Other subpersonalities may interfere with the work. We must then first work with the controlling subpersonality before we can get to the essence. Sometimes the resistance can be so powerful that we need a skilled guide to maintain a loving perspective, and to point out the disadvantages of maintaining the status quo.

d. Parental subpersonalities are told *they are not the true outer parent,* but a copy who has served as a role model. Now they should stop identifying with the biological parent and instead become an inner archetypal parent. This means that the inner parent has the same potential to develop as the client. When the inner parent realises it can become completely different from the outer parent, a transformation take place, changing how the client thinks about their inner parent and how the inner parent thinks about herself. These parental figures come in different forms developed at different ages. We should try to work with as many "versions" as we can find. These inner parents can be transformed into a nurturing archetypal parent that gives strength and support to all parts of the personality. Again, this approach to our inner parents strikes me as new and innovative.

e. When a subpersonality has agreed to co-operate, we tell it that *it will be integrated into the heart centre.* The heart centre is a key psychological point where the superconscious and basic unconscious are unified. This integration happens when the subpersonality escapes its time warp and enters the present.

When this is understood by the subpersonality a triangle of light and love can be created between the Soul, the self and each subpersonality. This triangle consists of the sun over the head, the sun in the heart centre, and the sun in the subpersonality's heart. Within this triangle we visualise light and invoke the Soul's healing powers. A wave of energy flows through each point of the triangle. We let the light do its work. The client must stay with the visuali-sation and not try to force the flow. In this way the subpersonality can be transformed; we can observe it being drawn into the heart where it finds its new reality.

When a subpersonality enters a new reality, we must be able to detect it and ground it. Subpersonalities create specific inner worlds based on their needs; some will be coloured by love, others by light. We should respect the subper-sonality's natural development in its new reality and give it everything it needs to develop. We tell it about its unique function and its place in a team of other subpersonalities, with the client as manager and the Soul as visionary. We then ask the client to talk to the subpersonality about the gifts it brings to the team. Finally, we tell the subpersonality it can ask for the client's attention, if additional needs arise. Then we guide the client out of the visualisation. The entire session takes place with eyes closed, preferably in an upright position.

If the transformation is successful, a little follow up work will be needed. Sometimes it helps to return to the transformed subpersonality and observe the inner process. We can include all of this work in the meditation, but usually it's best to leave the healing to the wisdom of the unconscious. Encouraging the client to write about this Soul process can also help to anchor the experience in the unconscious; I personally have befitted from this.

These are the essential elements of Soul Therapy. The process will vary depending on the individual. Painful emotions are released, but gently, and clients often experience joy throughout the process. A lightness arises, suggesting something has changed, and problems troubling the client gradually disappear. The subpersonality's perception of its identity and situation changes. The client's relationship to the subpersonality also changes and the two begin to co-operate. The whole process is guided by the creative river and its need to create harmony, balance and co-operation. It unites past (subpersonality) with the present (self) and the future (the Soul's life purpose and meaning).

An example from my own life may give you an idea of how it works.

"The past must be harmonized with the present, in order to meet the future positively"

From Isolation to Joyful Co-operation

In recent years I've worked hard to overcome my tendency to isolation and an overly serious approach to life. I wanted to relate to the world joyfully and spontaneously, qualities that the creative river and Soul Therapy can develop. During these years, I have grown enormously: friends say they can see new sides to my personality, different from my usual dynamic and dedicated nature; others, course participants and clients, say much the same.

I am more relaxed and can socialise more spontaneously. A new freedom and joy have come into my life. This may not sound exciting for those who are already easy going, but for me it's a revolution. Whereas I could have peak experiences in meditation, could easily focus, practice discipline and understand the meaning of spiritual literature, my tendency towards isolation was limiting my life. Now I am living my life more creatively, which is what matters most.

I discovered my tendency to isolation had deep roots. Working through many past lives, I was able to bring different subpersonalities into a warm inner community. Through Soul Therapy I developed an ashram in my heart, an inner world permeated with love, wisdom and meaning. This ashram gives the subpersonalities a unique place in the whole: there are temples with contemplating gurus, beautiful women, universities, colleges, and playgrounds for my inner children; there's a theatre ensemble that my inner mother loves to watch, a leadership academy where my dynamic subpersonalities can meet and discuss their plans; and there's a central hall where everyone gathers to meditate and receive inspiration from the Soul and the spiritual beings that guide the ashram. This sounds like a fantasy world – and it is – but I prefer this fantasy, which reflects my values, to the fantasies that my subpersonalities believed in response to things that happened many years ago and are no longer happening. As Proverbs 23:7 tells us: "For as a man thinks in his heart, so is he."

I bring my many inner children to this ashram. They are afraid of being rejected, and hate the boredom that comes when social connections lack life. I have been allergic to small talk, which in the past triggers in me rage, boredom and loneliness. I react less powerfully now, and see that small talk sometimes can function as a bridge to deeper connectivity.

These young subpersonalities are not sure who they are. Their confusion stems from the shame I associate with my sensitive nature. This has led to problems with self-esteem. When my teenage subpersonalities realised that sensitivity was attractive to women, I went through an emotional transformation and became comfortable with my masculinity. For one's true self to go unrecognised is painful, and leads to much inner uncertainty. Until I went through this transformation, the softer side of my character went unacknowledged.

Let me describe how meeting a subpersonality happens in practice. Here I work through the grief I felt because of the loss of intimacy in my life. This account is based on notes taken immediately after a soul therapy session.

We first build up power and send love to the subpersonalities that are in mourning. I focus on the heaviness in my solar plexus, the pain and sense of deprivation. I ask "Who suffers?" and a picture of myself as a 15-year-old teenager appears. He is lying on the floor in the basement of my childhood home, completely broken. He says he doesn't want to hear any "sacred bullshit", which suggests the spiritual character of his suffering. We accept him unreservedly and agree that his feelings of love and loss are entirely appropriate. He is upset because he lacks a woman's love. It is clear that he is not aware of his positive qualities as a young man. He believes he will never be loved by a beautiful woman. He is inhibited and lonely. He can't seem to reach the women he desires. A wall separates him from them. We start to talk about his good qualities, and why past girlfriends loved him. Could it have been because of his kindness and good heart? Can one really be loved for their goodness, he asks? We answer "yes" and it makes him happy. His sense of being un-lovable begins to fade.

I ask what he wants most of all. He says a girlfriend, and to make love to a beautiful woman. Through a loving, sexual intimacy he believes he will feel whole. This seems a good time to tell him that he is a subpersonality, that he is trapped in a past time and that many opportunities are available to him now if he enters the heart centre. He understands that he is stuck in time and says he would like to go to Copenhagen. The prospect of leaving his small town to head for the capital excites him. He thinks it is a great idea and says he would be happy to enter the heart centre if his chances for having sex are better in Copenhagen. We assure him they are.

We invoke the golden energy of the Soul. As this hits his heart, he becomes part of its love-wisdom. He grows firm and strong, becoming a 17-year-old on the threshold of adulthood. I see him spontaneously on a beach, as I have with other subpersonalities. He is a beautiful, strong, young man greeted by delightful girls playing volleyball. Self-confidence, joy and exuberance colour this meeting. Entering the ashram, he meets an older man, a mentor, who will help him to mature. His task in this new reality is to grow into a strong, wise and caring man who can contribute to a meaningful life. As the session ends, I feel joy, and am optimistic about my future love life.

Whenever my teenage subpersonality re-experienced pain, I repeat the process described above and my inner space widened. In this way I was gradually able to remain positive for longer stretches.

We can describe this process as bringing together the loving, wise intervention of the self and the good will of the basic unconscious, bringing the basic unconscious into closer co-operation with the Soul. In this way, the past is harmonised with the present in order to meet the future positively.

Creative Meditation is a powerful tool that develops our personality so it can express the Soul. It is useful for all personality types, even those who find it difficult to visualise for whom the focus can be on *feeling* the images. Creative Meditation is helpful for those who need to strengthen their will because it helps us to develop qualities that help us in our daily life. Creative types will naturally be attracted to this meditation, but we should be mindful not to leave our present reality behind and enter a fantasy world – and this applies to all types. I have met many people who have lost touch with reality and the fact that everything must be manifested on the physical plane. A creative imagination can make real changes in the world; it can also be a form of escapism.

Dynamic, mental, analytical and practical types can benefit from this meditation too. They tend to be dry and single minded, but this meditation can bring colour and vitality into their inner lives. As with all things, it is good to know the positive and negative qualities of this river, something that is important to remember as we now look at the scientific river and the development of the diamond light.

Chapter 9

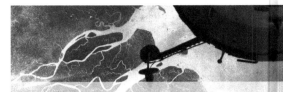

The Scientific River of Life:

The truth will set us free if we are ready to face it. This is the essence of what the scientific river is trying to teach us. We meditate in order to know ourselves and the energies of this river, the fifth, are an important part of the process. The truth can be uncomfortable and we often turn away from it, especially if we prefer to look at the world through rose-tinted spectacles. But when the Soul begins to awaken we soon realise that our lives are coloured by projections and wishful thinking. What we call love is perhaps just obsessive desire, our courage may be an expression of a powerful survival instinct, and our great visions turns out to be empty platitudes. People who are in touch with this river prefer to call a spade a spade; they want to discover and expose *facts*. Analysis and logic facilitate this river. Influenced by the dynamic and intelligent rivers of life, it stimulates deep and focused thinking.

Whether we study the physical universe or our inner psychic world, the energy of this rivers means our approach will be *methodical;* we test out all possibilities before reaching conclusions. A passion for truth motivates us and, with unlimited patience, we study every detail of that which we are investigating. This attention to detail differentiates this river from the intelligent river, where the focus is on the big picture.

The scientific river brings us the *light of truth*. People influenced by this river are not interested in faith – this is the domain of the idealising river – but in facts and truths. The light of truth is our inner Sherlock Holmes or Buddha mind. In the West, the influence of this river can be seen in our scientific and academic disciplines. In the East, people have used the same approach to map out the nature of our inner worlds. The West and East are now coming

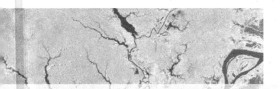

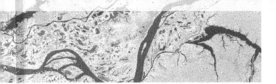

Your Way to Truth, Revelation and Knowledge

together and creating a scientific spirituality, with the scientific study of meditation being a good example.

Reflective Meditation

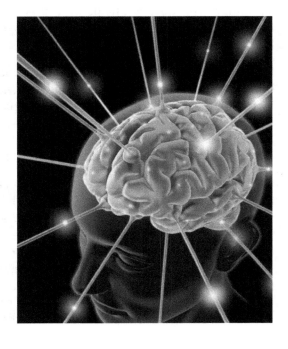

I discussed this form of meditation in the chapter looking at the intelligent river, where it is used to develop our abstract intelligence. Here we want to develop our intelligence as a practical tool, rather than as a means to discover new abstract ideas. Our research may lead to new discoveries, but these will be something concrete that we can sense and feel.

When we are influenced by this river we want to understand how reality works. Our life becomes a field study as we research and document our findings. Accordingly, we can use Reflective Meditation as a research tool. We can explore anything we like with this meditation. Personally, I have used it as part of my transformative practice in order to uncover and discover previously hidden aspects of my psyche.

Before I start meditating I centre myself and disidentify from my body, emotions and thoughts. Next, I anchor myself as the observer while focusing on my forehead (see Appendix). This puts me in an objective, aware state and I use the diamond light to explore my inner worlds – the diamond light is the light created when the Soul uses the concrete mind as a penetrating, analytical beam.

In Reflective Meditation we often alter between observation and exploration. We start by observing, accepting and embracing whatever we meet on our inner journey. Then we move on to explore relevant subpersonalities and their corresponding thoughts, images and desires. We speak to the subpersonalities (second person) and fully identify with them (first person). This manner of *investigative interview* is very effective: astute questions can penetrate to the core of a problem and uncover the experiences, strategies, needs and requirements of the subpersonality that are connected to the problem. Asking the right questions at the right time is an art in itself, and it is a good idea to prepare the questions in advance.

When I or a client experience pain, the first question I ask is: "Who is suffering?" This question helps us to disidentify and establish the observer. Keeping a journal to record our impressions during meditation can help us to build up our understanding.

I use meditation in my work as a psychotherapist to explore how we can free ourselves from constraints and inhibitions. That I am able to help clients who face complicated, chaotic and painful life situations fills me with deep appreciation. Together we are explorers mapping out and conquering unknown territories. This process is associated with the scientific river, and I have witnessed how the truth can free people from limiting perspectives.

One client was surprised by the insights that came to her in therapy. Her husband had cheated on her and she was deeply identified with a victim subpersonality. For six months he had apologised and repented in every possible way, and had almost stopped socialising. She still loved him very much but her heart remained closed to him and she could not forgive him. We used chair work (a technique ideally suited to the energy of the scientific river), whereby the client pictures or places a subpersonality in an empty chair, then speaks with it. My investigative interview with her uncovered a subpersonality who wanted revenge; the client wanted her husband to suffer until she was convinced he would never betray her again. When she saw that side of herself, a wave of love flowed through her, and she regretted bitterly that she had tortured him for so long. In realising the reason why she was so reluctant to forgive him, the truth came in and set them both free. The client's identification with a victim subpersonality meant she could only see the injustice done to her.

Some people are masters at uncovering the truth, using their crystal clear intellect to ask penetrating and precise questions. They are in deep contact with this river, and whether they are detectives, psychotherapists, chemical engineers or spiritual explorers they can throw light on something that has been hidden. My work with both clients and myself has given me insights into many psychological laws of cause and effect. In the spirit of the scientific river, I have translated the knowledge I have acquired into something specific, and I will now draw upon one of my own personal field studies to offer as an example.

For long periods I meditated on my desire for sex, and the pain I felt when my needs were not met. Soon after I started meditating, I met a group of subpersonalities, each with their own desires and passions. They showed me my longing and desire to surrender to the One. This made sense to me because my typology is dominated by the dedicated, idealising river. My desires were overly idealised and romantic, particularly with regards to beauty. So I understood that the energy was not purely sexual but also spiritual. My sexual desire was rooted in a longing for union: the merging of the feminine and masculine. I interviewed my subpersonalities and explored the relevant psychic centres, or chakras, that are located between the base of the spine and the top of the head. These centres contain different types of energies that can be connected to the psychological layers in the egg diagram.

These insights helped me to understand that I had acquired an unconscious connection between having sex with a beautiful woman and the spiritual experience of joy and happiness: This insight also explained the pain I suffered whenever such a union could not take place, such as when no partner was available or my partner was not in the mood. In order to free myself and mature sexually I had to find a way to break this pattern.

The quest for greater freedom and personal growth – and more enjoyable sex – motivated my meditations. During the first half hour I would visualise a positive and nurturing force field surrounding me. Then I directed the diamond light from my brow centre to the source of my pain. I looked deep into my desires and noticed a regressive force that wanted to return to the womb, as well as a progressive force that yearned to unite with the divine through beauty. The regressive force turned me into a dependent state, while the progressive force connected me to higher awareness, happiness, beauty and love. The former longed for a pre-rational surrender to the mother; the latter sought to transcend my ego self and connect to the One.

I have never practised tantra, and I don't even have a book about it, but somehow I seemed to intuit the essence of its teaching. Tantra teaches that powerful sexual encounters can arise out of a deep devotion between two people who love each other. Discovering these forces changed my relationship to sex by explaining why sex sometimes turned me into regressive states and at other times took me to a place of higher awareness. During Reflective Meditation it is possible to re-connect with the energies that are activated in the sexual act by tuning in to the images you have in your memory. In this way you can create a parallel process between your meditation practice and your sex life, which will give you new insights into the sexual energies at play and your own energy psychology.

Reflective Meditation has provided me with invaluable perspectives and insights into the forces that are at play in my life. My yearning to surrender to the divine feminine would sometimes dissolve my boundaries when I met a beautiful woman; unconsciously I believed she *was* the divine feminine. This insight was liberating. I was feeling insecure because I had projected this archetype onto the beautiful women I met. Reflective Meditation helped me to see my relationship to beauty from a bigger perspective and this helped me to withdraw my projections.

Meditating on beauty has released many of my emotional blockages. I am more open to the world around me and my relationships are freer. I feel liberated and independent, which is important for a healthy sex life. A loving and conscious sexual relationship between two people that both seek spiritual development can be profoundly transformative.

My meditations also had a positive impact on my therapeutic work. I have worked with several men who are unconsciously caught up in similar projections. When they turn a woman into the Goddess, they become very frustrated. A woman can of course represent the divine feminine, but it is important to distinguish whether one is seeing a woman merely as a symbol or as a human being. Many men have powerful spiritual yearnings that they transfer onto their relationships with women. But a woman cannot accept a role as the divine feminine, nor the man as the divine masculine, unless we are conscious of the forces at play. However, when both partners are conscious of the divine, sex can become a powerful tool for personal and spiritual love, an alchemical meeting place where man and woman become one body and Soul.

Exploring the World of Sex

The scientific river motivates us to engage in research, and that is why I am sharing my research on sexuality and sex. But this river is not about sex, it's about sincere research into a specific field. I have simply chosen sex as my research topic and, to reiterate, I offer it as an illustration of what research might look like in the hope it might inspire you in your own chosen field of study.

In order to carry out effective research we will first need a basic knowledge of the topic we are studying. I have previously pointed out that Reflective Meditation opens us up to the inspiration of the Soul (please be mindful of this as you read the following passages, which might prompt you to contemplate your own sexuality). We also need high quality *research tools*. Here my research tool is meditation. Next, I *investigate* – which in my case means having sex – and then I *reflect* on the experience with my partner. Finally, I *write down my findings* in a journal.

I cannot provide you with wonderful techniques that will improve your sex life because I do not know any. The only practice I know is devotion; I devote myself in love and I am fully awake in the meeting with the energies that arise. This is not so different from meditation. The sense of presence is intense and the act of union can lift the energy levels higher and higher. Throughout the act, it is possible to meditate on your partner.

Aside from wanting to offer you an example of scientific research, I have also included the topic of sexuality in this book on meditation because our sexual instinct is so powerful. Like our spirituality, sex is an expression of unity, which is the driving force behind the sensitive river. Individually we can connect to the Soul through meditation, and as a couple we can do the same through sex, but only if we are motivated by spiritual values. The incoming energies of the Aquarian Age are activating our relationship to sexuality in the collective unconscious, and this is another reason why I am including the topic in this book. The consequences of the internet and new technologies, which in my view have cheapened the sex act, show us that we must develop new perspectives.

Few other human interactions can expand our consciousness in the same way that a deep sexual encounter can. In the sex act, with love and spiritual awareness we can activate the body, our emotions, mind, Soul and Spirit, but certain conditions have to be present for this to happen. The couple must agree that sex is important to their spiritual development and they must be self-aware and willing to evolve and challenge their comfort zones. Very few people are ready for this kind of sexuality – for most of us, sex is a way to connect, play and have our basic sexual needs met.

Love, trust and commitment are required for sex to become a conduit for the healing powers of love. Only then can we access and release our deepest wounds. If we think we will be abandoned, the egocentric parts in us react and withdraw. A balance between detachment and attachment will help the couple to open up and show their most vulnerable sides. Sex alone will not give us the experience of oneness. It is the sum of the spiritual development of all our developmental lines that are united in the sexual act. Before the ideal meeting can become a reality both parties must have a dedicated spiritual practice that develops all aspects of their nature.

In order to begin a spiritually informed sexual practice two key aspects need to be in place. The *inclusiveness and acceptance* of the heart centre must be sufficiently developed so we can meet any resistance with loving empathy. The couple must also be totally *honest and transparent* with each other. This will help them to understand and define the energies at work. Scientific research is not possible if we withhold information. At times unpleasant energies will be activated, and to deal with the challenges they present we can also draw on the qualities of the dynamic river.

The use of Reflective Meditation as a research method when we study the sexual act is perfectly valid. The idea of researching and documenting our sex life sounds foreign to most of us, but this approach can prove valuable. We uncover many barriers that block our ability to experience genuine oneness. When our sex life is illuminated by the diamond light we have the potential for a *true* meeting between two Souls where everything is loved, held and lifted to a higher level.

The Seven Chakras and Sexuality

Medical science is interested in the physical body and its diverse physiology. The science of meditation is interested in man's energy body and spiritual anatomy. Next, I will connect sexuality with the study of the energy centres, or what are referred to as the chakras in the East. I described the eight basic lines of development in Chapter 4 and how they evolve through seven stages.

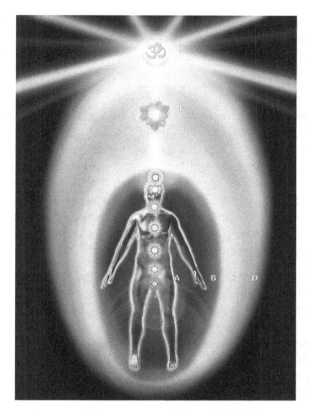

Figure 18. The inner man and the subtle bodies.

In this section, I will use the seven chakras as a reference and suggest how sexuality, or should I call it the process of uniting, is effected by the seven levels of consciousness.

Knowledge of these chakras will help us to *interpret* the energies we experience in the sexual process. When we use this knowledge properly we will know which level we draw our energy from.

For millennia the East has viewed man in terms of energy. They consider the physical body to be the Soul's most tangible body, the body it uses to sense and act in the world. Figure 18 shows how our physical bodies are surrounded by a number of energy fields, or bodies. Each energy body has a specific function.

The etheric body (a) is the vital body and consists of millions of energy channels (Nadis). The Nadis ensures the integrity and life energy of the body. In acupuncture we work with these energy lines. During Reflective Meditation we can learn to notice the quality of our energy levels. *The emotional body* (b) is the Soul's sensitivity that enables us to feel and identify emotional atmospheres. *The mental body* (c) is the mind, or intelligence, of the Soul. We can observe this body as the content and nature of our thoughts. These three bodies have their anchors in the physical nervous system.

The *Soul body* (d) is the Soul's own energy field and corresponds to the superconscious in the egg diagram. This body contains all the goodness, truth and beauty that the Soul has accumulated over lifetimes. In meditation we often experienced this body as boundless love and wisdom. The core of this body is the twelve-petalled lotus (e), which contains the spiritual spark or jewel. *The Spirit body* (sat-chit-ananda) is the innermost essence which is Spirit-in-Action (f), and contains the dynamic life that drives the Soul forward life after life in order to develop greater awareness. This jewel is illustrated as the star on top of Assagioli's egg diagram.

A number of psychic centres are located along the spine in the etheric body (Figure 19). These centres are the source for seven of the Soul energies and correspond to the seven ray qualities, although each centre can in fact express all of the energies at different stages of development. The level of consciousness of the Soul determines which energy type dominates the centre. Even if these centres are located in the back of the body, they open up as a flower in the front that expresses swirling energy. This swirling motion is why the energy centres are referred to as chakras, which means wheels, in Eastern literature, and also why they are described as lotuses with varying numbers of petals, which refer to the number of powers a lotus is expressing. Blueprints of these centres can also be found in the emotional and mental bodies.

The centres express seven different types of energy and receive corresponding energies from the environment. Hence there is a continuous exchange of energy deeply integrated in the nervous system.

Knowledge of the chakras provides us with a map of the different frequencies of our consciousness.

The level of development in each centre varies. Some centres are brilliant fountains of light and consciousness, while others are asleep, waiting for the Soul to awaken them.

The three lower centres are related to our primary energies and are therefore the most developed. They relate to the basic and middle unconscious, as depicted in Assagioli's egg diagram. Culture and education focus on the development of the type of consciousness that corresponds to these centres and the throat centre. Any imbalances here could prevent awakening in the higher centres.

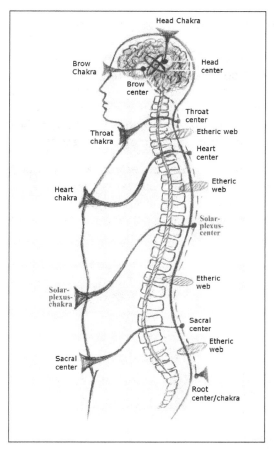

Figure 19: The inner man and the seven chakras.

In the following section I will discuss the seven chakras in relation to sexual energies and identify the themes which are relevant for each chakra.

Each chakra has a feminine and a masculine pole, but each chakra also represents either masculine (will) or feminine (love) energy. The first chakra is dominated by the will, the next by love, as follows:

First chakra: ▶	Root centre	– dominated by will
Second chakra: ▶	Sacral centre	– dominated by love
Third chakra: ▶	Solar plexus centre	– dominated by will
Fourth chakra: ▶	Heart centre	– dominated by love
Fifth chakra: ▶	Throat centre	– dominated by will
Sixth chakra: ▶	Brow centre	– dominated by love
Seventh chakra: ▶	Head centre	– dominated by will

Knowledge of these centres helps us to navigate the sexual journey more intelligently. For example, it is important to understand how we can develop the different chakras. The starting point is always sexual awareness and open and honest communication. The goal is the union of body and Soul through the sexual act. Soul therapy, general psychotherapy, Reflective Meditation and Creative Meditation are all important tools we can use to release the barriers we encounter. The primary method is the field study, where the couple, through the sexual act, work through all the stages and test what works.

As I explore the themes relevant to each chakra, I will differentiate between the genders, however it can be noted that each theme will be relevant to both women and men because we all have been both genders in past lives. That said, we each tend to identify most strongly with our current gender, which will bring particular experiences to consciousness.

The same principles apply to those who are LGBT, who must also polarise during sexual union in what might be termed the masculine and feminine roles in order to create the necessary tension.

Root Centre

The root centre is the first chakra and the seat of the survival instincts and the life force. It is closely linked to the physical body and our need for nutrients and protection. This chakra represents body consciousness and through its energies we connect to physical life. At this level of consciousness we associate sex with survival and reproduction.

A negatively activated root centre becomes a dominant theme in the sexual act usually due to unresolved blockages around survival needs. For thousands of years, sex has been associated with survival: we procreate for the survival of the species and so that our children can take care of us in old age. Women often have sex to receive protection and security from a man. If that is the case they will find it difficult to say "no" to sex. Men on the other hand can be possessive and may relate to a woman as their private property.

The root chakra is connected to the body's basic cellular consciousness and the attractions and repulsions that exist at this level. If we don't feel connected to our bodies we may find it difficult to generate sufficient vitality and potency required for sexual intercourse. It is therefore important to keep our bodies healthy. We can become aware of and heal this centre through the sexual act. If both parties can empathise and understand the barriers they encounter, they can consciously raise the awareness of the relevant subpersonalities. This will create new patterns of behaviour in relation to the body's needs.

When the root chakra in both partners harmonises, two vigorous and potent bodies can meet and the sexual act can generate the vitality required for energy to travel up the spine. An orgasm will then include the whole body and not just the genitals. From a spiritual point of view, we can transform even the survival instinct if we heed the heroic call of the Soul – this happens when the energies of the root chakra rise to the head centre, transforming body consciousness to unity consciousness. In such cases, we might find we are even able to put our lives at risk if it might further the spiritual cause – indeed, many spiritual explorers have found this to be true: one famous example is that of Jesus who entered Jerusalem even though he knew it would lead to his death.

Sacral Centre

The second chakra is called sacral centre, which is the seat of the sexual instincts. Related themes are concerned with *reproduction, bonding, security* and *sensuality.* This chakra is also connected to herd consciousness and our need to belong. As an emotional centre, this chakra controls basic emotions that are associated with the body and physical environment.

When the sacral centre is negatively activated you may feel concerned about security, intimate connection and sensuality. Traumatic experiences, such as the loss of intimacy and sexual abuse, have a negative impact on this chakra. Historically, through marriage and trade, women have been used as a commodity to ensure the family's survival and power. This abuse has resulted in prejudices existing in the collective psyche that block the free and sensuous expression of sexual energy. We need to work through such prejudices and barriers for total intimate surrender to be possible. Of course, we can repress these issues and still have a well-functioning sex life. But in a spiritually-orientated sex life, many of these repressed energies will be activated when the values of the heart centre collide with the more egocentric values connected with this centre.

Possessiveness is another theme for this centre. Our security and survival needs activate powerful energies that seek to attach us to our partner. To let go of these attachments is difficult, but that is precisely the purpose of a spiritually-orientated sex life: a sense of detachment is important. This detachment doesn't mean a type of isolation created by our defenses, but rather a sense of freedom and healthy connection controlled by the heart.

Another theme related to this energy centre is shame, in particular feeling ashamed of our bodies. This will obviously be a great barrier towards sensuality and merging, both on a physical and emotional level. Our bodies are different, and sometimes we have to work to attune them, but when we have experienced two bodies that are in tune and in love we will know what intimate surrender means.

When the sacral centre is developed (usually with the help of the heart centre) we experience pleasure, erotic warmth and playful sensuality, and the union of two bodies becomes a joyful journey towards higher and higher states of consciousness. It is also possible for the herd instinct to come under the influence of heart's values and be transformed into the group consciousness that connects us with the World Soul and all of humanity. When this happens, energies from the sacral centre move up to the throat centre where they can be verbalised so that we can become aware of them. This transformation from one centre to another occurs when we make the unconscious conscious.

Solar Plexus Centre

The third centre is the *solar plexus chakra*, which is the seat of our *assertiveness*. Here we develop *self-awareness* with the support of the throat centre. Themes associated with this chakra are *self-confidence, ambition* and *personal power*. The purpose of this energy centre is to support the development of independence, strength and personal boundaries that help us to master our lives. As a centre for emotions and desire, this chakra affects our personal preferences and biases, identity and unique role in a group.

This centre is also where we act out erotic play, which provides the opportunity to offer mutual confirmation of the each partners' attraction and value.

An imbalanced solar plexus chakra will lead to power struggles and problems with self-confidence. What should be healthy competition between the sexes turns into destructive power games. We see our partners as status symbols that will give us power and prestige in society. A man can use his power to dominate a woman and "keep her in her place", or the woman can manipulate the man to get what she wants. Such behaviour is, of course, devastating for self-confidence. When neither party is willing to surrender for fear of losing power, a deep union is impossible.

These sorts of power struggles can lead to humiliation and loss of reputation. When hurt, the ego becomes even more defensive and will shun real intimacy. This chakra is where we hide or repress our weaknesses or any qualities the ego deems unattractive or detrimental to power and status. However, it is important to acknowledge the will to power. If we can lift this energy up to the heart centre it can become a supportive force that helps the couple to grow in confidence with themselves and with each other.

When this instinct is being expressed healthily, governed by the ethics of the heart, the man wants to conquer the woman, and the woman wants to be conquered. We can also use sex to explore and build each other's sexual self-image and self-confidence. We can be playful and delightfully erotic when this centre is harmoniously developed. We feel good about ourselves and have the confidence needed to embrace our lives and the world. The man courageously conquers the woman, and explores new dimensions of her being. The same is of course applicable to the woman, and the couple can positively challenge and support each other. When the Soul dominates this centre the energies from the solar plexus rise up to the heart centre and self-assertiveness is transformed into spiritual dignity, self-worth and Soul-assertiveness. This enables us to manifest the good, the true and the beautiful.

Heart Centre

The fourth chakra is the *heart centre*. This is the seat of our higher emotions, the Soul's group awareness, and the development of group consciousness. Here our awareness is lifted beyond the needs of the ego and we can identify with the needs of others. The herd instinct is concerned with my own need for security, whereas group consciousness is concerned with the needs of my community.

The themes are *self-esteem, appreciation* and *connectedness*. Through this centre's exalted emotions and impersonal love we are able to accommodate and accept the energies from other centres.

When the energies are received from the other centres they can be activated through the heart centre to enable us to transmute our egocentric tendencies. We experience a heartfelt need to relate to our partner on equal terms, and to consciously connect with those we meet. We recognise intuitively the unity behind all separations.

The heart and brow centre are the most important centres for a spiritually-orientated sex life. These centres are instrumental to our sense of self-worth and self-esteem, as well as our ability to sense and appreciate another person's unique qualities. When the heart centre is unbalanced, the opposite will be the case. We will be unable to appreciate ourselves and others because we are not in touch with love. No amount of solar plexus confirmation can give us the deep inner peace that can arise from the heart centre. Devotion is connected to the heart chakra, and we will lose ourselves in the relationship if we don't have a sense of our self-worth – we will also lose the important tension created by the polarity between the two sexes.

A blocked heart centre blinds us to the other. We cannot see or appreciate the other's unique value, which is only possible when we can look at them in the light of our own beauty. More egocentric centres can also hijack this centre and abuse its sweetness and sensitivity – our speech might come across as sensitive and heartfelt, but we are motivated by deeply egocentric needs. We have seen many dubious spiritual teachers misusing the gifts of this centre.

When the heart centre is open an almost ecstatic union is possible. Duality dissolves and the couple is able to surrender to pure love and bliss. Devotion becomes pure compassion and we can meet and honour our partner when they risk showing their vulnerabilities. We can love the vulnerable, and what was separate and unloved can become whole again. This idealised depiction of the meeting of two hearts does not normally occur when we have sex, but it can happen when the couple is deeply motivated from this rather unselfish place, and this is why we make the effort. When we succeed in establishing a safe intimate relationship, our sex life becomes an important source of connection and power. The heart centre motivates us to make a difference, and we can heal our hearts and emotions through sex as a physical and meditative practice.

Throat Centre

The fifth chakra is the throat centre, which is the seat of intelligence. As a centre for knowledge and communication it is here we develop self-awareness and identity. Themes are *communication*, *clarity* and *truth*.

Blockages in this centre make it difficult for us to talk about our sexuality, and we struggle to develop our sexual identity. In order to find out who we are we must be able to accurately communicate our feelings. Communication and thinking around sex and sexuality may be so unclear and confusing that we don't know what we really feel. We may say what we think our partners want to hear so we can have our own needs satisfied. If we have felt punished after sharing our truth, it is understandable that we would become distrustful and withholding. Other blockages in our sexuality can make it difficult and painful to listen to when our partner is talking about sex.

The throat centre's primary task is to serve the heart by using intelligence in the service of love. In relation to the scientific river, this centre is the primary channel for the light of truth. This energy centre can make forgiveness and redemption possible. When a couple can talk openly about the energies that are activated in the sexual act wonderful revelations are possible. We can allow our curiosity to unfold so that we can explore together, studying and sharing what we find. When communication is precise and flowing freely, a couple can explore and experiment with a playful curiosity. Even telepathic communication is possible if this centre is sufficiently developed. A developed throat centre is also telepathically susceptible to the Soul, aligning our self-awareness to the consciousness of the Soul.

Brow Centre

The sixth chakra is the brow centre. This is where the purpose and wisdom of the Soul is integrated with the energies of the personality. The themes for this energy centre are *wisdom*, *integration* and *vision*. This chakra can translate sexual energies into their highest possible expression, always with the purpose of developing the

Soul's creative talents for the benefit of the whole. The sexual union and the transformative process, when it is controlled from the brow centre, will be guided by a desire to have a greater impact as a Soul in the world.

When the brow centre is imbalanced the sexual relationship will lack in spiritual depth and purpose; the direction of the relationship will not reach beyond the couple's own personal fulfillment and therefore higher universal energies will have difficulties entering the relational field. This lack of vision may also lead to illusions and deceptions: powerful desires and passions can be aroused that we might think are of a spiritual nature, but in the end enslave rather than liberate us. This is probably the greatest danger in this work, and therefore we must take care to be motivated by our highest values.

When the brow chakra is open, a couple can consciously represent the divine masculine and feminine and through the sexual act express the highest spiritual energies possible in human form. This requires that the couple stay at this level of consciousness throughout the sexual act. If the couple can access these states while meditating together, there's less risk of activating and being dominated by egocentric energies during sex.

Head Centre

The seventh chakra is the head centre. Here the will of the Soul is united with the universal will. This energy centre is associated with the dissolution of all boundaries and with the arising of cosmic and non-dual consciousness. I have only had a few, brief glimpses of what it means to be in touch with this centre, and these glimpses are not sufficient for me to draw any conclusions. Instead of speculating I will urge the reader to do their own research.

In Table 5, I have summarised the key findings and themes from my research into sexuality and the chakras. I hope this will inspire the reader to develop a joyous, meaningful and creative sexuality.

Sexuality and the Chakras

Centre	Consciousness	Theme	Unbalanced	Potential
Root	Survival instinct, awareness of the body	Survival, sensation, connection to the earth	Fear of death, impotency, possessive	Vitality, physical freedom, physical strength
Sacral	Sex drive, herd instinct	Intimacy, security, sensuality, comfort	Fear of Intimacy, sexually blocked, shame, addiction, control	Erotic warmth, joy, sensuality, sexually liberation
Solar plexus	Assertiveness, self- assertiveness	Self-confidence, ambition, personal power	Power battles, dominant-submissive relationships, isolation, fear of humiliation	Sexual confidence, affirmation, erotic play, conquering, vitality
Heart	Group instinct, holistic awareness, group consciousness	Self-worth, spiritual dignity, Soul to Soul connection	Inferiority, loss of self, poor boundaries, oversensitive	Equality, worthy, sweetness, empathy, intuitive connection
Throat	Curiosity instinct, self-awareness	Communication, clarity, truth.	Taboos, control, lack of clarity, manipulation.	Clear, open and exploring sexuality that can be freely expressed
Brow	Wisdom, awareness of purpose, integration of Soul and personality	Wisdom, integration, vision	Illusions, betrayal, seduction, selfishness disguised as spirituality	Visionary, Sexuality and the chakras. Sexuality, service to the whole
Head	Transpersonal will, non-dual consciousness	Transcendence, union, higher will		

Table 5: Sexuality and the chakras.

Conclusion

In this chapter I have taken a practical approach to Reflective Meditation and the scientific river. Meditation is in this case used to explore areas where we can experiment and develop a practice. In line with integral meditation the purpose is to translate insight into action. I chose sex as my field study, but I could have chosen medicine, engineering, management, education or abstract topics such as the nature of the Soul, wisdom or love. The same practical approach would apply. The purpose of this type of meditation is to develop new knowledge that can be implemented in practice.

Those who will most benefit from this type of meditation are analytical types whose Soul purpose is to research and discover new knowledge, with meditation being a valuable source of inspiration. I would also recommend that sensitive, creative and dedicated types practise this form of meditation; these types tend to be imprecise, overly emotional and unclear in their thinking, and this meditation will offer greater clarity. Reflective Meditation is an important part of any integral meditation practice it helps us to practice discrimination.

From these very practical and analytical explorations, we will now move onto the idealising river of life.

Chapter 10

The Idealising River of Life:

Your Way to Devotion, Purification and Perfection

In the early 1990s I moved into a flat share, which gave me the opportunity to develop my social relationships. During this period I also practised a forgiveness meditation where I consciously forgave everyone I felt had hurt me. It was a devotional meditation; I held the image of Christ in my heart and he radiated forgiving love to all sentient beings. For hours I could devote myself to this image and the sweet, mild energies the meditation created. I decided to turn the meditation into a 24-hour practice where I would systematically go through my life and send forgiveness to everyone I could think of. I added music and incense to the meditation, and I was fasting. The urge to purify myself of negative energies was strong, in that way Christ consciousness could descend on me. I wanted nothing less than pure perfection.

I directed forgiving love to the situation or person in question until I felt it was thoroughly purified. As the day progressed I thought of all the people I needed to forgive and I committed myself to Christ in my heart so I could become one with his consciousness. I felt lighter and that I had more energy because of all the emotional baggage I had left behind. One time, I remember feeling ecstatic and completely free, relieved of all darkness. I felt that Christ consciousness could descend on me and perfect me. But at the same time a strange sadness came over me: if I transcended everything, how could I now live with ordinary people? I felt empty but also grateful for what I had achieved. After this process, I decided to have breakfast. I sat alone in the kitchen, enjoying my serenity. Then one of my flatmates came in – a talkative Swede who took up a lot of space. He immediately started talking enthusiastically about some project of his and didn't stop. This quickly irritated me. His chatter disturbed my exalted state. He was oblivious, chattering on, unaware of my reaction. It soon became too much for me and my anger boiled. I wanted to tell him to shut up, but then it came to me: I still had anger in me. It was both a surprise and a relief to realise I still had something to work with. I was not yet purified; the Christ-nature had not yet filled me completely. I laughed, got up, said good morning and went to my room to contemplate this discovery.

This story illustrates the key element of the idealising river: *the devotional heart.* We can all have peak experiences, but it is our understanding of them that reflects our level of maturity. For some the energy that manifests during a peak experience could be too much and they will collapse; for others the experience will represent a step forward in their spiritual development.

The energy of the idealising river can cause imbalances and create illusions, as the above example illustrates. Strong ideals can easily lead to extremes, and this is especially so for types dominated by this ray. The idealising river combines the sensitive and dynamic rivers and through this it makes us passionate and focused. (This was also discussed in Chapter 3, where we discussed the psychological functions, and in Chapter 7.)

The energy of this river can bring us home to our source via the devotional heart. If we want to maintain an intensive meditation practice in order to overcome restrictions and challenges, we will need this river's help. It motivates us to strive for the good, the true and the beautiful. This is the heart's longing; it awakens in us when we realise humanity's higher spiritual possibilities and we see beyond our personal passions. In its lower expression as the ego's desire for ambition, this river is related to the solar plexus , and in its higher spiritual striving it is related to the heart chakra.

For some the heart centre's longing can be very powerful. They are drawn to a meditation aimed at devotion, surrender and dedication. Their passion is focused on a vision. They may want to follow in the footsteps of a saint or to devote themselves to God or some spiritual ideal. The great mystics have all learned much from this river. The call of the heart may not be religious in nature – one can strive to become the perfect leader, a great teacher or an artist. At the same time, there is also the risk that we will feel pain if we do not reach our ideal. In fact, this pain is inevitable because our ideal is most often so great that we cannot achieve it, at least not in one lifetime.

Passion is the psychological function associated with the idealising river. Here the desire, willingness and courage to follow our hearts and reach our goal is the only thing that matters. In meditation, this passion sparks the fire we need to reach the ecstasy of unity. As with the dynamic river, there is often a strong tendency when under the influence of this river to go to extremes. We are prepared to "go all the way". Our longing is so powerful that we are willing to sacrifice everything – family, friends, status, etc – on the altar of love.

The idealising river raises everything it flows through. When it motivates our meditation, we yearn for transcendence. While the intelligent river provides a higher mental perspective, this river works with the heart, enabling us to *feel* greatness and love. We want to realise an ideal, whether that is perfect power, love or enlightenment.

Creative Meditation with Surrender

Creative Meditation helps us to develop the qualities of the idealising river. Imagination and visualisation are the primary tools we use in Creative Meditation. When using Creative Meditation, the energy is different according to the river we are working with. For example, with the idealising river the energy will be intense and concentrated, often generating a single image, whereas for the creative river the energy will be lighter and we will pass through many stages with many variations of images being generated.

A central theme of the idealising river is surrender. We forget ourselves as

personalities and commit to something greater. We sacrifice our small self so we can become part of a greater Self. The meditation we do with the idealising river is the same as the method we use for the creative river – but the effect will be felt different. We begin by centring ourselves, then ascending the mountain, then focusing our attention on a specific theme. A common practice in many spiritual traditions is to focus on an enlightened master or saint or the Buddha (see Appendix). We visualise the master and feel benevolence radiating from his image. It is necessary to affirm and believe that the master exists in our inner world. In this way we create a link between our image and the real spiritual entity. Our devotion and clear visualisation magnetises the image and forms this link. We establish this connection through the heart centre or face to face in the mind's eye. We then surrender our small selves, letting go of anything that blocks a perfect union. A prayer or a mantra invoking the master will help, although later we may reach the contemplative stage of a silent union. Our success depends on the purity of our intent and the focus of our concentration. Remembering Christ's words, "Not my will, but thine," can assist us. The meditation succeeds when we merge with the master and we receive blessings and directions from him.

The image strengthens over time, becoming more vivid, and eventually the Soul uses it as a way to communicate with us. Through projecting onto the image all the goodness, truth and beauty of the master, our inner image of the master comes to embody the master's noblest qualities. At a certain point, the image becomes a kind of door that the disciple can open in order to meet the real master. In doing so, we are able to enter into the master's consciousness and learn about the master's role in the earth's evolution. When the disciple can raise his consciousness to the level of the master in this way, the master is ready for him: the disciple knocks on the door, and the master graciously lets him in.

These meetings are more frequent when there is a full moon because of the high frequency energy that the full moon emits. Sometimes we can feel ecstasy and feel like we have had a real encounter with the master. In my experience, however, these energies usually come from our own Soul, which uses these heightened images as a way of communicating with us. It is not always easy to remember that our inner images of a master are not the master himself. Here, as in all things, discrimination is key.

It is common to visualise Jesus or the Buddha because these images are familiar and easy to relate to. At the same time, they can flatter us and give us false messages if the ego projects what it wants to hear onto the image. Again, we must practice discrimination and be wary of revelations that inflate our little self and feed our pride. That said, communing with the image of a master can be deeply transformative because, as mentioned, the images contain all the master's qualities and we experience these. In real encounters with a living master, he or she may communicate a vision – a work of some service – that the disciple is charged with manifesting.

In 1989, I had an experience that set the direction for my future spiritual development. For some time in my meditations I had been visualising Christ and the sun in the heart. During one meditation, Christ appeared surrounded by a golden sun, which was his aura. The love emanating from him was so overwhelming and penetrating that I dissolved into tears and rapture. I felt infinitely loved and appreciated. Although this being was far more evolved than me, I somehow felt I was of equal value, as if I was a brother of Christ. As the figure approached, I felt a powerful love which was painful to the self-hatred I felt at the time. However, a gentle loving-kindness radiated from him and overcame my resistance. A fragrance like the finest rose had subtly found its way into the darkest chambers of my being. His love drew my shadow out from the darkness. The figure stood before me, then passed right through me, which was more than I could bear. Cleansing light and love flooded every pore of my being. I burst into tears, surrendered and gave myself over to it. I was dazed, disintegrated, overwhelmed, sobbing, helpless. I had no idea what I would do. I had never experienced anything like this before.

At the time I could not express the intensity of what had happened. I had been touched and healed by an all-embracing love. It was as if Christ had entered my shadow and given me hope. Love is real: this realisation came as revelation to the part of me that had turned its back on love. But the experience also left me in crisis because I did not know how to integrate this experience. The encounter had happened while I was visiting my parents in my childhood home, but I knew I could not share the experience with them – they would not understand. I felt alone.

Then good karma arrived. It seemed that everything had been prepared and organised because I was swept into a series of events that helped with the birth of this new consciousness. On impulse, I called a couple I knew, who are astrologers and psychotherapists. They had been my astrological counsellors, and I had attended some of their courses, but I couldn't say I knew them well. When I spoke to them, I tearfully explained that I had met Christ. They were very calm and explained they would pick me up – despite the fact they lived 50km away – and take me to their home. I could not believe it: two people I barely knew would actually do this for me! It was almost too much love to absorb.

I was a sensitive, confused young man, unsure of my identity and used to having to fend for myself. After they had collected me, I broke down in their car. But now "mother and father" were there. They told me quietly and calmly that I'd had a visit from "our friends on the first floor".

At their house I took some Bach's flower remedy, which seemed to help. Then they recommended some "love therapy", which involved a big hug from both of them at the same time. We would call this "holding". The technique was simple: they lay one on either side of me, making a "body love-sandwich" with me in the middle. I wasn't used to this, and found it uncomfortable at first, but it turned out to be very effective. I soon calmed down and could speak coherently about what had happened.

My Christ experience took several years to integrate. Looking back, it was clearly one of the most significant experiences of my life.

Purification and service run deep with this meditation. The heart's desire can lead to states of consciousness where transcendent realities are revealed. We can meet enlightened masters or know the cosmos as a great living being. Glimpses like these awaken the longing to unite with the ultimate being. But the experience soon fades, and we return to the harsh realities of an imperfect life. In the tension between perfection and imperfection the mystic is crucified. The beloved stands across a gulf that we can bridge only in our dreams. Each night the beloved whispers: "Let go of the heavy burdens of the ego so you can be with me each day." Through a catharsis of the heart you can transcend these limitations and be united. This is sweet music to the ears of the dedicated type, who yearns to sacrifice his life to a noble cause. With this burning zeal the ideal of perfection is born.

No-one will take the way of purification without the promise of a future reward. Traditionally, Buddhism and Christianity offered nirvana or heaven to the disciple who would follow the footsteps of Buddha or Jesus. The ideal was to become a bodhisattva or a saint who would help others to reach a higher world. This required hard work, daily cleansing, sanctification of the personality, and the disciplining of the ego through service to humanity. Despite the wish to help their neighbours, the disciple's ultimate motivation was to escape the world, transcend it and live in eternal peace.

Our modern world seems out of step with any notion of spiritual evolution. This is why we need the new spirituality. Sri Aurobindo points out that Spirit-in-Action, or Supermind as he terms it, wants to manifest in this world. Spirit is matter at its highest frequency and matter is Spirit at its lowest frequency. Our task is to help the highest manifest in the lowest. This gives us a new ideal to strive for. Our task is not so much to leave the earth and enter the kingdom of heaven, but to create heaven here on earth. Our awareness may be anchored in the highest consciousness, but it is useless unless it informs our actions. God, Brahman, whatever we want to call the ultimate cause, is on the way here, and we are the ones God's been waiting for.

The idealising river creates the goals of the new age, and these change rapidly. The ideal of purification and service remain, but our purification includes the basic unconscious as a spiritual partner. Service means that we will use our creative talents to live a meaningful life for the benefit of all. That brings us to our next form of meditation informed by this river of life: *Creative Meditation on Ideal Models*.

Creative Meditation on Ideal Models

An ideal model is a realistic picture of what we may be if we fully dedicate ourselves to our spiritual practice. It is a vision of our ideal personality. The work of the Soul and Royal Self is to create a personality that is large, spacious and intelligent enough to hold the highest spiritual expression. The ideal model helps us to create a whole new personality, stage-self, or role. Working with ideal models is typical of the idealising river, which enables the ideal to direct the transformation of our identity.

I have mentioned how the self and Soul co-operate through inspiration. The telepathic transmission of archetypes or ideal models is an example of this co-operation. This is similar to a composer who asks the conductor to perform his masterpiece as he had heard it in his mind. For the conductor to do his best he must first grasp the spirit of the music. Then he must inspire his musicians – our subpersonalities – to do their best. The entire orchestra must co-operate if the masterpiece is to be performed as the composer intended.

Ideal models and archetypes present the next step in our spiritual development. They embody the qualities and talents needed for the Soul to grow in our lives and in the world. This is key. The Soul wants power! We've seen this with the dynamic river, but here with the idealising river the approach is

*"We come home to our Source
via the devotional heart"*

more practical. The Soul wants power so it can bring love and wisdom into the world within what we can call our kingdom. This kingdom is where we are most creative. Subpersonalities often resist this, perhaps out of laziness, or fear of failure or loss of prestige, or a sense of inadequacy or inferiority. For whatever reason, the subpersonalities will refuse to co-operate. The resistance stems from a feeling of self-sufficiency, a selfishness that doesn't want to leave its comfort zone. It is as if the subpersonalities are thinking: "We can do good, we can make a difference. We have the power to make the world a better place. But we don't want to use this power." Why? "Because it is too difficult and we are too lazy."

The world is full of injustice and pain and there are powerful people more interested in increasing their power than in the values of the Soul. We will meet these people when we step into our own power. If we say yes to becoming kings or queens, we must expect struggle, battles and injuries for the sake of the Soul. The Bhagavad Gita shows us this. As Arjuna is about to enter a battle against his old friends, he hesitates. But Krishna – the Soul – says he must proceed because he is fighting for values that are beyond his rational mind, namely the laws of heaven, which should govern earth.

In our troubled world, it is not enough to meditate and send out positive thoughts of peace and justice, hoping this will help. Gandhi, Mandela, Martin Luther King and others could have done this; instead they chose to act. It seems that those in seats of power today either cannot or will not stop the exploitation of the planet's resources and the oppression of its people. This continues without a thought for the consequences. If we want a world that is good, true and beautiful, it seems we have to fight for it.

The essence of the idealising river is a vision of love and hope for a better world. Bringing together the sensitive (love) river and the dynamic (will) river, the idealising river manifests in activism and extroversion. The idealising river flows in the hearts of all who want to make a difference in the world. The question is: "How do we manifest the power to do this?" First, we must discover our sphere of influence. Where can we develop our creative talents most? That is, we must find our vocation if we do not already have one. The meditations already described can help: Dynamic Meditation, for example, can help us to focus on our identity, and with the help of the intelligent river and both Reflective and Receptive Meditation we can open ourselves to the Soul's inspiration and the ideal model that embodies our next step.

When we have a good picture of our ideal model we can begin Creative Meditation. The ideal model may change when we begin to meditate on it. But soon we can start a meditation where we visualise ourselves as the ideal model (see Appendix). We draw inspiration from the manifesting river in expressing our ideal model in practice. Here is another example of integral meditation, in which different forms of meditations can be used together to help us reach our goal.

When we have found an ideal model that embodies what we need, we work with it. We keep it in our consciousness and identify with it. We do this until we feel that we are merging with it and are absorbing the qualities it embodies. In practice it is often good to work with the three stages I discuss in Chapter 7, namely using first, second and third person perspectives; we can incorporate this approach in a single meditation or vary it from meditation to meditation. Here we should remember the three basic areas: I, We and the World. Here's an example from my own practice.

For several years I worked with an ideal model of myself as a yogi. I've come to believe this was connected to a previous incarnation because visualising myself in this way seemed somehow natural. The image came to me in meditation, and I immediately recognised the yogi's name as my own. I saw him sitting under a tree in a sacred place in a perfect lotus position. This image strongly appealed to me, as I am a dedicated type. At first I saw him from outside, in the third person perspective, observing his charisma and charm. I reflected on his name, and wondered about his life story and what had motivated him. Many things came to me and I began to shape this inner image, making it as alive as it could be in my consciousness. Soon I began to feel a devotion to Brahman. I only had to think of his name and I felt a blissful love and wanted to surrender to the transcendent being that is the cause of the universe. I had never before experienced this, and I saw that it was connected to the image of the yogi. In other meditations, I saw again him from the outside, how he interacted with people around him. Many insights came from this.

At times I identified with the yogi through the first person perspective, and visualised him in the middle of my head or in the centre of my heart. Sometimes I imagined myself as the yogi sitting by the Ganges, looking out over the ancient river. I listened to Indian ragas and burned incense to create a conducive atmosphere. I absorbed the qualities of the yogi and identified with the role he played. That I taught meditation and spiritual psychology in this life led me to believe that this was something I had always done.

At times I saw myself radiating wisdom and love to all the people in my life, and then beyond through the We and World perspectives. The ideal model became integrated into every part of my life. My yogi is now a living part of me, and I can draw on him whenever I need to. There is so much we can do when we have found an ideal model with which we can work creatively.

It is important not to rush our work with an ideal model. One should meditate on it for at least a month, preferably more, before going further. We need to observe the effects of our meditation, and to study them over time, which means we shouldn't switch from one meditation style to another too often. I have worked with one meditation for a whole year. In this respect it is a good idea to follow the cycle of the moon, starting at a new moon and ending with the next new moon. There is more about this in the next chapter.

Ideal Models of Power

Integral meditation involves all levels of energy, from the lowest centre to the highest. In the following section I will discuss how we can increase our power by developing an appropriate ideal model on seven different levels. We may need to increase our overall strength, or perhaps to strengthen a specific area. Using ideal models can help with this. In general, the Soul must be grounded at all energy levels before any kind of spiritual breakthrough can take place there. Spirit-in-Action works through our chakras and so we must keep them sufficiently strong and purified.

"The beloved stands across a gulf that we can bridge in our dreams."

The Root Centre and Power

This centre is linked to our vitality and strength, and ultimately to our survival. If our body is frail and feeble an atmosphere of weakness can form around us, and we will compensate for this elsewhere. We have to take the body seriously; we need strength and good health if we are to actualise our values in the world. Happily, we all have access to as much strength as we might need because we all carry within us archetypes from earlier times when physical strength was necessary for survival.

A strong, vital body radiates power, authority and mastery in our inner and outer worlds. It gives us the stamina needed for real work. Our own strength and health will be reflected in our surroundings. This does not mean having a muscular body, but a strong etheric body. We exude vitality when we are strong and healthy. The higher vision of the root centre is for us to have a vital body in service of the Soul.

Our body may be in such poor health that we cannot manifest the Soul's ultimate vision for us. In this case, we must instead create an ideal model of good health and work with this. We generate an image of how a healthy body should look, then we meditate on this and slowly include the physical exercises needed to transform our body into that of our image.

The ideal model here is the physically vital human being. The head centre, or "cave", is the best place for working with the ideal model in meditation. The body is related to the root centre, but we meditate in the cave because our work is to create a new consciousness using material from the three basic elements: body, feelings and thoughts. The cave is the alchemical workshop where we refine and raise the frequency of our physical and psychological energies.

The Sacral Centre and Power

Here we find the power linked to sex and our ability to create intimate relationships. Sexual potency can help us radiate a powerful presence, because when the sacral centre is healthy we feel happy and sexy. This erotic glow is attractive because it suggests vitality and the strength to cope with life. It is linked to the social world because the sacral centre is involved in our communal life. We do not have to be explicitly sexual; the energy is magnetic enough. Happy, confident people who have a healthy sensual life are always attractive. Also linked to this centre is our inner child; here we learn to play with the world.

If this centre is unbalanced we isolate ourselves, fearing and lacking the strength and confidence for intimacy. Others may suspect we are hiding something. Our inner child does not want to play. We cannot truly express ourselves; without a healthy sacral centre we do not feel safe and relaxed. As we relate to others in a separated way, our power in this centre fades. The higher vision of this centre is for us to trust out interaction with others; its ideal model is the playful human being.

The Solar Plexus Centre and Power

Here power is linked to self-confidence. Standing up for ourselves gives us confidence in our powers. When this centre is healthy we are proud of our accomplishments. We see them as true expressions of our self. We have the courage to trust the world. We are outgoing, spontaneous and enterprising. Our optimism and confidence make us attractive. A healthy and powerful solar plexus makes us resilient, able to withstand the challenges life presents. Life is hard, but we don't take it personally. We see every challenge as an opportunity to become stronger and better. This gives us power and people will have faith in us.

With a weak solar plexus we flinch from life. We become a victim and want others to second guess our needs. We feel powerless when those who are more powerful violate our boundaries. But we allow them to do so by not being responsible for our lives. We suppress our anger and do not assert ourselves. Unexpressed anger soon becomes hatred and we can quickly find ourselves isolated. We fear humiliation and defeat. We lack the energy to fight and avoid challenges. The higher meaning here is the courage to fight for our vision. But we must be careful. There is a risk we might over-compensate for our powerlessness and go in the opposite direction, provoking battles to prove our worth.

The ideal model here is the hero.

The Heart Centre and Power

Here, power is linked to our self-esteem and the dignity that comes from the good will. We feel our power and know that our being is essentially good, true and beautiful. We do not have to prove or demonstrate this. It is a fact. We are a unique being with an intrinsic value that cannot be replaced. Realising this we can access the power of unity and connection that stems from a heart appreciative of the unique value of others. Here our inner king and queen radiate generosity, magnanimity and nobility. We know that we come from the highest power and are representatives of the One Self. Knowing this, we act accordingly.

If the heart centre is weak, no one will be interested in our visions or want to join us in our cause. We lack what is necessary to inspire them. We are open to manipulation because we do not trust our source. We copy others and follow them, abandoning our own God-given kingdom. We ignore our worth and forgo our birthright. We lack the courage to stand up for ourselves and resist the tide when necessary. We fail to uphold the values we are here to actualise. The higher vision here is the power of love and dignity. The ideal models are the inner king or queen.

The Throat Centre and Power

Here power is linked to our knowledge and our ability to communicate this knowledge. Through this centre we learn how to express who we are and what we know clearly and precisely. Communicating our ideas effectively em-powers us. With clear communication we can tell the world who we are, what we believe in, and what we will stand up for. This will help us to relate to others intelligently, which means we can influence the world. We can't know everything, and what we do know is informed by the knowledge of others, so it is clearly essential that we learn how to communicate and dialogue effec-tively with others.

When the throat centre is weak we cannot make our case. We are invisible to others, even to ourselves. We don't know what we believe, so we adopt the opinions of the majority. Our lives are confused and chaotic; our mind lacks order, nothing is clear. Modern education address this by teaching students critical thinking and an ability to express our ideas. We need a healthy throat centre if we are to make our voice heard in the world. When the throat centre is inspired by the Soul, we can communicate values that reach out to the collective. When we speak for the common good we attract great power. The higher vision of this centre is to be a channel for the Soul's love and wisdom.

The ideal model is the illuminated communicator.

The Brow Centre and Power

Here power meets wisdom and our ability to harmonise the personality with the Soul's vision. Through this centre we are given a deep insight into the world and a sense of the forces directing evolution. We see everything from a spiritual perspective; everyday reality is informed by Spirit. We grasp complex relationships and understand the inevitable compromises that must take place between ideals and reality. We identify how we might manifest the will of the Soul. This wisdom brings the power to inform the greatest need with the highest good.

When we are weak in the brow centre it means our life is out of balance; it is not whole. We may be too idealistic or too materialistic; either way we are blind to what is essential to our reality. This centre opens relatively late in our development; for many of us this is yet to happen. Nevertheless we need to understand the importance of this centre for the Soul. The higher vision of this centre is the Soul-wise conductor in the world.

The ideal model is the wise woman or man.

The Head Centre and Power

In the head centre power is linked to a perfect and free identity. Here we are beyond personal interest and desires and have entered an eternal transcendent NOW. As we contain all meaning there is nothing we want. Being free of needs gives us the power to commit fully to the needs of the highest good. We are in the world but not of it. In the head centre there unfolds a twelve-petal lotus, releasing a boundless love that includes the whole planet. We are a direct representative of Spirit-in-Action, an incarnation of the divine in flesh. This is the self-sacrificing self, the no-thing containing everything.

Any desire for existence will limit this power. The slightest attachment to life will be threatened by loss. Yet if the energy of the root centre is brought to the head centre our consciousness will expand beyond any ideas of self. We live but without attachment: we are able walk with Jesus to Jerusalem, even if it will mean our own death. This is the ultimate freedom: wanting nothing for oneself, but to be the One Self. Any remnant of self will prevent us from crossing into this austere level; the smallest flicker of ego will keep us at the door.

The ideal model here is the perfect liberated human being.

Table 6 highlights some of the themes we have been discussing.

Power and the Chakras				
Centre	**Consciousness**	**Theme**	**Unbalanced**	**Potential**
Root	Self-preservation Body awareness	Survival, sensation, connection to earth	Physical weakness, inferiority	Power through physical strength and vitality, physical endurance Ideal Model: The vital human
Sacral	Sexuality, herd instinct	Intimacy, security, sensuality, comfort	Fear of others, isolation	Power through joy and resourcefulness, trusting interaction. Ideal Model: The playful human
Solar plexus	Assertiveness Self-reliance	Self-confidence, ambition, personal power	Power struggles, victimisation or conflict behaviour, loss of initiative, fear of humiliation	Power through self-confidence and pride, charisma and break-through power, courage. Ideal Model: The hero
Heart	Group instinct Holistic consciousness, group consciousness	Self-worth, dignity, appreciation of others, connectedness	Inferiority, loss of self, poor boundaries, oversensitive	Power through dignity, self-esteem, power of connection, integrity, moral courage Ideal Model: King or queen
Throat	Curiosity instinct, self-reflection	Communication, clarity, truth	Unclear, vague communication, not daring to speak freely, copying others' opinions	Power through intelligent and clear communication, higher perspective Ideal Model: The enlightened communicator
Brow	Wisdom, spiritual purpose	Wisdom, integration, vision	Focus is muddy, lacks comprehensive understanding and clear vision.	Power through profound spiritual wisdom and insight, ability to reconcile ideals with practice Ideal Model: The wise man or woman
Head	Transpersonal will Unity Consciousness	Transcendence, unity, supreme will	Reduced ability to surrender the personal will to the transpersonal will	Power through an extraordinary transcendent will, love and wisdom Ideal Model: The perfect liberated man

Table 6: Power and the chakras

Conclusion

In exploring the idealising river of life I have focused on the heart's desire and its longing for purification, perfection and transcendence. Most people can recognise this in the lives of the mystics and saints, yet we must all enter this river, mystic or not. What we aspire to deserves our passion and devotion. We need to free ourselves of old identifications and attachments so we might grow.

Everyone can benefit from Creative Meditation. Dedicated types will be especially attracted to it, but anyone who needs more passion can also make good use of this meditation. Those who are drawn to Awareness Meditation, whose meditations often lack a goal, can also benefit from Creative Meditation because it will introduce the element of purpose and goal. Mental and analytical types, whose meditation can easily become dry and dispassionate, can also benefit from Creative Meditation by introducing vitality.

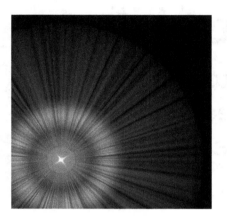

In the next chapter we move into the organising world of the manifesting river of life.

Chapter 11

The Manifesting River of Life:

Your Way to Creative Power, Effectiveness and Manifestation

The seventh river of life brings to the creative culmination of the other six rivers. It expresses our conscious or unconscious yearning for heaven on earth and is what drove the great kings and builders throughout history. Cathedrals, palaces, the pyramids and other great monuments are embodiments of humankind's powerful creative urge. Inspired masons gave form to Spirit in the soaring arches of the Gothic cathedrals; places like Chartres and Notre Dame de Paris still move us profoundly even now. The soaring arches of the cathedrals are a direct reflection of the vast inner sacred space revealed to the mystics. The greatness churchgoers experience in the cathedrals resembles the mystics' experience in their encounters with God. Bridges that cross our rivers and skyscrapers that tower above us are informed by the same energy.

From this perspective only what is manifested is real, yet this does not mean it is materialistic. This river represents the universal will to manifest its purpose through law and order. If love, beauty and truth are expressions of the universal will, we must allow them to inform the values and principles that guide our lives. The United Nations is an example of this. It expresses the ideal of a diverse humanity working together to address common challenges. Clearly, we are far from reaching this ideal, but we have taken steps in the right direction.

The purpose of the seventh river is difficult to realise. If we want to manifest Spirit-in-Action, we must integrate all the energies inherent in our nature and embody them. Our mental, emotional and physical energies must surrender to the central directing will of the Soul. Achieving this gives us Soul Power and love-wisdom. The seventh river aims to synthesise all aspects of the personality; it is, in a way, Psychosynthesis itself.

It is only the Royal Self which gives us the power and dignity to pursue such an ambitious goal. To embody our royal selves we must act impeccably and feel our connection to something greater than ourselves. As representatives of the One Life, we know that talk is cheap and that actions speak louder than words.

The manifesting river is composed by the dynamic, sensitive and intelligent rivers, so it carries the ability to manifest whatever is set in motion by the three primary rivers of life. The seven rivers can also be perceived through a sevenfold creative sequence, where each river plays an intrinsic role in the unfoldment of divine purpose. This process of manifestation follows certain natural steps, of which the following is an example.

Following the earthquake in 2010 which devastated much of Haiti, we can imagine that a wealthy benefactor decided to build a hospital for the poor in the country. He had the money and made the initial decisions. He represented the initiating dynamic river – the will that chooses to set something in motion. He contacted a developer with the understanding and skills needed to achieve this purpose. The developer's vision embodied the values that gave this project a special quality. The vision was attractive; it met an important need and there was love behind it. The developer represented the sensitive river.

When the vision was fully developed the developer contacted an architect. The architect represented the intelligent river. He drew a detailed outline of the hospital and arrived at a strategy for completing the project. The architect's task was to make concrete – literally – the ideas shaping the purpose and vision of the philanthropist and the developer.

So far this has mostly been an internal process, creating plans and sketches. This is the work of the first three rivers, preparing the ideal which the other rivers will put into practice. The architect now worked closely with the designer, selecting the right location for the hospital and the right materials for its construction. The task of the creative river is to ensure the harmony and beauty of the building, and to negotiate the practical decisions that must be made. This was part of the designer's role.

Next the builders and specialised craftsmen got to work. They had the knowledge and equipment needed for the job. This is the task of the fifth river. A marketing and communication strategy would ensure that everyone involved knew what they were working with and why. These ideals motivated the entire team during the hospital's construction. The Public Relations consultant fulfilled the function of the sixth river.

Next it was time for the project manager, who makes sure everything gets done in the right way and on time, to step in. She made sure that everyone worked together in a carefully orchestrated way. This required a systematic, well-organised approach involving targets, timing, and flexibility. This is the task of the manifesting river. Here we can see a natural sequential order, from the philanthropist's initial purpose to its fulfilment. The seventh river helps us to understand this process; with it we encounter a powerful creative force, one that helps us to be focused and practical.

Not all creative processes proceed in this order. We may have a vision or a plan before we start the meditation and, depending on what we want to manifest, certain stages may be more important than others. Nevertheless, we should know the stages because they can help and inspire us when we want to manifest something in our lives.

Integral meditation seeks to manifest Soul and Spirit; it is not content with only being present as a contented observer of life. We must be creators, in the way that the Universal Self is the ultimate Creator. It is not enough to acknowledge unity with the All; we must in some way demonstrate this. This puts demands on us greater than those required by past spiritual traditions. The ideal is to combine passive and active meditation, inner and outer work. I, We and the World constitute a whole that is involved in everything we do. This work arises from the manifesting river, motivating us to pursue greatness and make our mark on the world.

We have an opportunity to create a life that truly expresses who we are and what we are here to do. We will not achieve this through meditation alone. A systematic approach to spiritual development requires other practices too. Directing our resources toward actualising our highest possibilities brings happiness to ourselves and others. Integral meditation's practical, holistic approach to spirituality makes this synergy possible. Ken Wilber, who has written much around this idea, calls this the integral life practice. Meditation must not be isolated from our lives, but interconnected with it.

Integral Meditation and Life Practice

Let me give an example of how the manifesting river unfolds through the practice of meditation. According to esoteric sources our present time is increasingly dominated by the manifesting river, which is also known as the seventh ray. If this is so, then this type of meditation is relevant to us all. For the past 2,000 years, the sixth ray had dominated an era characterised by religious idealism. Over the last few centuries we have gradually moved into a time where we must put these ideals into practice through a creative union of science and spirituality. This is also what has been called the Age of Aquarius, but exploring this in more detail is beyond the scope of this book.

For years I have tried to follow an integral life practice, inspired by the work of Ken Wilber, Alice Bailey, Aurobindo and Lucille Cedercrans. In my own life I can identify five essential, interconnected areas of spiritual practice, and I have centred my meditations around them. In this section I will discuss these five areas in connection with the qualities of the manifesting river, which helps unite the disparate elements of our lives into an overall purpose. Let's look at these five essential life practices and see how the seven ray qualities are involved in the process of creation. The five life practices are:

Body work: The art of keeping healthy.

Shadow work: The transformation and transmutation of our emotions.

Mind work: Widening our perspectives and increasing our understanding.

Service work: Benefitting ourselves, others and the world.

Spirit work: Bringing the Soul and the personality together in meditation through the creation of the bridge of consciousness.

"We must be creators, like the One Self is a Creator"

You will notice that each of the five life practices focuses on one of the five elements of the personality and soul (ie body, emotions, mind, personality and Soul). Their interaction will bring in different types of energies and affect our meditation. Each life practice is also a type of meditation because each involves having an *awareness* of our whole life, including an examination of our dreams. Ideally, we should aim to reach the highest possible point of awareness in our morning meditation and then work to maintain this awareness throughout the day.

The manifesting river is linked to the dynamic river, specifically through the use of the will and practical creative force to develop our integral life.

The main purpose of my life is to promote energy psychology, either through my own living example, my teaching or other creative pursuits. Energy psychology enters into all areas of my life and this must be reflected in the way I live. In this way the purpose of my life is to manifest my Soul and Spirit as fully as I can.

Body Work

My body must be healthy so I have enough energy and vitality to carry out my purpose. The body's overall health is crucial if we want our meditation to bear fruit. The body is the temple of the Soul; we must take this metaphor literally and ensure our body is in shape. This means eating well and exercising regularly: such is the secret of body work.

The etheric body is linked to the nervous system. We can imagine the nervous system as the conductor of consciousness, bringing the Soul's messages to the brain. If our body vibrates at a low frequency, we cannot hear these messages. A healthy diet, good hygiene, fresh air and exercise all help to raise the body's vibrations. My daily health routines create new energy and increase my endurance. If I skip them I immediately notice a lack of energy and focus during meditation. Low vitality clearly affects meditation, making it harder to remain quiet and aware. During the initial process of meditation, we will quickly notice the condition of our body and what it needs. It is a daily reminder to maintain our energy levels at the physical level. I strive to live as healthily as possible, eating nutritious organic foods. A special diet or a fast may be needed on occasion to detox. Massage and body therapy can be helpful too.

Shadow Work

Emotional blockages and inhibitions prevent us from living the life of the Soul. Meditation can make us aware of our emotional reactions and help us to consciously choose our thoughts and feelings. Integral meditation will definitely raise our level of consciousness and how we respond to life. Ideally we should be able to respond wisely to all influences, but most of us have a way to go with this. Shadow work can help refine and cultivate our emotional life. Our emotions affect our thoughts, often unconsciously. We need to purify our emotional life, and meditation alone cannot do the job. Repressions and defense mechanisms can obscure the true cause of our emotional difficulties and may require the help of a psychotherapist to release them. The Soul ultimately wants to open us up to universal love and wisdom. Integral meditation requires more than peak experiences. We must manifest the energies we have contacted and the consent of our emotions is needed for this. As mentioned, I utilise my method of Soul Therapy for this, but many other approaches are equally valid.

An emotional life aligned with our life purpose will make us enthusiastic and Soul-driven. Shadow work helps us to stabilise our emotions, a necessary step in Self-realisation. An emotional life opposed to our life purpose creates resistance and depression. The inner resistance reduces our ability to attract the right people and, in general, what we need in life. Emotions are the *power factor of life*. Our emotional life needs to be healthy if we are to manifest our life purpose, otherwise our life can become one long uphill struggle.

A deep understanding of who we are and where we want to make our mark in the world is necessary. Our outlook determines how we interpret our experience and define our reality. What I have arrived at in this book is based on experiences that have been of great help and inspiration in my life. Our outlook on the world helps us to understand what we encounter in meditation and in our lives; it gives meaning and direction to our experiences. Our values enable us to confront challenges cheerfully because we know how to give meaning even to them.

Mind Work

To understand our lives and have clarify of purpose, Mind Work is necessary. We constantly observe and analyse our lives, and it is necessary to study the thought of others also. We live in a collective world with a shared reality in which we develop a common language and fruitful co-operative relationships. The many spiritual dialogues I have had with friends and colleagues have greatly aided my personal growth. From the perspective of integral meditation the mind is a bright light of discriminative understanding. With it we consciously choose our thoughts and feelings, which have an effect on the overall health of our body.

Service Work

Service Work is our focused engagement with life. We take what we have received in meditation and use it to help our community. A focused vision of life helps to integrate the personality by giving its disparate parts a unified aim. Making a difference in the world opens the heart centre and makes its healing powers available. We are each a part of a network that extends to all humanity. The Soul knows this and its primary motivation is to illuminate this connection. In some spiritual traditions service is seen as the first stage of meditation and precedes more advanced practice. In this way the energy that we develop during meditation is correctly channeled into life. We also avoid overstimulation and the psychic constipation that can block inspiration and lead to psychosomatic illnesses. Realisations not acted upon are a significant cause of illness and hamper growth. If we ignore what we know to be true, we create a dissonance between what we believe to be true and how we act. Establishing a strong focus and vision for our lives informs our meditation, and this leads to notable effects. Our service work shows us where we need to develop new skills and qualities in order to realise our vision and meditation helps us to do this. Our studies, shadow and body work do this also. Our life becomes a creative process, full of joy. To find a purpose to which we can dedicate our lives is perhaps the noblest form of self-expression.

Spirit Work

Spirit Work means meditation, which is the focus of this book. Indeed, integral meditation is precisely concerned with getting our five life practices to work together, like cogs in a well-oiled machine. Through this we get a sense of coherence and creative power because all our resources are aimed at the same objective: fulfilling our Soul's purpose.

When we use Integral Meditation during a Personal Crisis

Crisis can test our integral life practice to the limit. Crisis can be a barrier to growth, but it can also be an opportunity for growth. We can recoil from crisis, regressing to some earlier state until it passes, or we can use the crisis to shake things up so we can move forward. For example, a personal crisis in 2012 became a turning point for me. It was a challenge to free myself from old ideas and completely transform my life.

Analysis had revealed that I had certain problems with self-esteem that were preventing me from living my life freely. I needed to feel a greater respect for myself and feel more dignified in my masculinity. I began to meditate on the themes of power and grace. My Soul, I knew, had everything in its secret storehouse that I was looking for in the outside world. Soul Power became an important idea for me. For the first time in my life I deliberately sought greater power, aligning myself more consciously with the dynamic river, which is the river that be drawn upon to actualise the Soul's values. This was the power aspect of my meditation.

Equally important was my relationship with a certain type of beauty that had always fascinated me, namely an aspect of the divine feminine that can be found in dancers and other expressive artists. It is a lightness, a poise, a kind of elegant feminine dignity that lifts everything it touches. Great actresses have it. I call this grace. I desired this beauty which I perceived to be a kind of elixir, a single drop of which could lead to my surrender. I knew such attraction was dangerous if projected onto a woman. I had to assimilate this quality within myself, to integrate it as part of my personal power. If I could do so, I knew this would help to resolve my tendency towards over-work and isolation – both character traits of my type – so I would lighten up, my relationships would improve, and I would be less self-conscious. My isolation weakened me and formed a barrier in my social life and in the pursuit of my life purpose. The Soul realises itself through relationships so it is vital to improve our relationships if we are to develop our talents and make a difference in the world.

Working with power and grace guided me through 2012 and the following years, and this gave birth to many initiatives. One was to strengthen my work with the five integral life practices so I could bring more energy and conscious-ness into my life. I intensified my meditation; over a couple of years I spent three hours every day focused on the theme of power and grace. Character is created from the inside out, so as I brought power and grace into my inner work, they began to show in my outer life also. I used different methods of meditation, but always for the same purpose.

Shortly after beginning this work, I noticed that I mostly only observed sub-personalities who felt weak. I knew something was happening in my basic unconscious, so I began to ask "who suffers" every time I could feel pain inside. I discovered several subpersonalities who were lonely and isolated. I used the same approach with each one; I would observe them, speak with them, and accommodate their needs. When they were clearly realised in my mind, I did Soul therapy with them and had good results. We can call these Healing Meditations.

I also use the Creative Meditation method to explore power and grace. My aim was to satisfy my need for affirmation – which is located in our solar plexus – not externally, but from within. I meditated on the image of the sun god Apollo and observed a channel of light connecting my Soul to the solar plexus. I imagined this light radiating out from my own centre to the world. Sometimes I felt I was in the presence of the sun and could sense the Soul softening my emotional life. I did nothing besides holding the alignment; I knew the Soul would do its work if I was able to surrender.

My solar plexus was imbalanced, which made relationships difficult and weakened my personal power. It also prevented me from using my talents to the full. There were layers of fear, hypersensitivity and insecurity. Yet behind all of this lay the bright, ecstatic joy of a young Apollo who longed to be free.

When I meditated on grace a wonderful white light would appear. It felt divine and feminine, and it could see into the deepest recesses of my unconscious. Its effect on me was the same as certain women. It revealed what was hidden, and I had to surrender in devotion to it. I recognised landscapes in my sub-conscious and a deep longing for this type of inner beauty. I called this type of meditation "light work". Different qualities of light gradually coloured my emotions, softening their dark hues, and allowing power and grace to flow into me. I could now radiate these qualities more freely, and this was reflected in my life and work.

Meanwhile, I did more physical exercise, which helped to counteract the pain I felt. I knew it was important to keep in shape, and for me yoga was a graceful way. This generated a feeling of health and vitality that increased my confidence. I started wearing beautiful clothes and demonstrated a greater ease and gracefulness. I also decided to beautify my surroundings; I painted my apartment and brought fresh flowers daily. A painting by the esoteric illustrator Francis Donald invoking the full moon in Aries seemed to capture my theme of power and grace, and I put a print of it in my meditation space. My meditation and exercise seem to go hand in hand – knowing that my daily run helped create more power and grace was inspiring.

I now turned to shadow work, part of the Soul Therapy I had been pursuing for some time, and looked more closely at the subpersonalities that were preventing me from fully actualising power and grace. At one point I undertook weekly sessions with a guide. One session in particular was particularly powerful and presented me with a model for how to work with the solar plexus. During this session, I entered into a subconscious domain that had an atmosphere heavy with a kind of patriarchal energy. An old man (subpersonality) stepped forward into my mind's eye. He was isolated, living in a basement, and said he could not exist without beauty. He was petrified and held onto beauty as his only link with life. We told him he was a previous incarnation. We understood that he was stuck in a time warp, but knew there was a light within him that could free him. He saw he was in a prison but, with our encouragement, he became hopeful.

We performed the healing triangle and something astonishing happened. It was as if the sun had entered me as a powerful light swept through my body. I had never felt so vital and masculine. I laughed as the old man became a golden god. My solar plexus exploded into a sun of light and vitality. The golden man now told me he was Apollo, and I watched as his perfect body rose from the solar plexus and into my heart, then into my head and Soul. The body then returned to the solar plexus, and I understood what this meant. A channel had been made between my Soul's royal aspect and my solar plexus.

After this, Apollo became a focus in my meditations, and I strove to feel his presence. In the end I realised I had witnessed the birth of a Soul archetype that could serve as an ideal model for the development of my solar plexus centre.

In relation to women, my shadow work has given me greater authority, masculine power and ease. I feel more "manly" than ever before. This seems to affect my surroundings positive. Subsequent reading about Apollo had led me to marvel at the Soul's genius: Apollo led the nine Muses, the goddesses of inspiration, and is also connected to three Graces, the goddesses of beauty and creativity. When Apollo plays his lyre the Graces dance. We can see here a link between power and grace. Myths tell stories, but they also tell us something about the psyche. Understanding them can be a means to great power.

Something else manifested during this time: this book. I knew it had to be different to my previous books. It needed to be a personal, candid account of meditation as I understood it. I had to expose myself, to say how I saw the world without worrying about the consequences. I wanted it to be something I could be proud of, the very best I could do. It needed to be a practical manual for meditation and integral life practice that could inspire all those who choose to die daily. In this way, it would be a work of service.

Writing developed my mental skills. I discovered I knew things I didn't realise I knew. My thoughts became clearer as I explored the knowledge I had, which in turn led to new insights. I didn't refer to books; I felt that if I did not know something already, it wasn't important. This unlocked my writing – I felt I had whatever answers I needed. I vowed that my writing would only draw upon my own experiences; all I needed to do was depth and simplicity in how I presented this material.

In the process I have described above, all the rivers of life met in one creative work. A single purpose drove the process. Power was here, which is the influence of the dynamic river. My desire to expand my capacity for love and to end my isolation represented the sensitive river. My perspectives were broadened due to the influence of the intelligent river. Grace represented the presence of the creative river. Analysing and assessing my reactions brought in the scientific river. My work was based on ideal models inspired by power and grace, which drew upon the idealising river. Finally, I have been in charge of the whole process; I have directed and focused the creative expression, which is the work of the manifesting river.

With this in mind we can say that *integral meditation is a creative synthesis of different types of meditations that draw upon the seven rivers, seven levels of consciousness, seven meditation roads and seven spiritual types to work through the three areas of life using five life practices, the ultimate aim of which is to manifest Soul consciousness. We can formulate this as an equation: 7 x 4 x 3 x5.*

Group Meditation During a Full Moon

Lastly in this chapter, I want to describe the full moon group meditation. Working with a group is one of the most powerful forms of meditation we can experience. United by a common purpose, a group mind can generate a force far greater than any individual. In integral meditation, the focus is always on I, We and the World. By bringing these foci together the group can transmit energy to the world, something we can also do on our own if we try to telepathically link to other people in the world who are also meditating.

Group meditation is an expression of the manifesting river. It brings people together, aligning them with a common purpose. An example of this is globalisation, which is a response to the seventh ray/river. Group meditation is, of course, a part of many spiritual traditions. The groups I am speaking about, however, are not hierarchical, unlike with the church. In full moon meditation, participants meet as equals. The participants themselves create a bridge to spiritual energy and do not rely on the intermediary of a guru or priest. This allows for differences in individual development, and places much greater responsibility on each participant. We cannot leave the responsibility for our development to a spiritual teacher, from whom we can, of course, learn much, but we must also take on this challenge individually and communally. This makes full moon meditation more in keeping with the tone of our era, which is more individualistic than in the past. As we think for ourselves, religious dogmas lose their importance, allowing each of us to achieve an understanding that suits our unique spiritual path.

The aims of group meditation are twofold. One aim is to create a channel through which spiritual forces can become manifest in the world, anchoring the good, the true and the beautiful. This can be achieved through group spirituality wherein an equal partnership helps us to align our energies. The group forms a kind of psychic grail that can collect the spiritual energies we want to manifest. The process of channeling follows stages we have discussed: centring, ascending, receiving and anchoring.

The second aim is to forge a vertical link between the spiritual forces that inspire humanity and the telepathic sensitives in the world. Some see these spiritual forces as the collective consciousness, the group self or the Universal Authentic Self. Others speak of Buddha, Mahatmas or enlightened masters. In these matters we must discover our own language. In my experience, it is equally valid whether we understand these spiritual forces as impersonal energies or personal beings.

Before the full moon meditation begins, participants must ensure that their motivation and purpose is not self-centred. We meditate on behalf of all humanity and nothing less than that. The Soul works in terms of the world-centric perspective and so must we. If carried forward successfully, the meditation will gradually awaken us to the World Soul, the one consciousness and our sense of ourselves as separate egos dwindles.

At the beginning of the full moon meditation, the group leader unites the group around a common purpose. The role of the leader is vital. If leader fails in offering direction the group can fracture or the group leader himself or herself can become the centre of attention. The leader then takes the group through a series of stages integrating their physical, emotional, mental and spiritual energies, creating a unified meditative consciousness. A group energy field can then become available enabling spiritual inspirations to come through. This meditation follows the same stages as the individual work (see Appendix).

The leader can encourage the group to meditate on anything that will generate inspiration. It is often helpful to begin with a simple exercise in being present, which can create the calm necessary to receive inspiration. This is a challenge because without a specific focus for our meditation we can sink into personal thoughts and daydreams. But if we stay present and open to the group self, a quiet clarity can arise. Moving forward, a common focus for the meditation is the seven rivers or rays.

At the time of a full moon our openness to inspiration is considered to be at its fullest. Indeed, the manifesting river

teaches us to be in step with the natural cycles involved in creative work such as this. Timing is important in any creative process, and paying attention to the cycles of the moon is what is of significance here.

As the new moon begins a new cycle, it is a time for seeding new initiatives and harvesting those which are ripe. The energies at this time seem to me more earthy and material, something I feel in my meditation. If we want to start a new cycle of meditation with a new theme, now is the time. The new moon is also the time where we harvest the fruits from the former cycles.

Towards the end of the cycle, as the full moon approaches, the energies lighten allowing us to enter our meditation more deeply. This makes the days surrounding a full moon especially important. It is as if a door to planetary consciousness opens, connecting the spiritual and physical worlds. Two days before the full moon we make ourselves open and receptive; at full moon itself we receive. In the following two days we distribute the energies we have received to others. Then, in the period between a full moon and a new moon, we anchor the insights we received.

Having tuned into these planetary rhythms we can monitor the earth's ebb and flow, and working with these natural rhythms can strengthen our own personal creative force. So it can be very helpful to particpate in a full moon festival. But if we don't have such an opportunity, while meditating alone we can still reach out to others who are also tuning into the earth's rhythms.

Full moon meditations are an important part of my practice which have led to many breakthroughs. I like to arrange spiritual courses and attend retreats during a full moon. Depending on the astrological sign at the time, different energies are available.

Conclusion

Meditation influenced by the seventh river is a very potent meditation. It aligns us with the dynamic creative force which synthesises all available resources around a common purpose. The aim of this river is manifestation through organisation. Strengthening our ability to manifest our visions is important if we are to be effective in life. It also helps us to better understand the stages of the creative process and how to balance these with the different rivers. Life is a process – integral meditation helps to experience it dynamically. Body work, shadow work, mind work, service work and spirit work form the backbone of the spiritual life.

Everyone can benefit from manifesting meditation, but some types may make more use of it than others. It offers grounding to sensitive, creative and dedicated types. The practical type is drawn to this form of meditation because of the opportunities it provides, particularly in the present day which is an age informed by this river. Recognition of the qualities of this river is increasing and more awareness of it can only benefit us. Manifesting meditation is particularly beneficial to those drawn to the asceticism of the idealising river because it will help them to reconnect with the universal life stream.

We have now reached the last chapter of this book, which offers a natural continuation of the present chapter in offering an exploration of the unfolding integral holistic perspective.

Chapter 12

An Integral Vision for a New Humanity

Today a new consciousness paradigm seems to be emerging. More and more of us desire a greater meaning in life than what our consumer society can offer. We seek greater connections and wholeness. We look for happiness within, and books about personal and spiritual development sell like never before. We go to meditation retreats, embrace therapy, life coaching and other methods of self-help and personal development. At the same time we make new demands on our work and relationships, requiring that they are meaningful and relevant within a larger, spiritual context.

The Awakening of the World Soul

From a spiritual perspective we seem to be witnessing a worldwide awakening to the Soul. Around the world people who are well off materially are beginning to feel that something is missing. They feel a lack of inner wealth, an existential emptiness, and a longing for meaning and purpose in life – and this has brought them to a crisis. From an integral and energetic point of view, the human Soul is awakening to its freedom. In our hearts we are manifesting a living force for good.

Millions of people today are awakening to the Soul. This can happen through peak experiences, new humanistic values, or sudden feelings of universal love. We may experience the inter-connectedness of everything, feel a strong call

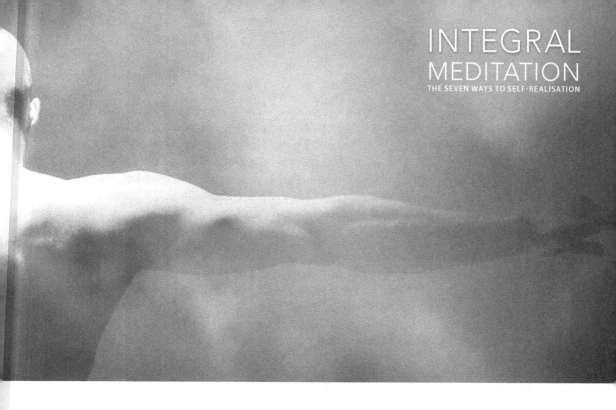

to serve humanity, or desire a life of greater meaning, one in harmony with our planet. However we look at it, it seems that the World Soul is awakening.

Souls conscious of their calling seek their true purpose within the whole and through this the development of their talents. This global awakening takes place on two different levels of consciousness: through the abstract mental holistic mind and through the intuitive group consciousness.

Many people today are encouraged to think holistically because of globalisation. Our economic and ecological crises involve the entire world and force us to find solutions from a global perspective. However, many ignore the bigger picture and continue to think only in terms of short-term solutions motivated by self-protection. This happens with individuals as well as nations, but, nevertheless, many people are working together to find answers that will benefit all of humanity.

I believe we are witnessing the birth of a new integral consciousness that is being expressed through psychology, spirituality, sociology, and even a new politics. Holistic thinking unifies the discoveries of the rational and practical mind. The slogan "Think globally, act locally" expresses this consciousness. Thinking that works through the holistic mind enables us to identify with the greater world. We see that our personal well being is deeply connected to that of humanity.

It is as if we are living through a revolution. Identifying with humanity's well being changes the centre of gravity of our consciousness, moving us away from self-interest towards a desire to embrace the entire world. Personal needs are secondary from a holistic perspective. When we understand the world from an integral perspective we recognise our place in a global reality – we see our own inner values reflect a universal consciousness; we see that our problems are not unique to ourselves but only individual stories reflecting collective themes.

This shift to a holistic consciousness is partly due to the problems caused by me-centred mindsets and partly due to the Soul's call to awaken. Part of this awakening is the realisation that in essence *we* are the World Soul – we are not a part of it, but its living expression. Grasping this powerful insight can change a person forever. It may come to some spontaneously, or as the re-sult of spiritual practice. But the thing to recognise is that it is happening all around us.

We tend to think of the Soul as an expression of ourselves; we talk about your Soul and my Soul as if the Soul is simply a finer version of our personality. But the Soul is something different. We can say it is an expression of the group consciousness, that is, humanity.

Group consciousness is not a simple awareness of the fact of inter-connected-ness grasped by the rational mind. Rather, group consciousness is an *identity* we awaken to. Paradoxically, we recognise ourselves as one consciousness unfolding in time and space but also as an individual part of a collective ex-pression of this consciousness, something we touched on in Chapter 2.

A New Map for New Challenges

We can no longer regard our individual development as separate from the larger reality to which we belong. We can see our relation to the collective and to ourselves as forming a kind of cross. The horizontal bar symbolises our social reality; the vertical bar represents our connection to the spiritual world. To orientate ourselves accurately, we need a map that covers both the horizontal and vertical aspects of life.

Søren Hauge and I have devised a map integrating our vertical and horizontal dimensions. We call it the Holo Map. But before I talk about this, let me first briefly describe the seven collective levels of consciousness that are an inte-gral part of its perspective.

In many spiritual traditions we can find the idea that consciousness, or being,

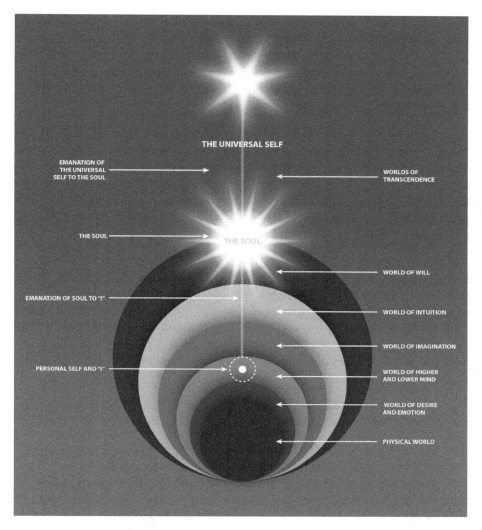

THE UNIVERSAL SELF

EMANATION OF THE UNIVERSAL SELF TO THE SOUL

WORLDS OF TRANSCENDENCE

THE SOUL

THE SOUL

WORLD OF WILL

EMANATION OF SOUL TO "I"

WORLD OF INTUITION

WORLD OF IMAGINATION

PERSONAL SELF AND "I"

WORLD OF HIGHER AND LOWER MIND

WORLD OF DESIRE AND EMOTION

PHYSICAL WORLD

Figure 20: Diagram to show how evolution proceeds through seven levels of consciousness.

exists at several levels, from our own awareness of a material world to higher, more spiritual spheres. Traditionally this is known as the Great Chain of Being. We find it in Buddhism, Hinduism, Kabbalah, Neoplatonism and Hermeticism. Some versions speak of three levels, others include many more. These levels of consciousness are real inner worlds that we enter through our feelings, thoughts and intuition. We explore these inner worlds as part of our journey from physical consciousness to unity consciousness. We have spoken of these levels in relation to Assagioli's egg diagram, but here let me say a bit more about them

Figure 20 shows how evolution proceeds through seven levels of consciousness according to Roberto Assagioli, each with its own experiences and opportunities. It is important to emphasise that these levels are collective. There are cultural expressions ranging from physical-emotional consciousness (primitive tribal society) to abstract mental consciousness (the globally-orientated intellectual avant-garde).

We locate the self at the physical level because consciousness is reflected in the brain. A mature adult's consciousness is anchored in the mental zone. Higher levels both transcend and include the lower; in this way we can observe energies of a lower level from the perspective of a higher one. Through the intellect we can reflect on our emotional life and so on. Higher levels of consciousness are reflected in the brain and will actualise on the physical plane when the self has awoken to them.

The Jewel in the Lotus, or pure presence of the Soul's core, is located above the superconscious, at the top of the egg-shape in the diagram. The Soul's radiating consciousness penetrates the intuitive level, along with our unity consciousness. Our Soul's core integrates energies from the abstract levels (holistic awareness), the higher imaginal worlds and the level of the will. The Universal Self and Spirit-in-Action, shown at the top of the chart, are an expression of true universal unity consciousness, which includes both the World Soul and the Cosmos.

Physical World: At the bottom of the chart we see the physical world and it is connected to the root centre's body awareness, as expressed in yogic philosophy.

World of Desire and Emotion: Through our emotions the Self experiences humankind's collective feelings and desires. We bring our own nuances to these collective energies, but the basic emotions remain the same. We can say emotions come in higher or lower frequencies. This, for example, is the difference between jealous possessive love and self-sacrificing devotional love; they are both love, but at different frequencies. (The same distinction regarding frequencies applies to the other worlds.) Through our emotions we can enjoy safety and security provided by our family and culture. The sacral, solar plexus and heart centre are all connected to the emotional world, each at their own frequency. Tribal consciousness is associated with the sacral centre, while the solar plexus fuels assertiveness at the level of self-awareness. The heart centre is related to the higher emotional life and in its higher aspect to pure intuition.

World of Higher and Lower Mind: Through the level of the mind the self gathers knowledge about itself through the family, society and culture. This is where the self forms its first ideas. The rational "I" awakens and we experience ourselves as individuals with our own needs. In the mental world it is important to be recognised for our individuality. This level is connected to the throat centre. Here we develop self-awareness and self-esteem based on our uniqueness.

World of Imagination: This is the picture-making faculty which, according to Assagioli, is a synthetic psychological function that can "operate at several levels concurrently; those of sensation, feeling, thinking and intuition". In the above diagram, Assagioli emphasises the higher aspect of imagination and that is presumably why he places imagination above the mental level.

The personality is made up of a mental, emotional, and physical body. When the self discovers the abstract higher mind the need for self-actualisation arises. The desire to become whole and integrated focuses us on Self-realisation. People who achieve this are prominent in their field; they become pioneers because they concentrate their energies on their goals. The discovery of the lower frequencies of this level motivates the self to synthesise the personality. The brow, throat and heart centres govern the personality's development.

The abstract field's holistic level (higher mind) resembles the first layer of the Superconscious in Assagioli's egg diagram from Chapter 2. Here we entertain universal ideas and first consider reality holistically. We see that everything is connected in different systems and contexts. Ken Wilber calls this field the "integral level" because here all levels are understood as parts of a larger, coherent whole. All philosophical or abstract thought draws from this field, but it becomes integral through integrating the evolutionary stages from body to unity consciousness. Our holistic perception is further enhanced by incorporating a sense of direction that is provided by our vertical, or depth, perspective. The brow centre is strongly linked to the development of a holistic consciousness.

World of Intuition: This level is also part of the superconscious and here a true group consciousness can develop. Group consciousness is not the same as solidarity; it is the experience of a common identity with all humankind. We experience a higher We, filled with an impersonal universal love. We gain insight into the inter-connectedness of creation expressed as true wisdom. Duality persists, and levels of development and functions of the Soul vary from person to person, but now all interactions are characterised by love and understanding. Love here is no longer subjective, given and received, rather we awaken to a love within and surrounding our being that we breathe and share. Our purpose is focused on life's fulfilment and participates in its evolution. Here we recognise the world of the Soul, but we are not yet identified with the highest level of consciousness. To achieve the highest level of consciousness is the Soul's natural harbour. The brow and heart centre are important in the development of shared consciousness.

World of Will: At this level we manifest purpose. We identify with the purpose of life and all its manifestations. We experience the One life of which we are all individual expressions. This One life is "being" on all levels of consciousness, since life expresses itself everywhere in the manifest universe. A sense of purpose, a powerful inner calling, speaks of the source of life and fills us with a purpose to unite with the One. Indeed, as we rise from the physical level up to that of Spirit-in-Action our longing for a deeper fusion with life increases. Beginning with a desire for physical well being, we reach for emotional happiness, then mental joy and intuitive ecstasy, and finally pure spiritual bliss. The centre most associated with the development of will is the head centre.

World of Transcendence: At this level, which is the highest spiritual level, we can attain non-dual consciousness through identification with the Universal Self. All dualisms dissolve. We come to understand that all existence, from the physical to the transcendent, is an expression of one consciousness and one life. We recognise this unchanging consciousness as a transcendent wakefulness. This consciousness is the perfect, motionless witness who is nevertheless responsible for all that exists. We are this witness and Creator.

This spiritual level is the first expression of Spirit-in-Action. It is pure essence.

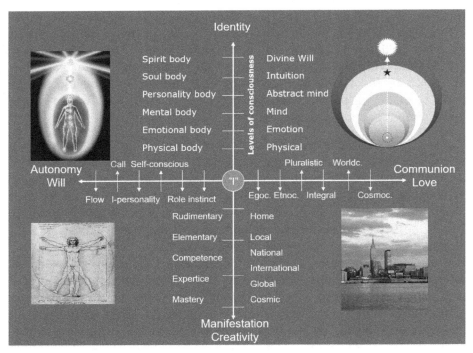

Figure 21: The Holo Map – an integral perspective of life.

We identify with the will of the Father, as Jesus does in the Gospel of John: "The Father and I are one." This is our destiny: to unite with the evolutionary impulse, with Spirit-in-Action. The head centre relates to this achievement.

The Holo Map (Figure 21) brings together the different perspectives we have looked at in this book, and shows some of the main routes for the journey to the Soul and Spirit.

We can see how the central observer (the "I") and active consciousness – the conscious self – develops along four cardinal pathways. The self occupies the centre of the diagram. Within it are the seven rivers of life and seven psychological functions. This means that the eight developmental lines unfold along all four paths.

In the diagram, each of the four developmental paths are divided into seven stages that trace an evolution from body consciousness to non-dual consciousness. The last non-dual, or transcendent, stage is not represented in the diagram (this is the seventh developmental stage). The four paths are called Identity, Creativity, Will and Love. Identity is about the self's development of identity through different stages. Creativity concerns the manifestation of that identity. The will is about autonomy and the self-in-action. Love works with social skills, fellowship and communion. These four ways are summarised in the formula I, We and the World, which owes its inspiration to Ken Wilber's AQAL model.

The left half of the diagram concerns individual expression at the inner and outer levels. The right half relates to the self's social dimension, its interaction with the collective. The top half concerns non-physical realms of consciousness, while the bottom half is anchored in the physical world.

The top left charts the different "bodies" or the sheaths of Vedanta needed to perceive our inner worlds as they pass through the seven stages of development.

In the top right we find the seven levels of collective consciousness through which all Souls evolve. This is the inner worlds – the great chain of being. In the bottom left corner, we have the physical body, with which we manifest our skills and talents, from the rudimentary to the masterful – these talents are in fact our seven psychological functions. As psychological functions they unfold naturally, but in this diagram we focus on their development for a specific purpose.

The bottom right corner shows us the operational range of our talents, our capacity to actualise them in the world.

We can understand the Holo Map as an overview of all that is involved in integral meditation. All seven rivers of life, meditation roads, stages of development, psychological functions and energy types are represented, radiating out from the Self as it passes through the seven stages from body consciousness to non-dual consciousness. This whole process incorporates the four development paths and five integral life practices.

Identity is an important theme in the Holo Map. Achieving our true identity is in many ways a journey towards greater transcendence, as it is rooted in Spirit. This is our "heaven within". Each stage is a step closer to the impersonal and universal consciousness that simply *is*. At the same time we also become more open to the transcendent will, which wants to manifest through our Soul on earth. It is a paradox that we lose our identifications while at the same time becoming more firmly rooted in the force behind evolution. It seems that in order to become someone, we must first become no-one.

The Soul has a dual nature, combining feminine love and masculine will. It is also creative. In the Holo Map we see these forces develop along the pathways of will, love and creativity. A fountain of these forces spring from the still centre of consciousness and life, and in turn these forces manifest as the three development paths that are universal to all people: Will-Love-Creativity.

The Path of Identity

As mentioned earlier, this path concerns the self-line. It consists of pure consciousness and will, as well as the identifications we adopt at different stages. I have called these our stage selves; they are not concerned with how we express ourselves in the outer world but how we understand our self in our inner world. This path is concerned with the level of reality our consciousness is able to embrace and identify with - how we anchor our experience of life. Our experience of identity will vary according to which of the five bodies is dominant at any one time.

The vertical identity axis is identical to the bridge of consciousness that links self/Soul to the universal Self. In Assagioli's egg diagram this is represented by a dotted line connecting Spirit, Soul and personality.

Will, love and creativity are the guiding forces behind three of the development paths. Accordingly, the vertical identity axis can be understood as showing pure consciousness at various stages of development.

The Path of Creativity

This path concerns the Self's manifestation in the body and the external world. It is controlled in particular by the development of the mental line, but the psychological functions of imagination, logic, passion and action are also significant.

Spirit-in-Action wants to manifest, and here we see its concrete expression through the seven psychological functions, which each have their core talents: leadership, empathy, innovation, harmony, knowledge, commitment and action. These talents provide us with creative skills in the context of our work and life. In this way, we create our own world in the same way that the eternal Spirit creates the universe. We can become masters of our skills and abilities, as we see with history's great geniuses, athletes and artists.

We can disseminate our talents in the world. We must remember that the Soul wants power to manifest its creativity. Basically the will to do good is actualised through our various abilities.

The Path of Will

This path is about the self's presence in the world as a sovereign, independent individual. Through this path, the personality develops authenticity and autonomy and the Soul follows its spiritual calling. Success generates the integrity and stamina we need to overcome challenges. The will governs this path and the development of the "I" through the stages. (It should be noted that although I speak of stages, this is not a rigid, step-by-step procedure, but something more fluid. Some stages can be entered earlier than one's overall development suggests.)

We are not born as independent beings able to exercise our will. In early life, will appears as instinct, which relates to body awareness on the identity axis. At the role stage of development our will is expressed through our ability to imitate behaviour and find our place in the group, also internalising the will of the group and its values, which is a development connected to the herd instinct.

We only begin to see ourselves as individuals when we reach the intellectual development of the self-conscious stage. At this stage we learn to think critically, focus on values, and find our place in life through education, work and friends. We are able to adopt our own attitude toward life and the world.

At the integral stage, the conscious will becomes active in the personality. Our strength of character and leadership potential emerge and we assert ourselves and our points of view. At this stage we find an interest in personal development, for example we might consider a change of career. We are becoming independent and autonomous and start to have an impact in our chosen field. This can lead to ambition and self-serving values that may nevertheless be spiritually-orientated. In any case, a strong character appears and with it a kind of holistic consciousness, albeit a lower expression.

At the next stage of call the self hears the Soul's call and comes under the influence of the transpersonal will, which is focused on humanitarian and spiritual action. Here we see the development of a dedicated personality able to achieve a balance between ethics and the will, exemplifying higher values and spiritual integrity. Such people are able to maintain their integrity, which is necessary if we are to realise the Soul's vocation. Here, holistic awareness, shared consciousness and a sense of purpose also appear.

At the flow stage of development, the Soul enlightens the personality, forming an extraordinary human being who can stand as a role model for others. The love and wisdom of the Soul provides such a person with an unshakeable determination. Gandhi is an example of such a character, as are several other cultural leaders who have shaped our lives through their actions and being. Here shared consciousness and awareness of purpose find their full expression.

Those who achieve the transcendent stage of development become founders of religion and pioneers of new ways of living. They are living emanations of cosmic energy, currents of a river of life. We call them avatars, enlightened beings or mahatmas. Here the non-dual consciousness appears.

The Path of Love

On this pathway the self finds itself through its relationship with the other. Feeling and Love dominate and the focus is on our capacity to extend our love beyond ourselves to the cosmos. How many beings do we really care about and commit ourselves to? This is the question on the path of love. We all have a divine Self within moving toward non-dual consciousness, and we must learn to love our neighbour and all sentient beings.

Egocentric love is self-love. With self-love our relationships concern us only with respect to what they can do for us. This may be natural for a child, but it is not how an enlightened adult will live. The challenge on this path is that inner wounds from childhood can trap us and prevent us from learning to love selflessly.

Ethnocentric love concerns the groups we belong to: our family, friends and broader social networks. This sort of love is still characterised by likes and dislikes. There are those you love and those you don't, and conflicts with those who think differently from you. Here ethnocentric consciousness dominates.

Pluralistic love is characterised by a sense of equality and tolerance. We tolerate others' values and ways of life, regardless of race, gender or other differences. The European Convention on Human Rights is an expression of this. The paradox of this sensibility is the belief that such tolerance is an absolute value, which is therefore more important than any other value. Here the self-aware stage emerges which celebrates diversity.

Integral love recognises the previous stages as part of an ongoing process. As mentioned earlier, higher stages transcend and include previous ones. This should inform how we understand cultural development in an evolutionary context. For example, some societies may begin as a religious, authoritarian regime before moving on to something more democratic (Ken Wilber has written about this in the context of Spiral Dynamic Theory). Integral love is more differentiated than other forms of love because of its deep understanding of development. Integral love contains more wisdom than other forms of love and a holistic consciousness has taken hold.

World-centric love unfolds as a realisation of the World Soul. When this love manifests, we no longer see ourselves as separate from others. Instead, we are all global citizens working to make the world a better place for all. We make no separation between nations because we understand that humanity's problems have no national boundaries. World-centric love is a global sensibility committed to humanitarian and spiritual work.

Cosmo-centric love opens the Soul to an awareness of purpose; through it we can attain a direct experience of the universe as one supreme living and evolving entity. This is the recognition of Spirit-in-Action and the community that exists between planets and galaxies. We are committed to a development that includes the whole universe; we each have a unique cosmic role within the whole. This love is not limited to earthly beings and includes the life that exists on the inner levels of consciousness.

Transcendent love is that which Jesus speaks of in the Gospel of John, where he identifies with the Father, which means the spirit of love, for God is love.

Such love gives all to all. It embraces the marginalised and those who have been rejected or ignored. It is an omnipresent selfless love without object.

These lofty perspectives can be gained from the everyday practices. The Holo Map attempts to capture this great vision in a single image, making it easier for us to remember. Indeed, the motivation behind this book is my wish that as many people as possible become aware to their greatness through integral meditation. It is written for those who already feel this call but who need something more to develop this calling. Let me end this chapter with some ideas on how to begin the journey of integral meditation.

Getting Started with Integral Meditation

The first step for integral meditation is to know why you are doing it. Why do you want to meditate, what are your needs, what is your purpose? Most likely you have already meditated, otherwise you would probably not have picked up this book? What is it that meditation has not already given you?

Perhaps you have heard the call to greatness and believe that integral meditation offers a clear path. I hope this is the case, but I must comment that adopting a new meditation practice is not enough – you must also change your life! Meditation is but one of five integral life practices all aimed at the same goal. Certainly, meditation is an important practice, which can provide great joy because it meets a valuable need. But integral meditation as a holistic practice is more than simple meditation that will take us beyond our comfort zones. But my experience is that the benefits far outweigh the inconvenience and the discomforts that we might encounter. So, at the outset, it is important to understand that this is a serious undertaking. For this reason, it is helpful to define your objectives and goals, and perhaps to seek help in doing this so that you can have them clear in your mind. Perhaps write them down so that they are there as a constant reminder and motivation.

Two important goals to set yourself at the beginning are a determination to expand your consciousness and develop your personality. This will help you to hear the voice of your Soul. Expanding your consciousness will provide a wider perspective and a broader outlook on life and, as a result, many of your problems will dissolve in view of the bigger picture. And when consciousness grows, the personality and the basic unconscious will very often revolt. So supplement the work to expand your consciousness with shadow work and meditations designed to transform your personality. This transformative practice is essential for helping you to realise your vision and purpose. Without this practice, higher levels of consciousness will not be able to manifest (see the spiral development in the egg diagram in Chapter 2).

Throughout this book I have highlighted some of the benefits of integral mediation. Let me summarise these here.

1. Physical benefits. These include relaxation, stress reduction, body awareness and increased vitality.

The meditations I have discussed are not directly concerned with the body, but most do have an indirect benefit in that the centring involved always includes relaxation. If you are looking for a more physical approach, then I would recommend meditations specifically designed for this. These can be found in most beginners' books on meditation.

2. Psychological benefits. These include the development of new qualities in your personality (through Creative Meditation), the healing of old wounds (Healing Meditation and Soul therapy), and fresh insights into the roots of your psychology (Reflective Meditation and Insight Meditation). Integral meditation can also strengthen your inner centre (Power Meditation).

3. Spiritual benefits. We become open to superconscious levels of consciousness. The Soul inspires us (Receptive Meditation) and we feel universal love energy (Unity Meditation). For those seeking deeper meaning or purpose in life, Reflective Meditation will allow you to contact your inner guru who has all the answers. You may choose to surrender to one of the countless inner Buddhas (Creative Meditation with surrender). You can expand your consciousness from the individual level through to the universal (Awareness Meditation).

In Table 7 I have summarised the different benefits offered by the 15 types of meditation that I describe in this book. Remember, it is possible to combine different meditations in order to achieve what you desire.

Five Life Practices and I, We and the World

Once you have defined the purpose of your meditation, you need to make it part of the larger perspective of I, We and the World in the context of the five life practices.

You can use body work to strengthen yourself to respond to the new energies that are experienced as a result of the five life practices. For example, it is a good idea to look after your physical health by improving your diet and exercising more. Also, you could beautify your home environment. You could

River of Life and Function	Meditation	Purpose	Effect
Dynamic River "Will"	a. Awareness Meditation b. Power Meditation c. Dynamic Meditation	a. Realising one's identity as universal awareness and power b. Realise one's identity as dynamic being c. Realise one's identity as dynamic power	a. Develops a centre of pure consciousness. Freedom, perception, detachment b. Develops a centre of dynamic being. Standing-power, dignity, greatness, the Royal Self c. Develops break-through power, strong will and freedom
Sensitive River "Emotions"	a. Healing Meditation b. Unity Meditation c. Insight Meditation	a. Healing through the transformative power of love b. Realising one's identity with the World Soul c. Developing wisdom and empathic understanding	a. Develops the empathic heart that can integrate painful emotions b. Strengthens identification with humanity through the great still heart. Develops empathy c. Develops the ability to observe, contain and to perceive and understand connections
Intelligent River "Thought"	a. Circle Meditation b. Reflective Meditation c. Receptive Meditation	a. Developing insights and perspectives b. Developing insights and perspectives c. Developing contact with inspiration	a. Develops group synergy, new perspectives, and contact with the higher "We" b. Develops concentration and realisations through reflective thinking c. Develops the ability to receive different forms of Soul communication
Creative River "Imagination"	a. Creative Meditation b. Soul Therapy	a. Gradual development of a new personality b. Developing co-operation between Soul, self and subpersonalities	a. Refines the personality with Soul qualities that makes it possible to manifest the Soul in practice b. Refines, redeems and transforms subpersonalities so they are a true expression of the Soul
Scientific River "Logic"	a. Reflective Meditation	a. Discovering the truth (within a specific field)	a. Develops the light of truth through research-based knowledge and new insights that lead to new practice in a field
Idealising River "Passion"	a. Creative Meditation with Surrender b. Creative Meditation on the Ideal Model	a. Union with a beloved ideal though focused surrender b. Gradual development of a new personality	a. Contact and unity with the Beloved. Ecstasy and service b. Manifestation of a new Soul archetype of personality and its expression in practice
Manifesting River "Action"	a. Integral Meditation	a. Manifestation of a vision through an integral life practice	a. Develops the ability to organise and coordinate power around a goal though the five life practices. Manifestation

Table 7: Fifteen meditations and how to relate to the seven rivers of life and seven psychological functions.

decorate your home with inspirational images, such as photographs of the universe taken from the Hubble telescope – this may help you to expand your consciousness into the cosmic realm. Meanwhile, plants and a fresh coat of paint may help create a more sensuous atmosphere.

At the same time, it can be very helpful to read about other people's experiences of the cosmic. The literature on this is vast. If you want to develop greater empathy, study topics related to it. When resistances to your meditation practice arise, take these seriously and consider seeking out a therapist to help you with shadow work. In addition, service work is important: you must find a way to bring the new energies that arise into your daily life through your relationships, work and social life.

The new moon is the best time to start a new practice. A good way to test the effectiveness of your practice is to continue the work for an entire full moon cycle, then evaluate the results. Keeping a journal of your meditations helps. Keep alert for any imbalances that arise from your practice. Once your purpose is fixed, you should have a good idea of the dominant river that arises in your meditation – and then you can work to balance this river. The shadow side of the river will show itself through aspects of immaturity that you start to notice. Once this comes into awareness, you can start to work with it. This topic was covered in Chapter 3.

Integral meditation is a journey through seven universal energies and seven levels of consciousness, taken by seven spiritual types following seven meditation roads. We do this through four development paths and five integral life practices.

Summary and Final Perspective

We have reached the end of our voyage. At the beginning I stated that the essential message of this book is: *"Meditate every day, love every day, and choose freedom every day."* I hope that through my writing you have seen how this can be achieved by using the practices I have described so that greatness can come into your life. The journey I have outlined requires adopting a new paradigm of consciousness. In the language of energy psychology, we come to learn that everything in the universe is made up of energy; we are each made of energy and our practice is essential a collection of techniques to help us to work in, with and through this energy. Meditation awakens universal energies, love develops them and freedom attunes us to higher perspectives. We awaken to the ultimate insight that we are the reason behind this universal presence. We are each Spirit-in-Action.

In parting, let me offer seven guidelines that will help you to be the captain on your voyage into the seas of energy. These keys will help you to master energy psychology and achieve greatness.

Energy centring anchors you in your essential being. It allows you to hear your life's purpose, which the key to your innermost identity. This purpose lives in your heart and prompts you to face the person you have always been, your essence. Energy centring is achieved by recognising the river of life that runs within you as your vital source, which is your true self. This is the gift of the dynamic river.

Energy understanding brings love to everything you encounter. Love enables us to understand everything we encounter: people, animals, plants, nature. Love sparks awareness and uplifts every it touches because the keynote of the universe is love or unity consciousness. Energy understanding develops through the heart and is the gift of the sensitive river.

Energy reading interprets and communicates different energies, combining and synthesising them. Much knowledge and a wide perspective is necessary here. Reading the energy of a situation allows us to adapt to change and get the best out of our situation. Energy reading develops through studying energy and is the gift of the intelligent river.

Energy harmonisation reduces conflict through the imagination. A lack of imagination perpetuates conflicts and blinds us to the benefits of co-operation. Through beauty we can integrate darkness and harmonise the energies we meet. Energy harmonisation finds peace in the midst of strife and is the gift of the creative river.

Energy verification identifies what is happening around you. It is your love of truth, your need to know things for what they are, and the joy you feel when the truth is revealed to you. Discrimination is a bright light cutting through a dense fog of uncertainty. The ability to verify energy develops through analysis and is the gift of the scientific river.

Energy Transformation lifts us from one stage of consciousness to the next. Knowing that all energies are really One raises our experience of life to a higher frequency. By grasping the inner potential of everything that happens we can transform basic psychological energies into spiritual ones. This transformation develops through seeing the perfect in the imperfect and is the gift of the idealising river.

Energy manifestation allows for the creative expression of our purpose. It requires organisation, practicality and ingenuity. Through energy manifestation we can turn dreams into reality. Energy manifestation develops by balancing the head and heart through a purpose that serves the world. This is the gift of the manifesting river.

Let these seven keys help you on your voyage. No doubt this book does not contain all the answers. Indeed, it is possible that this practice will create many new questions. But life itself is a question and our only hope of finding the answer is to live it. In doing so, may we learn that we ourselves are the answer to all our questions.

Safe journey to all wonderful Souls who chose to die daily so we might find freedom

May Maitreya be with us

The Dynamic River of Life
Awareness Meditation: "Mindfulness"

Dis-identifying from the body

Close your eyes and sit in a relaxed position. Let go of the body. Become the observer, noting your body's various sensations: your skin's contact with your clothes, your weight in the chair, the air as you breathe, the sounds you hear, any smells or taste. Now observe your breath without trying to change it. Just observe without interfering.

As you sink completely into your body, observe it and embrace it with affectionate appreciation...

That you can observe your body and its sensations shows that *you* are not your body but a consciousness using the body as a tool for experience and action.

Confirm to yourself: I have a body, I value it, but I am not my body.

Sit for a moment and let this realisation sink in.

Now move your observation to the emotions

Dis-identifying from the emotions

Observe your emotions without judgement. Do not judge whether the emotions are good or bad, only observe them as temporary and changing. Are they excited, depressed, neutral, or something else?

Accept your emotions and create a loving space for them to simply be.

If *you* can observe your emotions, they cannot *be* you. *You* are a consciousness using your emotions as a tool for experience and action.

Confirm to yourself: *I have emotions, I value them, but I am not my emotions.*

Sit for a moment and let this realisation sink in.

Now move your observation to your thoughts.

Dis-identifying from the mind

Observe without judgement your mind: the thoughts, ideas and images in your field of consciousness. You may think you have no thoughts, but *that* itself is a thought. See your thoughts as clouds drifting across an inner landscape.

Observe also the inner commentator, the voice inside you that you often associate with your own voice. Let it go. Accept your thoughts and create a loving space where they can be... and then release them.

That you can *observe* your thoughts shows that *you* are not your thoughts. Your thoughts are objects in consciousness. You are the thinker, not the thoughts.

Confirm to yourself: *I have a mind, I value my mind, but I am not my mind.*

Self-Identification

Who is observing your body, emotions and mind? It is the observer: you as pure self-awareness. *Who* is it that has intended and acted? You have, as will. You are, in other words, a centre of pure self-awareness and will.

Say to yourself: *I am a centre of pure self-awareness and will.*

Meditation as the observer

Now focus your awareness on the observer who is monitoring and noticing all your thoughts, emotions and sensations. Enter the here and now, which is always pure awareness. Nothing is more important at this moment than to experience this awareness.

Let everything be as it is and tune into the wakefulness of the moment.

Lovingly and *without judgment* let go of everything that enters your field of awareness: feelings, images, thoughts. No matter how beautiful or interesting they might be, let them go with determination and love.

If you lose focus or become identified with the contents of consciousness, let your breath be your anchor. Breathe through your body, emotions and thoughts.

Focus your awareness on this quiet state, allowing everything else to fade into the background. Identify with the loving witness and expand your awareness into the eternal Now.

Anchoring

To close the meditation, send awareness and positive energy out to your network.

Power Meditation:

"I am that I am"

Centring

Sit in a comfortable position and allow your body to relax. Become the observer noting your body's various sensations.

Observe your emotions and mood. Don't try to change anything, just observe. Step back; observe your thoughts and inner talk. Become aware of your thoughts and gradually let them go. The task is not to change your thoughts but to let them pass like clouds crossing the sky.

Observe your awareness and focus on its source. Recognise yourself as the observer.

Establishing the pillar of power

Move your attention to the heart centre and sense a brilliant sun of acceptance and being. This sun contains and illuminates all that you are.

Once you feel the presence of this acceptance, send a golden stream of energy from the sun in your heart to the centre of your brain, where there is also a sun. Allow this energy to enter and relax your brain cells.

Now connect with all the awakened Souls in the world. Observe that you've become part of a network of people and energies that are helping and supporting each other. Say internally: I am the conscious incarnated Soul.

When you have established this connection, draw the golden energy up to a wonderful sun just above your head. This is your Soul, your Royal Self, which contains all your love, wisdom and dignity

Now, in your own way, invoke your divine Self's loving power and open yourself up to its power and dynamic being. See how the pillar of being that reaches from your heart to the point above your head gently fills your whole mode of being.

Identifying with the silent will in the heart [1]

Now turn your attention to the heart centre, located between your shoulder blades and extending through the middle of the chest. Feel its softness and sink into its centre. Notice how this soft, powerful being slowly strengthens and fills your entire chest. Sense how it flows through your heart and connects you with all living beings.

Understand that your heart centre is an inner being of immovable power. It is your will to be who you are.

Stay with this sensation, anchor yourself emotionally in this powerful being. Say to yourself: "I am that I am."

Do not think about the affirmation, just hold it as an intention and an openness and allow it to sink into your deepest identity.

Anchoring

Decide that you want to step into life as your true self – in a true and authentic meeting with the world.

Send all your power out to your network and all living beings by saying OM three times out loud.

---

1. Alternatively you can direct your focus to the centre of your brain, which is the head's heart centre, while you stay with a sense of ease in your chest.

Dynamic Meditation on an Object

Centring

Find a comfortable sitting position, close your eyes and allow your body to relax. Become the observer noting the thoughts going through your mind. Be aware of your observations.

Now observe your breath without trying to change it. Follow your breath, and if any thoughts enter your mind simply return your focus to the breath – breathing in and breathing out.

Become aware of the silence in your breath and observe how your body slowly relaxes into your breath. Accept any tensions, restlessness or pain as a natural part of how things are.

Observe how the breath relaxes your emotions and notice how you are becoming calm.

Observe how thoughts and images fall into the background as you focus on the breath.

Observe how your personality becomes as quiet as a silent mountain.

Ascension to the Self

Put your focus into the centre of the brain, where there is a white diamond of light. Follow the light to its source about 30cm above your head where you see a sphere of brilliant blue-white light with a brilliant diamond in its centre. This is the essence of your Self's heart.

Dedicate your meditation to your Soul's service in this world.

See the light pouring into your head. Become one with this light. Notice its quality and remain still while the light does its healing work.

Meditation on the Essence of the Self

Focus your attention on the brow centre, about 5cm in front of your forehead. Gather the white light within you and direct it to the brilliant diamond that sits within a blue-white sphere in front of you.

As you focus this burning light towards the diamond, ask the question: "What is the essence of my true spiritual nature?" Know that the answer can be found in the heart of this diamond. Allow your will to penetrate into the diamond. In the silence, await the answer.

Anchoring

Visualise the blue-white light radiating out of your brow centre towards all living beings, inviting all Souls to awaken.

Anchor this energy by saying OM three times on an outbreath while you hold the intention: Let the light awaken in all living beings.

The Sensitive River of Life

Healing Meditation

Preparation

Before you start the meditation choose an aspect of your inner life that is in need of healing. This could be a general feeling of loneliness or anger, or a specific subpersonality that you are aware of.

Centring

Find a comfortable sitting position, close your eyes and allow your body to relax. Become the observer and follow your breath.

Move your attention to the heart centre, and visualise a sun in the heart region that is emanating acceptance and love throughout your personality.

Move your attention to your body as a whole, and embrace your body allowing a warm wave of acceptance and love to flow through your body.

Move your attention to your emotions, allowing all your emotions be exactly as they are, containing them by letting the sun's acceptance flow through them.

Move attention to your thoughts and mental images. Allow them to be exactly as they are, observe them as clouds drifting across the sky. Contain and embrace them with your heart.

Establishing the Healing Pillar

Visualise a sun in your heart region that is emanating acceptance and love throughout your personality.

Now visualise a golden light that emanates from the sun in your heart, up through your throat centre, and up to the sun in the centre of your brain, where this golden light illuminates and relaxes every cell in your brain.

Now make connection with all awakened Souls in the world. Sense how you become part of a network of helping powers that support one another.

Now draw the golden flow of energy up from the brain to the gentle healing sun that is above your head. This sun is your inner being that contains all the wisdom and love that is needed to heal any pain.

Invoke your divine Self's love and healing energies and pray that this meditation will generate the highest good for you and those in your surroundings.

Observe how you are quietly and calmly filled with the gentle healing power of the Soul that runs through a pillar of being that descends from the sun over your head, to the sun in the brain, to the sun in your heart.

Centre yourself in your heart while you are fully awake and present.

Now send a gentle stream of healing light out from your heart to the part of your life where there is suffering. Breathe in and out of the painful state while you embrace it with all your love.

Now ask the part of you that is suffering what it needs. It might be confidence, acceptance, courage or something else. If an answer is not forthcoming or is not clear, use your intuition. Once you have determined what is needed, let this quality flow through your heart and surrender to the instructions coming from your Soul. Step back mentally and let the Soul send a flow of energy, as much as might be needed.

Hold this intention and observe how the energy flows effortlessly from your heart to your wounding, then further out to your network where it will benefit whoever it touches.

Pay attention to any insights or releases of pain that spontaneously and effortlessly arise.

Anchoring

When you are ready, spend a few minutes sending healing energies out to anyone who shares your experience.

Close by saying OM three times while you breathe out healing to the world consciousness.

Unity Meditation:

"The Big Silent Heart"

Identification and Disidentification

Find a comfortable sitting position and allow your body to relax. Become the observer noting your body's various sensations.

Observe your emotions and mood. Don't try to change anything, just observe. Step back. Observe your thoughts and inner chatter, and gradually let them go. The task is not to change your thoughts but to let them pass like clouds passing across a clear blue sky.

Observe your awareness and focus on its source. Recognise yourself as the observer.

Identification with the Big Silent Heart

Turn your attention to the silence. Alllow your whole being to listen to the silence, sinking into it and giving it all your attention. Feel how the silence embraces and caresses your body, feelings and thoughts, like a big soft heart.

Move your attention, choosing either the heart centre or the middle of your head – and observe a deep blue indigo-coloured inner space, a silent loving ocean.

Sense how this great calm blue ocean expands to include your immediate surroundings.

Sense the empathetic sensitivity that exists in the silence and feel how this sensitivity expands to include the entire nation, Europe, the world and all beings in a single great loving embrace.

Identify yourself with this great silent heart that lives in the heart of all living beings – a soft universal field of loving, sensitive awareness – the great World Soul. Recognise that you are this silence.

Sink deeper and deeper into your identification with this silent embracing and awakened heart.

Anchoring

Send this embracing silence out to all living beings. With three out-breaths, say OM each time and send the blue loving ocean out to your network.

Insight Meditation

Preparation

Identify which aspect of your life you wish to explore and illuminate before you start the meditation. Prepare a few questions to ask this aspect of your life.

Centring

Close your eyes and sit in a relaxed position. Let go of all tension in the body.

Become the observer noting your body's various sensations. Spend some time allowing yourself to relax.

Move your attention to the heart centre. Visualise a golden, brilliant sun of impersonal warm love that illuminates all that you contain.

Draw a golden stream of energy up from your heart to the throat centre at the back of your neck, and see the sun relaxing your throat centre and your thoughts.

Draw this stream of energy up to your brow centre about 10cm in front of your forehead. Focus your attention on a golden-white sphere of light in front of you. Then prepare yourself to dedicate your personality to the Soul. When you are ready, say inwardly: "I integrate my thoughts, feelings and body and dedicate them to my Soul."

Draw the golden stream to the middle of your brain and focus here while you say inwardly: "I am the conscious incarnated Soul." Recognise that your awareness is part of a single universal awareness and that you are one with all awakened Souls.

Draw the golden stream up to a brilliant sun of love and wisdom that is 30cm above your head. Anchor yourself in the brilliant sphere of illumination that sits there.

Invoke your Soul's illumination by saying: "I invoke my Soul's wisdom and guidance with the intention to bring the highest good into life." If this affirmation does not feel right for you, offer an affirmation that better suits how you are right now.

Meditation

Move your attention to the brow centre. Bring into your focus the three methods of inquiry: observation, love and exploration.

Observe the energies you want to explore. Because everything is energy, you might want to explore the whole field. Accept all sensations and thoughts that are being activated.

How does it feel like? What thoughts and images are arising in the field? What meanings can you identify?

Ask the questions you have prepared, leaving a space after each one to telepathically receive the answer. Stay in the field, detached, accepting and curious.

Open yourself to the Soul's guidance. Know that your awakened loving interest will raise the frequencies in the field you are exploring.

Anchoring

Send the light of understanding that you have developed out to your network. Relax all parts of your head and allow all your light spread out in 360 degrees, allowing it to illuminate and inform all that it touches. Observe how you interact with your entire network via the mental plane.

Anchor the energies you have received by sending them out with three silent OMs.

The Intelligent River of Life

Circle Meditation

See the complete instructions in Chapter 7 and note that this meditation requires a skilled facilitator.

Reflective Meditation

In this meditation we reflect on love, but you can chose to focus on any quality. This is the same meditation we use in connection with the scientific river where the focus is more concrete.

Dis-identify from the Body

Sit in a relaxed position and close your eyes. Let go of any tension in your body. Become the observer noting any sensations in your body: your weight in the chair, the feeling of your skin against your clothes, any sounds you can hear, anything you can smell or taste. Now observe your breath without trying to change it. Just observe without interfering.

Who observes the body?

Now move your attention to your emotions.

Dis-identify from the Emotions

Observe your emotions without judgement. Do not judge whether the emotions are good or bad, only observe them as temporary and changing. Whether you are excited, depressed, feel neutral or something else, simply allow these feelings to be as they are.

Who observes the emotions?

Now move your attention to your thoughts.

Dis-identify from the Mind

Observe without judgement your mind, the thoughts, ideas and images in your field of consciousness. You may think you have no thoughts, but *that* itself is a thought. Therefore, observe your thoughts.

Who observes the thoughts?

Self Identification

You have observed the body, emotions and thoughts from a centre of pure consciousness. Now ask the question: *Who is willing this action?* Experience and deepen your contact with the observer and let go of all thoughts, images and sensations.

Who observes?

Ascension

Focus your attention in the centre of the brain. Open up a channel from your head centre to a blue-white sphere above you that is pouring a brilliant light down into your head. Dedicate your meditation to the Soul's service.

Reflective Meditation on Love

Reflect on the statement: "I love." Use the following questions to explore this statement: What is the real meaning of love? – What is love? – How many and what types of love are there? – In what way am I able to love? – How do I love? – Who do I love, and who do I succeed in loving? – Have I always succeeded in loving the way I would like to? – If not, why not? – What is blocking me? – How can I eliminate that which is blocking? – How is my love influenced by the people I love and how much does it depend on my own nature?

Anchoring

Anchor the energies you have awakened by saying three OMs while holding the intention: "Let all hearts open."

Receptive Meditation

Dis-identify from the Body

Sit in a relaxed position and close your eyes. Let go of any tension in your body. Become the observer noting any sensations in your body: your weight in the chair, the feeling of your skin against your clothes, any sounds you can hear, anything you can smell or taste. Now observe your breath without trying to change it. Just observe without interfering.

Who observes the body?

Now move your attention to emotions.

Dis-identify from the Emotions

Observe your emotions without judgement. Do not judge your emotions as good or bad, simply observe them as temporary and changing. Are you excited, depressed, feeling neutral, or something else?

Who observes the emotions?

Now move your attention to your thoughts.

Dis-identify from the Mind

Observe without judgement your mind: the thoughts, ideas and images in your field of consciousness. You may think you have no thoughts, but *that* itself is a thought. Therefore observe your thoughts.

Who observes the thoughts?

Self Identification

You have observed the body, emotions and thoughts from a centre of pure consciousness. Now ask the question: Who is willing this action? Experience and deepen your contact with the observer and let go of all thoughts, images and sensations.

Who observes?

Ascension

Focus your attention in the centre of the brain. Open up a channel from your head centre to a blue-white sphere above you that is pouring a brilliant light down into your head. Dedicate your meditation to the Soul's service.

Receptive Meditation

Imagine a brilliant star or diamond emanating a crystal clear light about 30cm above your head. This light symbolises the diamond mind and the Self and it shines a light down to the centre of your brain. Sense a clarity manifesting around your head.

Ask for inspiration, power or insight. Say to yourself: "I invoke the clarity of the Soul."

Stay still. Do not let anything other than what is relevant to your invocation enter your mind.

If any images, words or sensations come to you, make a note of them by writing them down. Then, in complete stillness, sink into the essence of your invocation.

Anchoring

Anchor the energies you have received by saying three OMs while you send the essence of your insight out to your network.

The Creative River of Life

Creative Meditation

Centring

Sit in a relaxed position and close your eyes. Let go of any tension in your body. Become the observer noting the various sensations in your body. Take some time to relax.

Observe your emotions and mood. Don't try to change anything, just observe. Step back; observe your thoughts and inner talk. Become aware of your thoughts and gradually let them go. The task is not to change your thoughts but to let them pass like clouds crossing a clear blue sky.

Observe your awareness and focus on its source. Recognise yourself as the observer.

Establish the self-Soul connection

Move your attention to the heart centre. Visualise a brilliant blue-white light in the heart centre that is emanating a gentle, feminine energy throughout your entire being.

Once you feel the presence of this being, send the blue-white stream of heart energy to the centre of your brain, where there is also a blue-white light. Let the light enter every cell in your brain, soothing them.

Now connect with all the awakened souls in the world. Observe that you've become a part of a network of beings who are helping and supporting each other.

When you have established this connection, draw the blue-white energy up to a wonderful sphere of light just above your head. This is your Soul, your divine Self, which contains all that is good, true and beautiful.

Now, in your own way, invoke the divine. See how your Soul is gently filled by the pillar of blue-white light that reaches from your heart to the point above your head.

Identification with the Lotus of Peace and Harmony

Now turn your attention to the heart centre, located between the shoulder blades and extending through to the middle of the chest. Feel the softness of the heart centre and sink into it. Notice how this soft, feminine being slowly strengthens and fills your entire chest. Sense how this being flows through your heart and connects you with all living beings.

Know that this inner being of beauty and grace radiates a love that opens all hearts through the gentle force of beauty.

Now visualise a beautiful white lotus bud at the centre of the pillar of blue-white light. Sense how this lotus contains the essence of peace and harmony.

Feel the lotus slowly open up, petal by petal, allowing a fragrance of peace and harmony to spread throughout your entire being.

Go deeper and deeper into your connection with this white lotus flower. Unite with its essence and become the spirit of peace and harmony yourself.

Anchoring

Send peace and harmony to your entire network and all living beings by saying OM three times loudly and clearly in three long breaths.

Soul Therapy

Choose a subpersonality to work with, or start the exercise by recalling yourself at a certain age or while playing a certain role. If nothing comes to mind, sit peacefully and allow an image to appear.

Centring

1. Become the observer, relax your body, be still and follow your breath.

2. Visualise a sun in your heart centre emanating acceptance and love throughout your personality.

3. Now visualise a golden light that emanates from the sun in your heart, up through your throat, and out through the top your head, where it rises up to a golden sun above you. This golden sun is your Soul and higher consciousness, containing all your wisdom. Ask your Soul for guidance and wisdom.

4. Observe how the sun of the Soul emanates a warm, loving light and wisdom throughout your body.

5. Notice how the sun's energy flows through your body, legs and feet, down to the core of the earth, Gaia, where you connect with the healing energies of Mother Earth. Gradually draw this energy back up through the same channel to the heart.

6. Centre the energy from the Soul and Mother Earth at the heart centre.

7. From your heart, send a warm, loving energy to all your subpersonalities. Accept them and ask for their co-operation. Direct this energy towards your solar plexus.

Identification of the Subpersonality

1. Now focus on a problem, situation, feeling or subpersonality, allowing it to emerge into the light of the mind's eye.

2. Explore the subpersonality's situation, environment, strategies and needs. Approach it as a living being with whom you can have a dialogue.

Transformation of the Subpersonality

1. Hold the subpersonality in your heart's loving atmosphere and send it love and light.

2. Let the subpersonality know that it is a valuable and loving part of you and your inner family of subpersonalities.

3. Let it know when it was created – at what age – and explain that it is stuck in a time warp and that you will now bring it to the present. Check to make sure the subpersonality understands what you mean.

4. Explain that it has the same Soul and purpose as you: to live a meaningful life in greater love and growth – chose your own formulations – and ask if it understands.

5. Let it know it can be what it wants through the light it carries in its heart.

6. Explain how it can find its way to the heart through the light bridge connecting your two hearts. Visualise this light. Then ask if it can also see the light. Explore the quality of this light together.

7. Ask if the subpersonality wants to enter your heart so it can discover the transpersonal potential to become the best version of itself (perfect inner child, teenager, etc).

8. See the light flow from your Soul – the sun above your head – to your heart, then from your heart to the heart of the subpersonality, then back again to your Soul. Let the light flow in this triangle.

9. See the subpersonality gradually enter the centre of your heart. Surrender this process to the Soul and watch the transformation unfolding.

10. Anchor this inner reality by talking to the subpersonality about its new situation, liberated from the time warp

The Scientific River of Life

Reflective Meditation
(Investigative Interview)

Chose an area of your life that you want to explore with the intention of gaining fresh insight understanding. Prepare a few questions to ask the relevant subpersonality or energy that you want to explore.

Dis-identify from the Body

Sit in a relaxed position and close your eyes. Let go of any tension in your body. Become the observer noting any sensations in your body: your weight in the chair, the feeling of your skin against your clothes, any sounds you can hear, anything you can smell or taste. Now observe your breath without trying to change it. Just observe without interfering.

Move your attention to your emotions.

Dis-identify from your Emotions

Observe your emotions without judgement. Do not judge your emotions as good or bad, simply observe them as temporary and changing. Are you excited, depressed, feeling neutral, or something else?

Move your attention to your thoughts.

Dis-identify from the Mind

Observe without judgement your mind: the thoughts, ideas and images in your field of consciousness. You may think you have no thoughts, but *that* itself is a thought. See your thoughts as clouds drifting across an inner landscape.

You have observed the body, emotions and thoughts from a centre of pure consciousness. Ask yourself: *Who is willing this action?* Experience and deepen your contact with the observer and let go of all thoughts, images and sensations.

Ask yourself: *Who observes?*

Ascension to the Self

Put your focus into the centre of the brain, where there is a white diamond of light. Follow the light to its source about 30cm above your head where you see a sphere of brilliant blue-white light with a brilliant diamond in its centre. This is the essence of your Self's heart.

Dedicate your meditation and any results of your meditation to your Soul's service in the world.

Align yourself with the blue-white light by visualising it pouring down into your head. Notice the light's qualities, and be still. Let the light carry out its healing work.

Scientific Exploration

Focus your attention in the brow centre, about 5cm in front of your forehead. Direct the diamond light from your forehead towards the area of life you want to explore. Stay in this position in the role of a neutral observer scientifically examining the field.

Next, observe the frequencies of the area of life you want to explore. What do they feel like? What thoughts and images arise from them? Accept all that they are without trying to change anything. Try to get a precise picture of the situation by analysing and collecting data.

When you are ready, start the investigative interview using the questions you have prepared.

Conclude the interview by identifying with any energies or subpersonality that have emerged and feel what it is like to have these energies.

Anchoring

Anchor the energies that have emerged by writing about them in your spiritual journal. From the data you have collected you can develop new questions which you can use for your next scientific meditation.

The Dedicated River of Life

Creative Meditation with Surrender
(Christ-Maitreya meditation)

According to some spiritual traditions, Maitreya is the next world teacher. Maitreya is also known as Buddha-Maitreya, Christ, Messiah, Imam Mahdi, Krishna, etc.

Centring

Sit in a relaxed sitting position and close your eyes. Adopt the standpoint of the observer and calmly accept all states.

Direct your attention to the heart centre, and sense a brilliant sun of pure acceptance and containment that emanates peace throughout your being.

Direct your attention to your body and let a warm acceptance flow through your entire body.

Direct your attention to your emotions, allowing them to be just as they are. Let the sun's light of acceptance contain and flow through your emotions.

Direct your attention to the images and thoughts in your mind, allowing them to be exactly as they are, not trying to change them, but observing them as you allow them to pass like clouds crossing a clear blue sky. Contain any thoughts with your heart's embrace.

Establish the self-Soul Connection

Move your attention to the heart centre. Sense a brilliant sun of pure acceptance.

Now visualise a golden light emanating from the sun in your heart up to the middle of your head, where you also see a sun. Let this sun in your head illuminate and relax each cell in your brain.

Now connect with all the awakened Souls in the world. Sense how you are part of a network of helping beings who are supporting one another.

Next, allow the golden stream of energy to rise up from the sun in your head to a gentle kind sun above you. This sun above your head is your inner being filled with love and wisdom. In the middle of this sun you can see Christ-Maitreya emerge with his right hand held up high to bless all living beings.

Meditation

Let Christ-Maitreya gradually descend down into your head centre, then into your throat centre, and then into your heart centre – all the time allowing his blessing to pour out with the right frequency for each centre.

In the heart surrender completely to Christ-Maitreya and merge with his being. Surrender your will to his will. Say a prayer to anchor this process of surrender.

Anchoring

Send the Christ energy you have received out to your network and all living beings while saying OM out loud.

Creative Meditation on the Ideal Model

Centring

Sit in a comfortable position and let all tension leave your body. Become the observer, noting your body's various sensations. Accept all sensations with a calm mind.

Observe your emotions and mood. Don't try to change anything, just observe. Step back; become aware of your thoughts and inner talk, and gradually let them go. Do not try to alter your thoughts, but simply let them pass like clouds crossing a clear blue sky.

Observe your awareness and focus on its source. Recognise yourself as the observer.

Move your attention to the heart centre and sense a brilliant sun of pure acceptance and space that emanates peaceful being to all parts of you.

Direct your attention to your body, and let a warm acceptance flow through your entire body.

Direct your attention to your emotions, allowing them to be as they are. Let the sun's accepting being contain and flow through them.

Direct your attention to the images and thoughts in your mind. Do not try to change them, just allow them to appear and disappear like clouds crossing the sky. Contain your thoughts with your heart's embrace.

Establish the self-Soul Connection

Move your attention to the heart centre. Sense a brilliant sun of pure accepting being.

Now visualise a golden light emanating from the sun in your heart up to the centre of your head, where you also see a sun – let this sun illuminate and relax each cell of your brain.

From this point you can connect with all the awakened Souls in the world. Sense how you become a part of a network of helping beings who are supporting one another

Now let the golden stream of energy rise up to a gentle kind sun above your head. This sun is your inner being filled with love and wisdom. In the middle of this sun you can see your ideal model, your Soul archetype, that which you realistically have the potential to become.

Meditation

Now you let the ideal model descend down to your head centre, your throat centre and your heart centre.

In your heart surrender completely to your ideal model and merge with its being. See yourself in different situations able to express yourself as your ideal model. Be still and sink deeper into its essence.

Anchoring

Send the love energy you feel out to your network and to all living beings while saying OM out loud with three long out-breaths.

The Manifesting River of Life

Integral Meditation

With integral meditation you combine a number of meditations to help you to manifest your vision. The meditations are selected purposefully to address your own specific needs. At the same time, in order to achieve optimum results, the meditation work is combined with body work, shadow work, mind work and service work. The process, which is described in detail in Chapter 11, offers each individual a uniquely tailored spiritual practice to help achieve a specific goal.

Full Moon Meditation

Choose a theme for your meditation that is linked to the meaning of the astrological sign of the sun for the time of year you will be meditating. In this way, you will be co-operating with the planetary cycle of inflowing and outflowing energies that exist between the earth and the solar system.

Group Centring

Make yourselves comfortable, close your eyes and establish yourselves as observers. Let go of all the events of the day and be fully present in the Now.

Move your attention to the heart centre and connect with the sun in the heart. Feel it softly and gently embracing everything you are. Sink into and rest in this loving being that empathically contains your personality.

Feel how your own being transforms into a group being that flows from heart to heart and from Soul to Soul. Sense the entire group field as one large heart and its warm, impersonal empathy.

Draw a golden stream of energy from your heart centre up to the centre of your head. Here you see a sun that illuminates your inner consciousness. Now associate yourself with all the awakened Souls you know in your inner spiritual world. Let your consciousness extend across the global network of Souls.

Now let the energy from the head centre rise up to a brilliant sun of love and wisdom that is over your head. This sun is your innermost being. Connect with the heart of your innermost being in complete self-forgetfulness.

Be completely still and sink into the heart of this sun, this solar being that is who you are.

Meditation

Focus on the theme of your meditation and remember the three stages, 3+2+1 (third, second and first person perspectives), and connect fully with these energies.

Connect with the silence and open yourself up to the astrological energies that are available to humanity at the time of year you have chosen to meditate. In the silence, know that you are humankind, the World Soul.

Anchoring

In your mind's eye, see how the sun and the earth are connected by a pillar of golden light that links the heart of the sun and to the core of the earth. Visualise how solar power and spiritual energies are flowing into the world consciousness through this pillar of light.

As a group, say OM three times while visualising these incoming energies from the sun.